Life Skills

Katie Fforde lives in Gloucestershire with her husband and some of her three children. Her first book, *Living Dangerously*, was selected for the 1995 WH Smith Fresh Talent promotion. *Life Skills* is her fifth novel. Her hobbies are ironing and housework but, unfortunately, she has almost no time for them as she feels it her duty to keep a close eye on the afternoon chat shows.

Praise for Katie Fforde's previous novels

'Joanna Trollope crossed with Tom Sharpe'
Mail on Sunday

'Warm and cheery . . . delicious'
The Times

'Fforde is blessed with a lightness of touch, careful observation and a sure sense of the funny side of life'
Ideal Home

'Deliciously, horribly recognizable – a stunning début'
Sue Limb

'I really enjoyed *Living Dangerously*. It was the perfect holiday read. A real tonic and great fun'
Marika Cobbold

'Old-fashioned romance of the best sort . . . funny, comforting'
Elle

'Freshness, good humour and a willingness to entertain'
Elizabeth Buchan, *Sunday Times*

'The innocent charm of Katie Fforde's unashamedly romantic début belies a perceptive wit'
Sunday Express

KATIE FFORDE

Life Skills

Century · London

Published by Century in 1999

1 3 5 7 9 10 8 6 4 2

Copyright © Katie Fforde 1999

Katie Fforde has asserted her right under the Copyright, Designs and Patents
Act, 1988 to be identified as the author of this work

First published in the United Kingdom in 1999 by Century
Random House UK Limited
20 Vauxhall Bridge Road, London SW1V 2SA

Random House Australia (Pty) Limited
20 Alfred Street, Milsons Point, Sydney,
New South Wales 2061, Australia

Random House New Zealand Limited
18 Poland Road, Glenfield
Auckland 10, New Zealand

Random House South Africa (Pty) Limited
Endulini, 5a Jubilee Road, Parktown 2193, South Africa

Random House UK Limited Reg. No. 954009

A CIP catalogue record for this book is available
from the British Library

Papers used by Random House UK Limited
are natural, recyclable products made from wood grown in
sustainable forests. The manufacturing processes conform to
the environmental regulations of the country of origin

ISBN 0 7126 8080 2

Typeset by SX Composing DTP, Rayleigh, Essex
Printed and bound in Great Britain by
Biddles Ltd, Guildford and King's Lynn

To Susan Watt,
with much love and gratitude

Acknowledgements

To Mike, Sam and Rhiannon Adams, for up-to-date information about important things. To the owners and crew of *Hart* and *Hind*, Guy, Helen and Nigel, for reminding me about Hotel boats and giving us a really lovely holiday. To Steve Marshfield for being the nicest health inspector ever. To Alexander Watt and Desmond Fforde for various sorts of technical advice, and to my late mother-in-law, Audrey Fforde, for being herself.

Chapter One

'I just don't understand you, Julia!'

Discreetly, Julia wiped the spit from her eye and tried to get out of range. If she'd realised Oscar was going to be quite so upset when she broke up with him, she wouldn't have done it in his car. She would have invited him in for coffee and he would have been spared hitting his funny-bone on the steering wheel, which he'd done twice already, and she could have avoided the more physical manifestations of his distress.

'And all this wanting some "fun" nonsense!' he went on. 'You're a bit old for that, aren't you?' A droplet of indignant froth landed on her sleeve.

'I'm only thirty-four, not exactly over the hill,' she said quietly, burrowing in her pocket for a tissue.

'It's pretty old to have children! And Mother offered us so much help with them!'

Julia began to lose sympathy for him. 'You mean when she offered to drag your old nanny out of her retirement home so they could be potty-trained the moment they're out of the womb! Hasn't she heard of disposable nappies?'

'She offered help with school fees too!'

'Only if we have a boy who's bright enough to get in to dear old Sandings!' She referred scathingly to his Alma Mater, the last place on earth she'd send her children to, if she ever had any.

'Well of course. Private education is expensive. You could hardly expect her to fork out thousands of pounds for a gir – someone who's not very bright.' He fell silent,

1

aware, possibly for the first time in his life, of how crass he had been.

Julia took a moment to swallow her rage. There was no point in ranting at Oscar. He was sexist and élitist in every fibre of his being and he could no more change that than he could change his blood group. Why had it taken her so long to spot it?

'I do appreciate it was kind of her to offer help with school fees' – she fixed her gaze on his walnut dashboard so he wouldn't see she was lying – 'but I'm still breaking off our engagement. Children aren't my first priority right now, and we'd just make each other miserable.'

'Then why did you agree to marry me in the first place?'

It was a fair question, but while she knew the answer, it wasn't one she could give Oscar. 'You're very attractive. I was flattered by your attention. And I do love Sooty.'

This last was a mistake. Her spot of ego-restoration was undone by the reference to his half-grown black Labrador which had been a puppy when they first met.

'Sooty!' Oscar blinked. 'What has Sooty got to do with it?'

'Well, nothing really. It was just that anyone who has a dog seems like good marriage material.' She'd gone off course. She was trying to soothe Oscar, not make him feel like a refuge for unmarried potential mothers, which, sadly, he was. 'I was flattered, Oscar,' she repeated. 'But I've realised I could never be the sort of wife you need.'

'What do you mean?'

'You said,' she explained quietly, 'when I was passed over for promotion, that it didn't matter because I'd be giving up work anyway when we got married.'

He'd worked out by now that that had been a mistake. 'Then why did you leave? If your job means so much to you?'

This time Julia's anger was harder to suppress. 'I did explain. They gave Darren *my* department, that *I'd* built

2

up, for nearly *five years*, just because he's a man and plays golf! He's not even competent!'

'But a lot of people prefer to deal with a man and golf's not only about the game, you know. A lot of business –'

'I built up the lettings department without being a man, or spending my spare time in the bar at the golf club!'

'Well, they wouldn't let you in unaccompanied . . .'

'I persuaded that Finnish company to use us to handle their relocation rather than one of the big Oxford firms –'

'I know, Peter was very pleased to get the business. He told me –'

'And did your golfing buddy also tell you why he didn't give me the department?'

'Only what he told you, darling.' Oscar, unnerved by Julia's anger, tried to pacify her. 'That he thought that while Darren was young, he had a lot of potential . . .'

Julia concentrated on keeping calm. If she let herself think about what Oscar was saying she'd explode and make a nasty mess on his leather upholstery. 'This is all old ground, Oscar, and not getting us anywhere. But I think you must realise now that we're not suited.' Seeing him about to prove her wrong, she hurried on. 'There are lots of super girls out there who would . . .' She faltered. Was there anyone willing to be a 1950s wife at the beginning of the new millennium? 'Who would – appreciate your many good qualities – and recognise what a catch you are. You're very attractive and supremely eligible, Oscar, it's just me you're not right for.'

She picked up her handbag and fumbled for the door-handle.

He put out a hand to stop her getting out. 'And this canal business? What's that all about? You've walked out on a perfectly decent career working for a very sound chap, and behaved very badly while you were about it, may I remind you . . .'

Julia wanted to laugh. At the time she'd been too angry,

but in retrospect, her departure from the office had had its funny side. Having heard her extremely toned-down version of her reasons for leaving, Peter had reached out across the desk to pat her, saying, 'There, there.' This patronising gesture had knocked over his coffee mug, which had been full. Coffee had spread all over his desk (which he kept clear, to prove how efficient he was) and on to his trousers. He'd been distraught. 'This suit is brand new! My wife'll go mad! Do something before it stains, Julia, please!'

'Why don't you ask Darren?' she had replied coolly. 'He's got a lot of potential.'

'But he won't know anything about coffee stains!' Peter had gone on. 'He's a man!'

'So he is. Shame.' Julia had smiled with mock sympathy and walked out.

Now she said mildly, 'I don't think I behaved that badly. You can't blame me for not wanting to scrub away with tissues at Peter's crotch, now can you?'

'Don't change the subject! You know nothing about this woman, or canals for that matter.'

'I'll know more about them both when I've had the interview. But I would have left Strange's anyway. I'd been there too long.' Six years too long, she now realised.

'You don't even know how much this woman is going to pay you! How will you make ends meet? Thought of that, have you?'

'Of course! I'm not an idiot.' Julia bit back her irritation. 'I shall let my house. That'll cover the mortgage and the bills. Whatever I get paid will just be pocket money.'

'Pocket money! Huh!'

'I'm young and single, Oscar – well, youngish. I've got my feet on the housing ladder. So as long as I can pay the mortgage, I don't need to earn vast amounts. Anyway, perhaps the pay is good.' She thought this as unlikely as he did, but since neither of them actually knew, she thought she might as well say it.

'If people don't pay you, they don't value you!'

'I was paid well at Strange's, and what did that prove? But I don't value myself by my salary, and I don't expect anyone else to. Now I really must go.' This time she actually got the door open and her foot out before Oscar jumped in again.

'My mother will be very disappointed about this, very disappointed.'

'I think she'll be heartily relieved,' said Julia, who had overheard an unflattering conversation about her age and her child-bearing potential on the one occasion she and Oscar's mother had met. 'This leaves you free to find someone younger and more biddable.' Oscar flushed to hear his mother's words echoed. Julia kissed his cheek. 'I'm sorry it didn't work out, Oscar. But I know I could never have made you happy, not for long.'

Julia got out of the car and made her way into her house feeling sad and guilty. Although she hadn't recognised it at the time, she reflected, it had been Oscar's inherent dullness and his heavenly Queen Anne house (she blushed with shame) which made her agree to marry her.

I was just so tired all the time, she thought, putting on the kettle, working my socks off getting the lettings department going. She'd spent hours on the phone to Finland convincing a very high-tech firm that she had at her fingertips, in sleepy Oxfordshire, plenty of very high-class accommodation for its top executives, and more hours convincing people who owned said accommodation that their Cotswold gems would be safe in her hands. She'd set up a team of gardeners so no rose would go unpruned or bindweed unchecked and even got a firm of furniture restorers ready to remove the merest scratch on the Chippendale furniture. She remembered now how scathing Darren had been when he'd discovered these details, saying it was a waste of time. She had had great

5

satisfaction in telling him that anxieties about their chairs were what stopped a lot of people letting their property. He had just muttered about insurance and cast-iron contracts as if Julia had never heard of them.

Working such long hours had affected her social life, and Oscar, introduced to her by her boss, seemed pleasant and undemanding. His idea of fun (apart from a challenging game of golf) was taking Julia to excellent country restaurants and showing off his knowledge to the wine waiter. As he hardly drank at all himself (his classic Jaguar was as precious to him as his Labrador puppy), Julia found herself on the business end of some excellent vintages. Not requiring much in the way of conversation, Oscar was quite happy if Julia just nodded and murmured at him, and wasn't offended if she caught up on some much-needed sleep in the car on the way home. He had asked her to marry him when her mind had been on something quite else and thus she had found herself engaged to a man she didn't really know at all, and who knew even less about her.

Somehow there'd never been time to get to know each other better, and Julia, still rushing about, began to see the prospect of a life of being well fed and watered in a beautiful setting (Oscar had some wonderful antiques to go with the house) as rather attractive. But when the promotion that was hers by right was given to Darren, young, arrogant and inefficient, just because he was male, she realised she needed to do some serious reassessment and, she also realised, downsizing (the Queen Anne house had seven bedrooms). Working so hard had allowed her to make a serious error of judgement and it wasn't worth it. Perhaps she should feel grateful to Peter Strange for inadvertently showing her the light.

After she had stormed out of the office, she had bought a copy of *The Lady* in preparation for her new life. For although part of her wanted to fill a rucksack and go hitchhiking round India that very minute, another, better developed part wanted to earn some sort of living.

Not even waiting to get home, she turned straight to the back pages and read as she walked, wondering why she had given so much of her life to a company like Strange's, who would always see women as little more than glorified secretaries, whatever they achieved.

Narrowly avoiding a puddle, and banging her hip on the garden gate, her excitement grew. Every 'Situation Vacant' seemed like a shining window of opportunity, beckoning her to a new world, exciting, glittering, totally different from the stress of the past six years. It was so nearly too late. Thank goodness Oscar's mother had wanted them to be married in an extremely fashionable church, which had a nine-month waiting list.

The narrowness of her escape caused her to be a little rash as she circled advertisements. She only just managed to retain enough sanity not to apply for jobs as a nanny (*Chance to travel with family*) or groom (*Must love large dogs*), when she had little experience of children and none whatsoever of horses.

But there had been one job which was not only intriguing but which she felt she could do. And it was this which had her one cold February lunchtime, just over a week after finishing with Oscar, outside an old coaching inn on the outskirts of the town.

Chapter Two

Julia opened the door and went into the pub, suddenly nervous. Oscar's right, she thought. I'm mad, I should stick to what I know and not meet strange women in pubs which are so dark I can't find the bar. Stumbling through tables and chairs and peering round agricultural machinery and under original oak beams, she was eventually led to it by a murmur of prosperous voices.

Three silver-haired men paused in their gentlemanly one-upmanship about sit-on lawn mowers as Julia appeared. They knew that these days it was perfectly acceptable for a woman to enter a pub on her own, but none of their wives would do it. Julia, familiar with the species, relaxed and smiled sympathetically. One of the men got to his feet and called through to the kitchen: 'Madge! Shop!'

Julia ran her tongue over her teeth in case there was lipstick on them. She wanted this job so badly. Having to admit that Oscar was right, and to trawl through the appointments section of the *Daily Telegraph*, would be a terrible disappointment.

She distracted herself by studying the comforting list of nursery food on the blackboard until 'Madge' appeared, wearing a light dusting of flour over her stripy apron. Julia ordered a glass of red wine, took it to a table by the window and stared out into the car-park. Rain was beginning to spatter into the puddles, making little exclamations of surprise at Julia's recent spate of life-style changes.

She should really have brought an updated c.v. with

her, but when she had walked out of her office so dramatically, she had cut herself off from proper secretarial facilities and, apart from a barmaiding job she'd had as a student, fifteen years before, there was nothing she could add to her résumé which might help her current application.

Athletic, outdoor type, good cook, good with people, wanted for work on the canals. No canal experience necessary . . . Julia didn't feel she was particularly athletic, but after Oscar's recent comments about her age she thought it was time she became so. She was a good cook and definitely good with people, which was one of the reasons, she now reflected, she was so livid when Darren got her job; he was *hopeless* with them.

She had reached the end of her glass of Fitou and was debating whether another would be wise when a very young woman arrived.

Slender enough to get away with her tight leather trousers, white T-shirt and short jacket, she was wearing expensive-looking boots and a devoré scarf which could have paid for Julia's entire outfit. Gold glinted on her wrist and at her ears and she was stunningly pretty. Her hair was short and thick and had at least three colours of blonde highlights in it. It was the sort of style which would need trimming every three weeks, and 'lifting' every four, by the sort of fashionable London stylist who, if you wanted an initial consultation, would, like Oscar's mother's fashionable church, have a waiting list nine months long.

Julia was wondering if she could possibly work for someone who looked so much like a celebrity deb and if she should slip out of a back door before she was noticed, when the young woman turned and saw her.

'Julia Fairfax? Suzy Boyd. Sorry I'm late, I got hopelessly lost. What are you drinking? Red wine? Is it nice? I'll join you.'

Julia found herself responding to the wide, ortho-

9

dontised smile which followed the greeting, but felt dowdy in her sensible jacket and trousers. Suzy Boyd was so glossy and well groomed, like a highly bred young racehorse, prancing with health and good breeding. She made Julia feel like a shaggy old riding-school pony.

Suzy returned with two glasses, passed one to Julia and took a sip of the other. 'I've never interviewed anyone before. I've got a list of questions.' She rummaged in a leather sack with a designer's name in gold on the outside and a lot of clutter on the in. 'Here.' She glanced at it. 'I wonder if we ought to chat a bit first, or get right on in with the questions?'

Julia, who was warming to Suzy, in spite of the leather trousers and minimal thigh-spread, said, 'The questions would give us a starting point.'

Suzy was obviously relieved to have this decision made for her. 'Right, let's see. You're thirty-four' – she glanced up quickly as if checking for signs of maturity – 'and you've had cooking experience?'

'I cooked in a pub one summer holiday, when I was a student, but it's been just dinner-party cooking since then.' If you discounted a couple of dainty little suppers for Oscar, and the one horrible occasion when she had cooked Sunday lunch for his mother. Julia had felt she was in a gravy advertisement and getting lumps in it.

'But you've cooked for quite large numbers?'

'It depends what you mean by large.'

Suzy put her head on one side, allowing a fall of straw-coloured hair to swing free of her cheek. 'Well, we take ten passengers, and three crew, so if we were full, that'd be thirteen. Could you manage that?'

'I expect so.'

'Good,' said Suzy. 'I'm not sure I can. I've never cooked for more than six, and then it's been a nightmare. I did a cookery course when I left school. My parents thought it would be useful.'

Julia felt compelled to ask. 'And was it?'

Suzy seemed doubtful. 'It might be now.' She referred to her list again. 'What about canal experience?'

'None at all.' Julia badly wanted this job, but she didn't want it under false pretences.

'Never mind. Uncle Ralph said if I insisted on experience I'd never get anyone.' Suzy took a gulp of wine. 'And we've got Jason.' She looked at Julia, and Julia saw uncertainty in her prospective employer's face. 'It was – is – Uncle Ralph's business. He'll sell it to me – on easy terms over a few years – if I can make a go of the first season. Otherwise, he'll sell to someone else.'

'How . . . nice.' Personally, Julia had had her fill of responsibility.

'It might be. Uncle Ralph has always been on my side. Against Mummy and Daddy, anyway.' Suzy wrinkled her nose. 'I didn't quite mean that like it sounded. I mean, they love me so much, but they don't seem to want me to be happy. Ralph has always understood how suffocated I feel.'

'Mmm.' Julia tried to sound non-committal and sat with what she hoped was an open, receptive expression on her face. She hadn't been to an interview for years, having worked for Strange's for so long, but she was sure it was a bad idea to comment on her prospective employer's parents. It hadn't done her a lot of good when she'd allowed herself the merest breath of criticism of her ex-fiancé's mother, even if that breath had included the word 'cow'.

'And as I said, we've got Jason.' Suzy wrinkled her nose. 'Which I suppose is a good thing.'

'Only suppose?'

'He's a bit patronising. I met him last summer, when I went on the hotel boats with Ralph. He taught me a lot and he said I was "quite good". But he obviously meant "good considering I was a Daddy's Little Princess".'

11

Julia felt herself flush. She had been having the same thoughts about Suzy herself.

'Which I was,' admitted Suzy cheerfully. 'But not any more. From now on, I'm going to manage without my parents' money and their outdated ideas.'

'Good for you.' Julia had suffered from outdated ideas herself lately.

Suzy referred again to her list. 'Uncle Ralph said I was to ask you why you applied for the job. He said it was very revealing. Not quite sure how.'

Julia decided to give it to her straight. 'I've just broken off an unsuitable engagement and left my job at the same time. My boss and my fiancé were best friends. I've decided I need a complete change and to do something fun.'

'That's sounds a good enough reason. In a way, that's why I'm here. My parents wanted me to marry and settle down too.'

'Aren't you a bit young for that?'

'Of course. But they think I have unsuitable tastes in men. Just because I had an affair with the pool boy!' She made a face. 'But it was never serious. I don't know why they made so much fuss.' She grinned, and a pair of dimples appeared in her delicately made-up cheeks. 'It was after that they rolled out the heir apparent to Daddy's empire. Bor-ring! Tell me about your ex-fiancé.'

'He was boring too, only somehow I managed not to notice. He – well, his mother really – wanted us to have children right away so his old nanny would still be alive to look after them.' She saw the question 'Why did you let yourself get involved with a man like that?' form on Suzy's lips and avoided it. 'He had a heavenly house and a sweet Labrador puppy. Sooty really was the best thing about Oscar.'

'Boring name though. Sooty. For a black dog.'

Julia considered. 'You're right. It does reveal his total lack of imagination.' Julia remembered she was being interviewed and brought herself back to the point. 'Apart from all that, I felt I needed a break from – office life.' Julia was deliberately vague. She didn't want to scare Suzy. 'This job seemed very appealing.'

'Did it? Ralph gave me the advert he always used. I thought it might be a bit *old-fashioned*.'

'Did you want someone younger?' Oscar had given her a complex. Her child-bearing years might be diminishing, but surely she wasn't yet old as an employment prospect?

'Oh no. At least, I don't think so. I mean, you are fit and everything, aren't you?'

'I think so.'

Suzy winced. 'I'm going to have to give up my member-ship of the country club when I leave home, so God knows what will happen to me. Flab City, I expect.' Suzy rearranged the beer mats with long, French-manicured fingers. 'They have a delicious trainer who actually looks good in Lycra. Made it worth the effort of going.'

Julia swallowed. 'Mmm.'

'Would you like another drink?'

'I'm not sure . . .'

'Did you drive here?'

'No. It's not far. I walked.'

'I've got to start doing that soon. Daddy's going to make me give back the car. He thinks by taking away all my toys he'll make me "see sense".'

'Would your parents *make* you marry a man you didn't love?' Julia's own mother delivered some pretty heavy hints, but she hadn't used force yet.

'To be fair, I don't suppose they would, but they want me to do something sensible: i.e., something they want me to do. They think this whole canal thing is ridiculous and won't give me a penny.'

'Well, why should they? What's in it for them?' Suzy seemed a little startled, but Julia persisted. 'I mean, you are grown up. Why should they give you money?'

Suzy looked bewildered. 'No reason at all, really. Except they always have.'

'Lucky you.'

'Lucky in some ways but stifled in others. The trouble with being a "Daddy's Little Princess" is you never know what you can do because you don't ever have to struggle. I don't even know if I can earn my own living, and I'm twenty-four.'

'You mean you've never had a job?'

'Oh yes, I've had jobs – as a receptionist, a demonstrator, a bit of modelling, things like that – but I've never had to live on my salary. Uncle Ralph says' – Suzy took a breath – 'that even living on one's salary isn't really earning a living. He reckons you have to go out and find customers to do that. Being given a salary doesn't really count.'

Julia buried her fingers in her hair. 'I never thought of it like that.'

'No, but he's right. And if I can prove to my family that I can run this business, get it to make money, they may stop trying to groom me into being a company wife. And Uncle Ralph will let me buy it, if I want to. Otherwise, I'll have to go home at the end of the season with my tail between my legs.'

Julia shuddered. 'Tell me about the business then. What is it, exactly?'

Suzy took a breath. 'It's a narrow-boat hotel. Only we have two of them. Narrow boats, that is.'

'Narrow boats? Like barges, you mean?'

'Never say that word!' Suzy was horrified by Julia's unintentional blasphemy. 'They hate it if you call narrow boats barges! Barges are much wider! These are less than seven feet across! Seventy feet long though,' she continued more calmly. 'They used to carry cargo on canals. Almost all the carrying trade has gone on to the roads now, so the canals are almost entirely for recreational use.' Julia had the impression that Suzy was quoting someone else's

14

words. 'Hotel boats are for people who don't want to hire their own boats and do all the lock work and the cooking and stuff.'

'So why do you have two of them? Wouldn't it be easier to just have one boat?'

'Well, there are a couple of hotel boats who just have the one, but they can only take about five passengers. Most of the others are pairs and take ten or twelve. Some of them have en-suite facilities, though Uncle Ralph's don't. His pair take ten, less cost-effective than twelve, of course.' Suzy took a breath and carried on. 'The passengers sleep in the butty, that's the one without an engine, towed by the motor. The motor has some staff accommodation, the galley, the saloon where everyone eats and stuff, and a well-deck where they can sit and look at the scenery. Hang on.' Suzy dived into her bag again. 'I've got last year's brochure somewhere. There's a picture.'

Julia examined the bird's-eye plan of what looked like two elongated railway carriages with pointed ends. The cabins were shown with washbasins and hanging space, the motor boat had a fairly large-looking galley, saloon and sitting area. Everything was telescoped into the narrowness with remarkable ingenuity. 'They look quite spacious.'

'They do on paper. In reality things are pretty tight. But neat, you know? A place for everything and everything in its place and all that.' Suzy frowned. 'Let's have another drink.'

'I've never had much to do with boats,' said Julia, when, on her suggestion, they had blotted up some of the alcohol with shepherd's pie.

'Mostly, it's being able to catch ropes, being strong, and not minding heights,' said Suzy.

'Oh.' Julia didn't like heights, didn't know if she could catch ropes, and didn't, just at that moment, feel terribly strong.

'But don't worry about any of that. There'll be time for you to learn all you need to know before the season starts. The boats are at a boatyard having some work done on them at the moment. It would be good if you could come with me and help get them ready. Then Ralph said he'd help us take them down to Stratford, for our first lot of passengers. Once we're at Stratford, we're on our own. Except for Jason, of course.' Suzy wrinkled her nose again at the mention of his name, giving Julia the distinct impression that Jason was a mixed blessing.

Julia felt she should come clean about her misgivings. 'I'm not sure I'm going to be terribly good at boating. Do you really want to offer me the job? You might have more – more athletic people to see.'

'You're the only one I liked the sound of. One of the others had just finished being a cook on a round-the-world yachting trip – seriously scary. And there was one who sounded a complete airhead with no experience of anything, let alone cooking.' Suzy regarded Julia steadily. 'Uncle Ralph told me I must get someone with common sense, whatever else they didn't have. Besides, all the others were men, and I had to have a woman because we have to share accommodation. Uncle Ralph wouldn't like it if I shacked up with the crew straight away.'

'I suppose not,' said Julia, reassured that she was the best of a bad bunch of candidates. 'And what are they called? The boats, I mean?'

'*Pyramus* and *Thisbe*. It's out of *A Midsummer Night's Dream*. Appropriate as we go to Stratford-upon-Avon such a lot. So' – Suzy gave Julia a look of entreaty which had melted stonier hearts than hers – 'will you come? It's terribly hard work but such fun. And the canals are so wonderful. I'm sure you'll just fall in love with them, like I did.'

Julia felt it must have been love which made an apparent social butterfly willing to give up all the comforts her father could provide. 'I'd really like to. It sounds just what I need at the moment, but hadn't you better check my references and stuff?'

Suzy shook her head. 'Uncle Ralph will meet you and if he doesn't like you, he'll say.' She frowned. 'The wages are crap, I'm afraid. I should have said, but I didn't want to put you off straight away.' She named an extremely meagre sum. 'Will you be able to manage on that?'

Julia gulped, grateful that Oscar need never know how little she was going to be paid. 'I'm going to let my house which should cover my standing orders, council tax and whatever.'

'That's all right then. Will you have any money over?' Suzy spoke with an ingenuousness which revealed that she had never had to think of anything so mundane.

'No.'

It occurred to Julia that if common sense was why she had been employed she ought to show some of it now. Suzy had had three large glasses of wine. 'Tell you what, why don't you come back with me and have some tea? Or even stay the night. I don't think you should drive.'

Suzy shrugged. 'Daddy's going to take my car away anyway, it won't make any difference if I get done for drunken driving.'

'Yes it will. Leave your car and come back with me. I'm not doing anything special tonight – just packing to go and see my sister tomorrow. You can pick it up in the morning.'

'A girls' night in? That would be fun.'

As Julia supported Suzy along the road on her platform soles she realised that a 'girls' night in' was as foreign a notion to Suzy as council tax. But they spent a very pleasant evening sitting in front of the fire, eating pasta, drinking the wine Suzy insisted on buying. They ended their time together as very good friends.

Suzy had offered to give Julia a lift to her sister's, and as they walked back to the pub together the following morning, to retrieve Suzy's car, she took hold of Julia's arm confidingly. 'I feel so much less scared about the whole thing now I know you're going to be with me. It's great to feel I've got a grown-up on my side.'

Julia didn't know what to say. She had just given up Oscar and a well-paid job so she could have a break from being grown up, but she was flattered by Suzy's confidence. 'Thank you. I'll do my best not to let you down.'

Suzy laughed. 'Of course you won't.' She clicked open the doors of her bright scarlet hot hatch, which might as well have had the slogan 'Stop me for Speeding' emblazoned on it. 'Now hop in, and we'll see if I can get you to your sister's without getting lost.'

Angela lived in a pretty village near Oxford, less than ten miles away from Julia, which they reached via a couple of wrong turns. Once Julia had got out, Suzy sped off without waiting to be introduced, having executed a dazzling three-point turn, shouting promises to send Julia details of where and when they would meet again. Julia felt that whatever else working for Suzy might turn out to be, it wouldn't be dull.

Her sister, two years younger than Julia, opened the front door with Petal, three months old and gorgeous, draped over her shoulder.

'Hello, Ju. How'd the interview go?'

Julia embraced her sister. 'I'll tell you in a minute. You look awful! Don't this lot let you have any sleep?'

'Not so's you'd notice.' At this moment Ben, an energetic two-year-old, thrust a toy in Julia's direction as a gesture of well-meaning, and then ran back into the kitchen, overcome with sudden shyness.

'Did you get the job?' asked Angela as they followed Ben.

Julia nodded. 'I did, but don't ask me how much I'm

going to earn because it's probably less than Ben's pocket money. But I think it'll be fun.'

'So what's she like? Your new employer?'

'V. glam, but really sweet and very good fun. Hello, Grace.' Julia addressed the eldest of her nieces and nephews. 'Cool shoes. When you grow out of them, can I have them?'

'If Petal doesn't want them,' Grace agreed. 'I've got a Tamagotchi.'

'Let's see then.'

With her children clamouring for attention, it was some time before Angela had the opportunity to pump her sister for more details about her new job. But eventually they reached the kitchen and she dumped Petal on Julia's lap. 'Here, have your niece for a while and I'll make some coffee. I've had to carry her around all morning.'

'Oh, why?'

'Wind. Last night wasn't so much broken as shattered, into twenty-minute slots. And when Petal finally got off, Ben had a nightmare.'

Julia glanced across at her sister. Never plump, her children had turned her into a wraith. 'I don't know how you do it, Ange.'

'I don't actually have a choice. If you've got children, you have to look after them. Unless you've got a high-powered job and can afford a nanny.' Angela took a restorative draught of coffee. 'So, tell me about yours then.'

'About my high-powered job?' Julia chuckled. 'It won't be as demanding as children, that's for sure, but it's just what I need – different and fun.'

'I never did think Strange's appreciated you.'

'But does anyone appreciate *you*?' Petal had started to grizzle so Julia handed her back, looking on in awe as her sister hefted Ben up, one-handed to share her lap with the baby. 'I can't imagine ever feeling brave enough to have a baby. All that pain, and then no sleep for months and months.'

Angela laughed. 'When the time is right you'll want them. You just haven't found the right man yet. Talking of which, how is Oscar taking it?'

Julia shrugged. 'As you'd expect. He's furious about this whole canal thing.'

Angela looked suddenly sheepish. 'And so's our distinguished brother, by the way. It just slipped out . . .' She held up a defensive hand. 'And having dumped you in it that far, I also tossed in about you and Oscar breaking up.' Angela sighed. 'I'm sorry! But I was tired. Children do scramble your brains rather.'

'Well, it gave him another reason to disapprove of me, I suppose. Something he likes doing.'

'You and Rupert always rub each other up the wrong way, but he's very fond of you. He even suggested you might be able to sue Strange's for constructive dismissal. He said to let him know if you wanted to.'

Julia smiled, touched that her stuffy-solicitor brother should have been so thoughtful. 'I don't suppose I've a hope in hell, seeing as I walked out, but it's kind of him to offer. And have you heard from Our Mother lately?'

Angela nodded, used to being the member of the family who kept the other members in touch. 'She had some hippy staying with her, chopping wood and putting up wind chimes in her garden. You must tell her how you got on. She's mad keen on this boating idea.'

'She would be. In some ways, she's really cool, as Grace would say.'

Angela broke off the corner of a chocolate biscuit. 'Mmm. To everyone except her daughters. Think of all those young men she attracts!'

'And tries to pass on to me,' said Julia grimly. 'I swear the only reason she didn't like Oscar was because she didn't find him for me, and it meant she had to stop matchmaking.'

'She'll be free to do that again now,' said Angela. 'But have you heard about her latest alternative therapy?'

'What? Radionics?'

Angela nodded. 'She asked me to send a lock of Petal's hair so she could "put it on the box" and work out why she isn't sleeping through the night yet.'

'Oh goodness. What did you do?'

'I told her Petal wasn't sleeping because she was only three months old and that she hadn't any hair to spare.' She stroked her daughter's down-covered pate.

Julia shook her head. 'It's funny, Dad wasn't all that stiff and conventional. I don't know why Mum went so New Age hippy when he died. Does Rupert know about the radionics?'

'Oh yes, but you know Rupe. Mum can't do any wrong in his eyes. Maybe he'd feel differently if she suggested he tried colonic irrigation every time he confessed to being tired. I like coffee, but not as an enema. Let's have another cup.'

Angela poured more coffee for them both and they sank into silence. Their mother was one of those people whom everyone felt they were lucky to have. And while they were both devoted to her, they would have found it easier if she'd been someone else's mother. To the rest of the world she was 'charmingly eccentric' and extremely charismatic. To her daughters, she was highly critical, with standards they could never live up to. But it was hard to moan about a mother who was on the surface so wonderful.

Later that day, when Julia phoned her, she found her mother was indeed full of enthusiasm for the canals. 'I've just had a young man staying with me who lived on a narrow boat while he was at uni.' Julia's mother was prone to picking up the slang of younger, if not current, generations. 'He said the vibes were far out.'

Chapter Three

Two weeks later, in the fluorescent gloom of the coffee shop at Reading station, Julia was wondering if she had made a dreadful mistake. She had drunk three cups of coffee and twice asked the woman behind the counter to mind her bags while she visited the Ladies' Room. Still Suzy had not appeared.

True, she was not actually due for another five minutes, but a station coffee shop was rather a vague location. Supposing there was another one, bigger and more prominent, that Julia had somehow missed?

Perhaps Suzy was too young and flippant to work for. Perhaps the things about her which were so attractive, her unconventional attitude to men, her ignorance about the harsher realities of life and her cheerfulness, would drive Julia mad when she was having to take orders from her.

But now Julia's cottage was filled with dried flowers and incense sticks and someone else's photographs. A friend of a friend of her sister was installed, sucking up to Julia's cat, growing organic vegetables in the garden, keeping an eye on Julia's elderly and very dear neighbours, and paying handsomely for the privilege. There was no going back there until the end of September.

Julia had just decided to buy the current edition of *The Lady* in case she needed another job in a hurry, when Suzy appeared. She had with her a large quantity of expensive leather sports bags and a handsome young fogey who had 'eligible suitor for the daughter of a Captain of Industry' written all over him. He had only just avoided wearing a tweed jacket and brogues.

'Hi, Julia!' said Suzy. 'Love the highlights! They make you look much – They give you a lift.' Having told the world that she was not naturally sun-kissed and golden, Suzy embraced Julia in a cloud of something pungent and expensive. 'This is George, who very kindly gave me a lift up. Only' – she turned towards her consort – 'is it a lift when you're not actually going there? Anyway, George, this is Julia.'

'How do you do?' George gave Julia a polite smile. Perfect manners, good teeth and better prospects. Julia, who had been told that George was the young man picked out by Daddy for his Little Princess, easily understood why Suzy didn't want to marry him. He was a younger, more easy-going version of Oscar.

'Well, Suzy-pooze,' he said. 'I'll be in touch. Must get off and see my old lady – my mother,' he explained to Julia, who, being so much older herself, might not have understood. Julia forced a smile.

'Thank you so much for bringing me all this way, George!' Suzy hung on his neck, and then gave him the sort of kiss which would ensure that his affection for her would endure as long as she needed it to.

Having got rid of her suitor, Suzy got down to business. 'What time is our train?'

Julia found herself smiling. Suzy used people like other people used tissues, and yet somehow it didn't affect her charm.

'Ten past three. Platform three. We'll have to cross the bridge.'

'Will we? Oh shit. I should have kept George. I'll never get all my stuff across.'

'I'll help you. I haven't got a great deal,' Julia went on reproachfully. 'You said not to bring much.'

'Oh, I know, but I didn't want to have to crawl back home for something vital I'd forgotten. I'll have a sort-out when we get there and give away what I don't need.'

'We'd better move. The train'll be here in four minutes.'

'OK.' Suzy hung as many bags as she could on her arms and then looked reproachfully at the remaining one, as if it had tagged along uninvited.

It was the size of a small body-bag and, when Julia heaved it off the floor, it felt as if the body were still in it. 'You don't go in for weight-training, do you?'

'Far too much like hard work. Why do you ask?'

'I just wondered if you'd brought your weights with you, that's all.'

'Is it heavy? Sorry. It's just some shoes, my stereo, radio, stuff like that.'

Stuff which Julia had reconciled herself to doing without. 'Right. Well, we'd better go.'

They stumbled across the bridge and arrived on the platform just as the train pulled in. Somehow, they managed to get on to it before it pulled away, and while Julia stuffed bags into the luggage compartment, Suzy found seats. She also found a young student to flirt with, who would be useful, Julia realised, when they came to get off.

Uncle Ralph was on the platform to meet them. He opened the door and fielded the bags as Julia and the student handed them out to him.

'Thank you so much for your help,' Suzy said to the student as she squeezed past him. 'We couldn't have managed without you. What did you say your name was?' She kissed his cheek and then turned her attention to her Uncle Ralph.

He was a good-looking man in his early seventies. Of medium height and fairly stocky build, he had a lot of thick grey hair and a wide smile. He wore corduroy trousers and a faded polo shirt. He embraced Suzy as she stepped off the train in the wake of her luggage.

'Hello, girl! What do you want with all that junk? There

won't be room for half of it. What the hell is it anyway?'

Julia got off the train in Suzy's wake, and waited for Ralph to free himself from Suzy's bear-like hug. When he did, he shook her hand and grinned. 'So you're the girl idiot enough to work for my dizzy niece? Well, I'm glad to see you. She doesn't know her arse from her elbow.'

'Uncle Ralph!'

Julia couldn't tell if Suzy's indignation was at her uncle's comment or his choice of language.

'But she means well and she's got guts, so she should be all right. Come and meet Jason. Suzy and he are old friends.'

Jason emerged from the back of the platform. He was wearing an oil-streaked boiler suit and a surly expression.

'Hello, Jason,' said Suzy. 'Lovely to see you again.' Suzy's smile was the full thousand watts of charm, dimples thrown in.

Jason gave Suzy only the smallest of nods in recognition that they knew each other, and Julia wondered if he was shy.

'And this is Julia,' said Uncle Ralph, his hand on her shoulder. 'I gather she's a first-rate cook.'

Jason's expression indicated that he existed entirely on engine oil. First-rate cooks were nothing to him.

'Hi!' Julia smiled with what she hoped was sincerity and comradeship and got nothing in return. Jason wasn't shy, she decided. Just rude. He regarded their luggage with the utmost distaste and shouldered the body-bag.

'Come on,' said Ralph. 'Let's get all this into the car.'

Neither woman spoke as they huddled together in the back of Ralph's ancient Volvo, surrounded by their possessions. Suzy's probably nervous at the prospect of having to give orders to Jason, thought Julia. And she's got more to lose than I have. I'm just nervous in case Jason bites my hand off when I try to feed him.

Jason leaped out of the front seat when Ralph turned

into the boatyard, and hurried round to the boot. He heaved out Suzy's body-bag and loped off.

'He's a good lad at heart,' said Ralph, trying to convince himself. 'But he's not used to seeing women as people.'

Well at least I'll be on familiar territory there, thought Julia.

'And he knows everything there is to know about boats and how to work them,' Ralph was saying. 'Can you manage, Julia?'

Julia nodded, looking around her, fascinated by the variety of boats which filled the crowded yard. They ranged from cruisers, paint peeling and glazed with a fine layer of moss, which lurked under ripped tarpaulins, to smartly varnished, clinker-built river craft, restored to museum standard, and many stages in between. They all looked huge out of the water.

'The butty – that's the one without the engine, where the passengers sleep, called *Thisbe* – is in the dry dock,' said Ralph. 'She's due out tomorrow but we've got to get a coat of black varnish on her first.'

'Is that the Royal "We",' said Suzy, 'or do you mean us as well?'

'You as well. Actually, you two on your own.' Ralph grinned. 'There's nothing like painting the sides of a seventy-foot boat to get an idea of how big she is,' he added to Julia.

'I'm sure,' she muttered.

'Come on to the motor. That's *Pyramus*, she's tied up a little way along the tow-path. Did you get lunch on the train? No? Well, hurry up and we'll get something at the pub. You can see the motor later.'

The General Custer was the sort of pub which relied on the lunchtime trade of the local firms. Ralph found them a seat in a section which seemed to be full of people he knew. They all looked at Suzy and Julia with blatant curiosity and, in Suzy's case, barely disguised lust. Jason hadn't come with them. Because, Ralph explained, the landlord had recently banned boiler suits.

'This is my niece Suzy and her friend Julia,' Ralph explained to the group of men who, Julia assumed, all had connections with the boatyard. 'What would you girls like to drink?'

Julia discovered that although she'd hated being called a girl by Peter Strange, she enjoyed being lumped in with Suzy. Oscar had always made her feel like a lady, recently of declining years.

'Oh, Campari and soda for me, Ralph.'

Ralph regarded his niece. 'You can't drink Campari on the cut – that's another name for canals,' he explained for Julia's benefit. 'Have a decent drink.'

Suzy made a face. 'I'll have a half of lager. I suppose I can't have lime in it?'

'No. Julia?'

'I was going to have a Dry Martini with a twist of lemon, but I'll settle for lager too.'

Ralph grinned, glad that his niece had had the gumption to employ someone with a sense of humour.

'So, you're taking on Ralph's hotel boats,' said a small man with a large beard to Suzy. 'Must be mad. You'll never make money out of them. My name's Ted, by the way.'

'And I'm Donald,' said another of the men, who had a Scots accent and a jumper hanging six inches below his bomber jacket. 'How are you going to like working with Jason?'

'Jason's very good with the boats.' Suzy glanced at her uncle, who was still at the bar.

'Oh aye,' agreed Donald. 'None better. Just don't let him near the passengers.'

'I don't remember him being that bad. And he's worked for Ralph for two years, so he can't be.' Suzy was looking anxious.

'Aye, but he had his girlfriend with him, didn't he? She kept him sweet. But she ran off with a lock-keeper towards the end of last season. Before that he just hated most people, now he hates everyone.'

'Here we are.' Ralph set a battered tray on the table and Donald and Ted claimed their pints. 'There are some sandwiches on their way. I hope you haven't been scaring my little girl,' he said to Donald and Ted.

'Oh no,' said Ted. 'Just telling her about Jason's disappointment in love.'

'Yes, well, he's got over it now. And there's no one better than Jason for teaching you about boat-handling, Julia,' said Ralph firmly. A waitress appeared with a tottering pile of cheese and pickle. 'Tuck in, girls. And when you've had something to eat, I'll show you what you've got to do. Better not to visit the dry dock on an empty stomach.' He winked, and lifted his pint glass. 'Here's to a successful season and me not having to sell the boats before the end of it.'

'What!' Suzy put down her lager. 'What are you talking about?'

'Nothing, really,' said Ralph. 'Just a temporary hiccup with the overdraft. New manager at the bank, but I'll get him sorted. No need for you to worry about it.'

Julia, who would have instantly become paralysed with anxiety, noted that the small frown which had wrinkled Suzy's brow disappeared immediately.

'And here's to Julia not running off with a rich American passenger,' said Donald.

Julia gave him a reproving look, but inside she was glad to note that in spite of all Peter Strange and Oscar had done to her, there was life in the old girl yet!

Nevertheless, it was with some trepidation and a twinge of indigestion that Julia prepared to inspect her new home.

'This is the Grand Union Canal,' said Ralph as, having

all used the pub's facilities, they crossed the road bridge to the boatyard. He spoke about the canal as if he were introducing an old friend. 'It goes all the way from London to Birmingham and it's wide.'

'Not very, surely?' said Julia, looking at the strip of water which ran under the bridge, trying to see the magic which was so obvious to Suzy and the others.

'It's not to do with the width of the cut,' Ralph explained. 'But the locks. The Grand Union locks are wide enough to take a pair of boats, like ours, breasted up, i.e., side by side, at the same time. With narrow canals, the locks are only seven feet wide and you have to put the boats in separately.'

'I see,' Julia lied.

'I'm sorry there's not time to tell you a bit more about it before you start work, but there isn't. Your stuff will be fine in the motor for now.' He paused on the arc of the bridge to admire his proudest possession. 'She looks grand, doesn't she? Joan and I used to take her cruising on the canals in the winter, when there's not much else about. You get the mist on the water, the hoar-frost on the trees; it's a real picture.'

'Chilly though,' suggested Julia, not quite convinced.

'Not at all! With the stove going and the central heating, it's cosy as anything. Now,' Ralph jolted himself out of his lapse into lyricism, 'you've got to black varnish *Thisbe*.'

'Is that the butty? The one without the engine?'

Ralph nodded. '*Butty* is Welsh for "mate". I'll let Suzy show her to you while I go and sort you out with some varnish.'

'Well,' said Suzy when she had led Julia to the dry dock. 'What do you think?'

Chapter Four

They were in a cavernous, tin-roofed shed lit by a series of fluorescent tubes which gave everything that wasn't already black a sickly green hue. A long, coffin-shaped section with wooden gates at one end had a wooden boat which looked as long as a football pitch in it. Water ran along the bottom echoing eerily against the brick walls of the dock. It was freezing cold and smelled of wet dog. No one, not even the most romantically inclined, could see it as anything but hell on earth. Julia struggled to think of a positive comment.

'"Dry" dock seems to be something of a misnomer,' she said, trying to sound cheerful. 'I'm glad you warned me to bring wellies.'

'That was Uncle Ralph. I had to buy some.' Suzy pulled several rings off her fingers and tucked them into her cleavage. 'Thank you for not walking out. The dry dock is such a hole, I wouldn't blame you. But I promise you, in daylight, in the water, in the sunshine, with her doors open, *Thisbe* is really pretty.'

Julia tried to make the leap of imagination, and shivered instead. 'I'll take your word for it. Perhaps it'll look better when we've painted it.'

They negotiated the slippery steps which led down to the bottom of the dock and looked up at the task before them. They had been issued with rubber gloves, old cotton scarves to tie round their hair and boiler suits, already stiff with the black varnish from previous jobs. Even in these unpromising clothes and fluorescent light, Suzy, Julia noted, still managed to look attractive.

Ralph had delivered an enormous tin of paint and two four-inch brushes. Suzy handed Julia one of these. 'Here. We'd better get going.'

Julia took the brush. 'I don't suppose you could use a roller,' she said doubtfully.

Suzy shook her head knowingly. 'No, you've got to work it really well into the seams. It's a hell of a job. Trust bloody Jason to say he's allergic to black varnish' – Suzy levered the lid off the can – 'so we have to do it on our own. I bet he isn't at all.'

Julia inspected the substance which gleamed sinisterly in the gloom of the dry dock. 'I don't know. It smells terribly strong. It's making my nose run.'

'It's got bitumen in it, so try not to breathe,' said Ralph from behind them. 'And if you get any on your skin, wash it off immediately. And let me know when you run out. I'm just mixing up some challico.'

'Trust the men to give themselves the nice jobs,' said Suzy. 'I'm sure we'd rather mix up challico than paint a mile of boat.'

'I doubt it, m'dear.' Ralph chuckled. 'Challico's made out of horse shit and tar.'

'And what on earth do you do with that?' asked Suzy.

'Pay the seams, after you've caulked them. A sort of nautical equivalent of grouting,' he added for Julia's benefit. 'Jason's going to do the bit round the front end where we had the new plank. Now, get going. You've got about seven hundred and fifty square feet of boat to paint. And you've got to finish it today.'

'Oh God!' Suzy was aghast. 'Why?'

'Boat's due out first thing tomorrow. It's got to have tonight to dry.' He went off, whistling cheerfully.

Suzy and Julia looked at each other in horror.

'Here goes then,' said Julia. She dipped her brush into the can of varnish and drew it along the top plank. It

31

glistened satisfactorily. 'It does look nice, I'll say that for it.'

'Huh!' said Suzy.

The women had finished one side, and were not looking forward to starting the other, when Ralph, Donald and Ted came clattering into the dry dock to join them. After the whole party agreed that Ralph whistling songs from the shows was less than inspirational, Ted got Suzy's CD player going, put on Oasis, and turned up the volume. The work went much more quickly and they finished painting just before eight o'clock.

Julia had rarely been as tired, and never as dirty. Her face glowed from proximity to the varnish and, in spite of wearing gloves, her hands and arms were speckled with black. Her newly highlighted hair was black where it had escaped from its protective scarf. Her days of foreign clients, business-class travel and lap-tops seemed to belong to another life. And Suzy was as dirty. They staggered out of the dry dock feeling like miners at the end of a long shift and made their way stiffly along the tow-path to the motor boat which Suzy promised would be 'really warm and cosy'.

'I've never worked so hard in my life!' said Suzy, leaning on the bow of the motor.

Jason, comparatively clean, in spite of his personal oil-slick which seemed to be a permanent feature, expressed satisfaction at this state of affairs. 'Don't suppose you have. But you can't come into the saloon in your boots.'

Suzy swore mildly and starting kicking them off, using one to prise off the other. She abandoned both in the area outside the doors to the cabin which Julia had learned was the well-deck, before going into the saloon.

Julia was having difficulty getting aboard. Her usually agile limbs were shaking with fatigue. 'Give us a hand, Jason,' she snapped, in no mood to ask nicely.

Jason reluctantly steadied Julia as she stepped over the side of the boat and landed in the well-deck with a thump. Too tired to move, she looked about her.

The front of the boat was arranged as an outdoor sitting area for, possibly, six people. There was an iron framework over it that had canvas covers, which, presumably, came down if it rained. The seats had lockers underneath and one of these was open. It was full of tins of paint.

'Paint!' she groaned to Ted, who'd followed her aboard, lured by promises of fish and chips and beer. 'I couldn't lift so much as a fork to my mouth, let alone a paintbrush, ever again.'

'We'll put your dinner on the floor for you then. Either that, or you could ask Jason to help you.'

Julia regarded him weakly. 'Jason won't let me in with my boots on, and they're terribly tight.'

Ted grinned. He picked up one of Julia's feet and pulled. Eventually, after a lot of tugging, the boot came off. He did the same with the other. 'There you are. Free to enter.'

Julia smiled and patted his arm in gratitude. If only Jason and Ted could swap personalities, just for the summer, she'd feel a lot happier about the whole venture.

She opened the double doors and was welcomed by warmth and light. She smiled involuntarily. 'Heaven!' she said to Ted behind her. 'It's wonderful!'

'It's got really efficient central heating,' said Ted, catching her arm as she made to sit down. 'But unless you want Jason after you, get your boiler suit off before you go near the upholstery. He's the only one who's allowed to make anything dirty.'

Julia wrenched at the poppers which held her boiler suit together and stumbled out of it, then she collapsed on to the banquette by the door, looking around her. It was extremely narrow, yet it seemed comfortable and homely. Quite how it would accommodate ten passengers for dinner, Julia assumed she would find out. Suzy was nowhere to be seen.

Ralph, who had finished work earlier than the rest of them, on the pretext of having some urgent business, emerged from the stable doors behind which was the kitchen – or should that be galley? Julia made a note to ask Suzy.

'Cup of tea, or alcohol?' said Ralph.

'Alcohol,' Ted and Julia said together. 'Neat,' added Julia, not caring if Ralph thought his niece had employed an alcoholic. 'A tumbler of it, please.'

Ralph chuckled. He took two glasses from a concealed cupboard and poured into them not quite a tumblerful, but a respectable three fingers. 'You've gone through a baptism of fire today. It'll be downhill from here. Suzy's gone to Donald's boat to wash her hair.'

Julia sipped her whisky and contemplated Suzy's skewed priorities. Even if she had an atom of energy left over, Julia wouldn't waste it on her appearance. It was such a relief not to have to look business-like and professional any more.

'Sorry I can't offer you a shower on this boat,' said Ralph, handing Julia a packet of crisps. 'We're short of water and there's a problem with the pump. We had to order a new one in the end.'

Julia looked up at him pathetically. She hadn't minded Suzy having clean hair when her own was crisp with paint, but the thought of going to bed in all her dirt was too awful to contemplate. Like a paintbrush, unless she was thoroughly cleaned after use, she would be rigid and unworkable in the morning.

'Jason's been trying to fix it all day.' Ralph was obviously trying to show Jason in a good light.

He failed. It might have been unreasonable, but Julia couldn't help thinking that if Jason had got anything like as cold and dirty as she and Suzy, he would have got the pump going somehow. She took a gulp of whisky and closed her eyes.

She opened them again as Suzy and Jason appeared in

the galley, presumably having got there from the stern of the boat. Whether their relationship had improved at all, Julia couldn't tell, but they both looked a lot cleaner than she did.

'Black varnishing has to be the worst job in the world.' Suzy sank down on to the banquette next to Julia.

'Wait till you've emptied the toilets a few times,' said Jason, sprawling into a chair opposite with far less excuse.

Suzy scowled at him, accepted the glass Ralph handed her and took a gulp. 'Yuck, whisky. I hate whisky.'

Ralph made to take the glass back, but Suzy held on to it. 'No, I need it. I am completely shattered.'

'Jason'll go out for fish and chips soon,' said Ralph soothingly. 'I was explaining to Julia about you girls not being able to have showers. Still' – he brightened up – 'I expect you'd've been too tired to have them anyway.'

Suzy, with clean hair, and more accustomed to the vagaries of boat plumbing than Julia, was philosophical. 'You're probably right. Where have you put us? In the crew cabin in this boat?'

'No, no. Jason and I are in here. We thought you girls would be better off in the back cabin of the butty.'

There was an uncomprehending pause. 'But the butty's in dry dock,' said Suzy.

'You noticed.' Jason helped himself to more whisky.

'But I read a sign about not being allowed to live on a boat in dry dock,' went on Suzy, ignoring Jason.

'That's why it's very important you don't let Terry Merchant know you're sleeping on it. It means you won't be able to light the stove, I'm afraid.'

'Uncle Ralph! That's like condemning us to sleep in a fridge! It'll be icy.'

'Dark too,' said Jason. 'The batteries aren't connected.'

Julia and Suzy regarded Ralph with disbelieving horror. 'I'm used to being dirty on the boats, Uncle Ralph, but not dark and cold.'

35

'I'm sorry, girls. We tried to get the boat ready earlier, but what with one thing and another, we didn't.'

Ted laughed. 'When I see a boat that's ready before the absolute last moment, I'll shave my beard off.'

'Is there somewhere else we could sleep?' asked Julia. 'Just while it's in dry dock?'

Ralph shook his head. 'All the passenger accommodation is on the butty too, and me and Jason are in here. It's only for a night, and you won't really need the stove, will you? If you get straight into bed?'

'It's the middle of winter, Uncle Ralph! It'll be freezing!'

'It's the middle of March, if a bit on the nippy side. But I'll find you some extra bedding and you'll be fine. Just think of it as camping. In permanent darkness.'

Suzy groaned and held out her glass to Jason, who was nearest the bottle. 'Whisky's all right when you get used to it.'

The two girls were standing on the side of the darkened dry dock contemplating the plank which led from the side of the dry dock to the boat. Their only illumination was provided by a torch Uncle Ralph had given to Suzy and, although they were both exhausted, neither of them was exactly eager to make the short journey to bed.

'I've never been camping,' admitted Suzy, shining the torch into the water at the bottom of the dry dock. 'We were going to once. At one of those sites where the tents are already put up for you, so I'd have other children to play with. But when Daddy realised how near the other tents were, and that he'd have to walk miles to the loo, he took us off to a hotel.'

'Did you mind not having anyone to play with on holiday?'

'I coped. I think it's why I developed a passion for pool boys so early, though. Would you like to go first?'

'Not particularly. I'm not all that good with heights and

36

narrow planks. I have been camping, though,' she added, so as not to appear a complete wimp.

'Nor am I, actually,' said Suzy. 'But I'm not staying here all night. And I'm not asking bloody Jason for help. Here goes.'

She swung her leg over the rail which surrounded the dock and crossed to the boat. She held out a hand to Julia. 'It's only about three steps. Come on.'

Julia decided that if she fell into the dock she would only break a leg, which, although very painful, would mean she could go home, have a bath, and get a proper job. In seconds, she was holding Suzy's hand and clambering down into the tiny well-deck, which was hardly big enough for both of them.

'Mind your head on the tiller. Let's go in.'

Only partially aided by Uncle Ralph's torch, the two girls examined their surroundings. Suzy had seen the back cabin many times, but in spite of the intense cold, Julia found it fascinating. There was a stove – tiny, but big enough to cook on – a lot of brass which caught the light of the torch, and a row of lace-plates. Every flat surface seemed to be painted.

'There are bits which are traditionally rose panels, and castle panels. There's always a castle on the front of the table-cupboard.' Suzy shone the torch at the picture of a romanticised castle, with mountains in the background and a river in front. 'But it's too late to have the narrow-boat painting lecture now. Besides, you'll get it from Ralph later. Now, we can either sleep separately, one on the side bed' – she indicated the narrow bench running along the side of the cabin which was digging into the back of Julia's legs – 'and one in the cross bed, which is meant to be a double. Or, as we've got sleeping bags, and it is the Arctic, we can both sleep in the double. Then we can share the duvet Ralph gave us. You poke your legs into that hole. It's just about long enough if you're not very tall.'

Julia, who until that moment had thought she could quite happily sleep on a rail, decided the side bed was just too narrow. 'I'm not very tall. If you don't mind – it is freezing – perhaps sharing the double would be best.'

'We'll die of hypothermia otherwise,' Suzy agreed. 'Fortunately, Uncle Ralph goes in for really good sleeping bags.'

Somehow, after much banging of elbows, bruising of shins and apologies for squashing each other, they managed to get their teeth brushed. Mouths full of foam, they simultaneously decided that the best way to dispose of their toothpaste was by spitting it into the dock, taking care not to splatter on the newly varnished hull.

'Disgusting,' said Suzy, wiping her mouth. 'But what else could we do?'

'It'll all be washed away in the stream by morning,' said Julia, 'but even if it isn't, the boat's coming out at eight o'clock. They won't notice a bit of toothpaste.'

'I don't usually get up much before ten.'

It was seven o'clock when Uncle Ralph appeared in their cabin with two half-empty mugs of tea. 'Come on, girls, rise and shine, the sun's splitting the rocks.'

'You may say that,' said Suzy, taking a mug, 'we couldn't possibly comment. Uncle Ralph was a sailor before he came on the canals,' she explained to Julia. 'He's got a colourful expression for every occasion.' Suzy didn't make this sound like a compliment.

'Thanks for the tea,' said Julia, looking into her mug. 'You really shouldn't have bothered.'

'Sorry I spilt most of it. But I wanted to make sure you were up and dressed before Terry Merchant appears. He's usually here about half past seven.'

'Ohmygod! Why?' Suzy withdrew her legs, still in the sleeping bag, and, after a brief tussle with the duvet, swung herself into a sitting position.

'So he can make sure there's no rubbish in the dry dock before he fills it. Don't dawdle.' Ralph clambered out of the double doors, leaving them open so what little warmth had accumulated during the night was lost.

Julia stumbled past Suzy in order to shut them again. 'That Terry person'll see the toothpaste. He might shout at us.' But Julia's plaintive cry fell on deaf ears; Suzy was busy cleaning her teeth again.

It was exciting watching the water fill the dry dock, gradually coming up the sides of the boat until it floated free of its railway sleepers. It was even more exciting seeing it emerge into daylight, poled by Jason, who stood on the roof, and pulled by Ralph. While the sun wasn't exactly hot, it was shining, and for the first time, Julia could see *Thisbe* in her full glory.

Jason had repainted the stern-end with traditional diamonds and lozenges. The name had been done with all the proper shading. It was as smart as the proverbial paint.

'It looks wonderful,' Julia said to Jason when he jumped back down on to the tow-path, having poled the boat alongside. 'You are clever to do all that intricate brushwork, and those flowers.'

'Roses. All it takes is a steady hand and a good eye. And the proper paint, of course. None of these new fancy finishes.'

Julia, who wanted to get to know Jason in a more positive way, prepared to listen to a lecture.

'Everyone thinks they can do traditional canal painting nowadays. Or they use transfers.' He spat out the word. 'I use the traditional, lead-based paint, like they did in the old days.'

Ralph came up behind them, having secured the boat. 'When I first came on to the cut, twenty-odd years ago, everyone used those modelling paints. Traditional! My elbow! No boatman worth his salt would have used lead-based paint if he could have got something easier.'

Julia, seeing she was in the middle of a conversation about paint which was only marginally more exciting than watching it dry, drifted away to let them pole the butty into position alongside the motor. She wanted to inspect the inside of *Pyramus*, where the galley was, in daylight and when not half dead with fatigue.

The saloon had pairs of wooden steps leading down from double doors in the side with storage space underneath and wide enough to sit on.

The galley was concealed from the public gaze only by a stable door and a pair of top doors, which were hooked back, and obviously never closed. Julia could see that it enhanced the feeling of spaciousness, which was considerable, considering the boat was less than seven feet wide, but she didn't really fancy cooking under observation. She hoped that people would stay on the banquette, up by the doors.

There was a table which hung flush with the wall, with, presumably, some way of supporting it when it was in use. Folding chairs were stacked in between the steps and a small desk, which doubled as a bar area. Wine glasses were suspended from wooden pegs above the bar and there were bottles on the top. The tumblers, she discovered, were kept inside the cupboard on the top step. A card-index box indicated that people helped themselves and wrote down what they'd had, which was a relief to Julia. It would be bad enough cooking where the paying public could see her, without being expected to tot up bar bills at the same time.

With some trepidation, she pushed open the stable door to the galley. Given Ralph's *laissez-faire* attitude to their sleeping arrangements last night, he might easily expect Julia to cook for thirteen people on a camping-gas stove. But no. There was a full-size cooker, presumably run off bottled gas, a fridge, and a catering-size liquidiser, powered by she knew not what. There was a full-size sink and a working surface, which, if not exactly lavish, might be adequate if one was really well organised. Julia realised that her unfortunate tendency to spread herself in the kitchen would have to be curbed. But basically the galley was light and attractive, and promised to be pleasant, if somewhat cramped, to work in.

Beyond the galley was a bathroom with shower and washbasin, crammed into something the size of a broom cupboard. There was a long list of instructions pinned up above the loo. Why? Julia wondered. Were loos on boats really so complicated? As there was no one about to find out if she did it wrong, Julia had a practice run, including a much-needed wash. All it needed, she decided afterwards, was some good quality air freshener to make it almost acceptable.

'Hi!' Suzy appeared just as Julia was reversing out. 'Can you put the kettle on? We're going to set off up to Stratford in a minute and Ted and Donald are coming with us – for the first bit, anyway, and they want a cup of coffee while Ralph and Jason argue about the dry-dock fees. It's so exciting!'

Suzy's enthusiasm was catching. Julia made coffee and brought it up to the others, where they sat about, Ted and Donald terrifying Suzy and Julia with tales of boats springing rivets in tunnels and other horrors. By the time Jason and Ralph had returned and the party was ready to leave, some of Julia's keenness had turned to nerves.

There was a crowd of critical onlookers watching their departure. Both boats were untied, and Jason, on the motor with Suzy, set off slowly, picking up the butty by grabbing first one and then the other short looped rope which hung from its bow.

Ralph, who was on the butty with Julia, exchanged rude remarks with the audience until Jason completed this manoeuvre and they were pulled out of earshot.

The huge wooden tiller, which Ralph referred to as an

41

'ellum, had been turned over so it curved downwards, and could now move the enormous rudder.

'You push the tiller the opposite way to the way you want to go,' said Ralph. 'But in fact, on cross-straps like this, when you're so close to the motor, you don't have to do much, unless you're going round a really bad bend. On a snubber or a snatcher, you have a bit more to do.'

Julia decided if she needed to know what snubbers and snatchers were, someone would tell her, and concentrated on pushing the tiller in the right direction.

'Think of it as a pencil: if your nose goes in one direction, your rear end goes in the other.' Ralph had jumped up so he was sitting on the roof of the back cabin. 'If you sit up here, can you see to steer? When the stove's lit, it's very cosy.'

Julia, shorter and less agile than her seventy-year-old companion, wriggled herself up. 'I can just about see, but I couldn't move the tiller very far over.'

'That won't matter for a while.' Ralph indicated a guide book which was open on the sliding hatch. 'I'll show you where we're going. Look.'

Julia followed the line of his finger as he turned the pages. 'I see. So what are all those little arrows?'

'Locks. We'll be all right for today. It's the Grand Union all the way, which, as you'll remember, is broad, so we can put both boats in at once. But after we turn off here' – his finger stabbed the place – 'they're single locks. We have to go in one at a time.'

Julia was about to ask how they got the engineless butty along without the motor when she became aware of a commotion in front of them.

'Oh my God,' said Ralph. 'What's happened now? The motor's stopped. It must be stemmed up.' He shot her a quick glance. 'Stuck on the bottom.'

The noise of the motor died away exposing some very colourful language from Jason directed towards Suzy.

'Don't you swear at me!' she hurled back at him. 'It's not my bloody fault there's a mattress in the cut! I can't see through the water seventy bloody feet ahead of me! Any more than you can!'

Even seventy feet away, Julia wanted to duck. Ralph climbed on to the roof and strode down the butty to the motor. He jumped down on to the counter and disappeared into the engine room. Julia didn't know whether to go and give Suzy moral support, or keep out of the way.

Opting for the latter course, she was just wondering if she should try and light the stove, when she became aware of shouting behind her.

'Would you mind getting your boat out of the way?' It was a small, fierce woman in a navy-blue track-suit, who had overdosed on assertiveness training. She was standing on the bow of a tiny plastic boat, which, in spite of its size, had as much attitude as its owner. 'Just because you're four times bigger than anything else on the canal, it doesn't give you the right to block it!'

Before Julia could apologise, explain, or make any other gesture of submission, the woman took another breath and carried on. 'Those boats are far too big for little canals like this. You shouldn't be allowed to have them. My husband's ringing British Waterways on the mobile right now. He'll get you out of the way! Well, don't just stand there with your mouth open! Do something!'

Chapter Five

Deprived of forward motion, the butty's rear end had drifted across the canal, blocking the way. Only briefly did Julia consider shouting for help. This was her chance to prove she was as boaty as anyone.

The woman's continual screaming didn't help. Trying to ignore it, Julia scrambled up on to the roof of the butty and spotted the long pole which lay there, resting against the side rails. She picked it up and stabbed at the opposite bank against which the butty's stern was now resting. She pushed and, to her surprise, *Thisbe* moved quite easily. Julia pushed again, harder this time, and got the butty back to where it belonged, directly behind the motor boat.

'I think you'll discover,' she said with dignity to the red-faced woman, slipping back into calming-down-indignant-client mode, 'that canals were designed for boats of these dimensions. You will also notice there is now ample room for you to pass. I am so sorry for any inconvenience.'

At that moment, the woman's husband emerged from the cabin holding a mobile phone. 'Waterways say they can't get here until this afternoon at the earliest.'

'We can get past *now*, you silly man!' said the woman, who, having been put in her place by Julia, now turned on her husband. 'Why do you always have to make so much fuss?'

Julia watched them chug by feeling pleased with herself. There'd been a problem with the boat, and she'd solved it on her own.

'You all right?' asked Ralph, a good quarter of an hour later. 'Went over a bloody mattress. Took a hell of a time to get the prop free.'

'I've been fine. Admiring the scenery. It's really pretty out here, isn't it?'

Ralph gave the fields a cursory glance. ''T's OK. Better further up though. Shall I light the stove? You look frozen.'

The first lock had been made ready for them by Donald and Ted. Two large gates were open to a brick-built structure which, although described by everyone as wide, looked a tight fit for a pair of boats.

'Now we're going to breast up,' said Ralph. 'Watch. Jason can't brake to slow down the motor, so he's got to go into reverse to stop his forward thrust, but the butty will carry on, and come alongside it.'

Jason had cast off one of the straps which caused the butty's nose to swing over. He then flicked the other free while Ralph kept the tiller steady, so the butty wouldn't swing into the bank. There was a loud engine noise and a lot of bubbling water as Jason put the boat into reverse, and the butty slid in close to the motor.

Ralph climbed on to the roof of the butty and ran along to the bow. Julia watched him pick up a rope and throw it over the tee-stud at the front of the motor, while Jason picked up a loop of rope from the stern of the motor boat and dropped it over a convenient hook on the butty.

'What do you want me to do?' Julia asked Jason politely.

'Stay out of the way,' he snarled and picked up a short length of rope, which, after putting the engine ahead again, he secured to the towing dolly by looping it to and fro several times. Then suddenly the boats were moving as one, going at what seemed a terrible speed, into the jaws of the lock. There wasn't an inch to spare, but the boats didn't touch the sides. Julia could see why Ralph put up with Jason: he was brilliant.

45

'No need for you to move,' said Ralph, 'we've got so many people helping. But think what it must have been like in the old days, with only a husband and wife working the pair.' Pretty stressful, thought Julia, especially if you were married to Jason. 'I'll take you through what's happening,' went on Ralph, 'and let the young things work up a sweat. When Donald and Suzy get the gates shut behind us, or before if I know Jason, Jason and Ted'll start winding paddles. That'll let water into the lock to bring it to the level of the canal beyond. Like turning on the taps in a bath. See? They're using windlasses.'

Water surged into the lock, causing the boats to move back and forth. Ralph laughed at the concentration on Julia's face. 'You'll soon get the hang of it.'

After five locks, Julia did feel she'd learned quite a lot about boat-handling. She'd opened and shut gates, used a windlass and, painfully slowly, raised a paddle.

She liked being on the butty with Ralph who explained things in a quiet, relaxed way, and wondered how Suzy was faring with Jason, particularly after their spat over the mattress. Although she and Suzy had opened lock-gates together, walking backwards with their backs braced against the balance beam, there hadn't been much time for intimate chat. She saw Jason hand Suzy the tiller and then duck down through the engine room.

'Probably wants a pee,' said Ralph. 'Or he'd never let her steer. It's in honour of you ladies that he isn't peeing off the back of the boat.'

But when Jason reappeared, he was carrying a tray of coffee. 'I maligned him,' said Ralph. 'He must think more of Suzy's steering ability than I realised. Grab hold of this, I'll get our mugs.'

Julia felt quite confident hanging on to the 'ellum while Ralph brought two mugs back from the bow of the boat, and kept hold of it while they drank their coffee. Ralph took the mugs back and left her steering. She was happy on her own, the heat from the stove warming her lower half, watching the countryside go by. Slowly, almost against her will, the magic of the canals was filtering through to her: a narrow strip of water moving through fields, wooded valleys, residential areas, or along the backsides of factories, with the same dogged determination. Now, the rural idyll was becoming more urban and Julia was watching distant children in a school playground when Ralph returned.

'Here's where your apprenticeship really begins. There's a couple of really sharp turns coming up.'

All Julia's confidence melted away. 'You do them.' Setting up a watertight tenancy agreement was one thing; if you messed up nothing or no one got damaged. Physical things were a lot more dangerous.

'Nonsense. You've got to learn, and if you're going to put the butty up the bank, you'd better do it while I'm here to protect you from Jason.'

Julia buried her nose and mouth in the collar of her coat and squeaked.

Ralph ignored this evidence of cowardice. 'Now, wait until you think you're going to hit the bank, and then swing the 'ellum right over, the opposite way to what you normally do. That way your nose pushes the motor's stern round the bed. Think of it as a hundred and forty feet of articulated lorry.'

'First it's a pencil, and now it's a lorry,' muttered Julia. 'I just get used to putting the tiller the opposite way to the way I want to go, and now I have do the reverse. I might have a nervous breakdown.'

'We're planning to go round the bend, so that'll fit in nicely.' Julia gulped in horror at Ralph's pun but they negotiated the bend safely. Ralph climbed on to the roof of the butty. 'Right, I'll leave you in charge now. There's another sharp bend here.' He stabbed at the page in the guide with a grimy finger. 'And we're here now.

47

Can you cope, do you think?'

'No,' she said to his departing back. But actually, she did.

'Hatton can be done in under two hours,' Jason said, his mouth full of sandwich, referring to the flight of locks which were in front of them, dauntingly climbing the hill like a staircase on steroids. 'You can go up the whole flight breasted. We should manage it with four of us, even if two of us are girlies.'

Only extreme hunger and consideration for Ralph's feelings prevented Julia from throwing her sandwich at Jason. And by the look on Suzy's face, she felt just as angry. They were only allowed time for a snack because they needed to fill up with water. Donald and Ted had abandoned them some time ago, having hitched a lift back to the boatyard on a small cruiser.

'Just a tad sexist, don't you think, Jason?' said Suzy.

Jason drained his can of lager and belched. 'If you girlies would like to set the locks, I'll finish watering up.'

Julia and Suzy exchanged glances which swore revenge. 'Jason might be an ace boat-handler, but his interpersonal skills make Neanderthal man look like Sir Lancelot.' Suzy swung her windlass menacingly. 'I'm not surprised his girlfriend ran away.'

'Have you found out what happened?'

'Apparently she was the crew girl and awfully good, but Jason was absolutely horrible to her one day. She went off lock-wheeling – what we're doing – on a bicycle, and a lock-keeper found her crying. She refused to get back on the boat and Ralph lost the best cook he'd ever had.'

'He should have sacked Jason.'

'That's what I said, but Ralph said people as good at the boats as Jason is are like gold dust. It's much harder to get good boat crew than good cooks . . . Nothing personal,' she added, belatedly.

48

The rest of the day fled by in a welter of ropes and locks, shouting, pulling and pushing. Jason didn't let up the pace, in spite of Ralph's call for moderation. Jason was in charge of the motor boat, and having the whip hand, used it.

'Anyone would think,' Suzy said to Julia while they struggled with a particularly difficult lock-gate, 'that we had to get to the base tonight. Ralph says it's a two-day journey at least. After the junction, the locks are narrow. And we have to go through them separately,' she added, in case Julia hadn't yet got the point.

'I wish Ralph would say these things to Jason.'

'Oh, he has. But Jason takes no notice.'

Julia didn't comment, but she did wonder whether, if Jason took no notice of Ralph, it was likely he would ever take any of Suzy.

The junction through to the Stratford Canal was negotiated. Ralph steered the butty for the right-angle bend, much to Julia's relief. It was then that Julia found out what they meant by narrow locks. They looked barely wide enough for a canoe, let alone seventy feet of narrow boat.

They tied up the butty in a safe place, and concentrated on getting the motor down to where they wanted to spend the night. Because, Suzy explained, then they could get a decent mooring, and without having to bow-haul (which meant 'pull', Julia discovered) the butty along, they could all work the motor. 'Then,' Suzy went on gaily, 'having parked the motor – don't tell Jason I said "parked" – we can all four of us get the butty down. Faster that way,' she finished.

After seeing how efficiently the others were managing without her, Julia took refuge in the galley. This was partly for a rest, and partly to keep the others fed and supplied with caffeine or cans of lager. It was also an opportunity to find her way round it on her own and see if she wanted to change anything. Sadly, no matter how she rearranged it, mentally and actually, she never managed to make any more working surface.

When she heard the boat go into reverse, she put her head out of the centre doors. It was pitch dark.

'We're going to tie up here for the night,' said Suzy, who loomed up out of the blackness. 'We've left the butty a few locks back. We're going to get her now.'

'Do you need me to help?'

'Not really. But as we're all starving and there isn't a pub within walking distance, Ralph says can you rustle up something to eat?'

Julia could, but not without some difficulty. Any bread had been eaten at breakfast and there was no milk, which meant they couldn't eat the huge box of Crunchy Nut Corn Flakes. There was nothing in the fridge remotely edible except three slices of ham, some very hard cheese and a few rotting tomatoes.

Fortunately, the store cupboards under the crew bunks had more promising offerings, including dried milk, dried onions, pasta and tinned tomatoes. With these and the end of a loaf, considered too stale to toast, Julia filled a large gratin dish which she covered in grated cheese and breadcrumbs and thrust into a very hot oven. A day in the company of Ralph, Jason and co. was enough to warn her that they would expect to eat the moment they got through the door, even if she had had barely half an hour to produce a meal.

She was just opening a tin of baked beans, the nearest thing she could find to a vegetable, when Ralph appeared. 'God that Jason is a slave driver! Mmm, something smells delicious. You are clever finding something to eat. I know there wasn't much. I meant to go shopping before we set off, but there wasn't time.' He produced the whisky bottle. 'Drink?' He grinned. 'There's always time to buy the real necessities.'

'I noticed,' said Julia. 'And yes please.'

Julia peeked into the oven. Her dish was just the right side of burned and bubbling like a hot spring. With difficulty, she cleared a space on the draining board so she could take it out of the oven and bent to do so. Too late, she discovered the oven glove had a hole in it. She was just about to dump it down and spare her hands from third-degree burns, when Jason appeared and stood in front of her precious space.

'What's that?' Jason demanded, regarding the dish with the utmost suspicion.

'Very, very hot! Could you just –' She elbowed him out of the way and dropped it with relief.

'What did you say it was?' Jason ignored Julia's flapping fingers and peered into it suspiciously.

Julia hoped his nose would burn. 'Macaroni cheese,' she said on impulse.

'Oh. Thought it was pasta. I can't eat pasta.'

Julia wondered if she should tell him what macaroni was but decided to quit while she was ahead.

Jason dried his hands on her clean tea-towel while she put margarine on cream crackers. Everyone was starving, but although she'd done her best, there was not a lot to eat. It wouldn't be her fault if Jason got up from the table hungry, but it would be her misfortune.

Ralph had raised part of the folding table and found knives and forks. Suzy, who'd found time to brush her hair and change her jumper, came into the kitchen.

'Smells yummy. I'm starving. Shall I take this?' She carried off the plate of cream crackers. 'You haven't got a bottle of wine stashed in there, have you, Ralph? I can't drink whisky with pasta.'

Fortunately, Jason never listened to what Suzy said. He sat by the stove with his legs stretched out in front of him, so Suzy had to step over them as she spread the knives and forks round the table.

'Bloody man. If I had the energy, I'd kill him.' Suzy picked up the pile of plates and the saucepan of beans and stumped back to the saloon. Julia followed with her pasta dish.

'I hope it's all right,' she muttered under her breath, and went in with a spoon. When everyone was served, Ralph raised his glass.

'Here's to a good season and a first-rate team. Jason, Julia and Suzy.'

Julia and Suzy picked up their glasses and drank. Jason didn't bother. It'll never work, thought Julia, we'll never become a team, not without one of us at least having a personality transplant.

They did, however, become more of a team over the next long day when, at last, they brought the boats to their mooring, a little way away from Stratford Basin. The tree-shaded locks, barrel-roofed lock cottages, and cast-iron split bridges, which enchanted those with the leisure to notice, had turned into the secret world behind a bustling town.

It was not only the scenery that was different. Julia no longer felt like a novice. Pulling the engineless butty about had become second nature to her and Suzy's steering was now expert. But while boat-handling became easier, they began to resent Jason's attitude more and more.

'He's going to have to realise that I'm the boss,' said Suzy. 'He may know a hundred per cent more about boats than I do, but he had no right to shout at me when I scraped the aqueduct.'

'He didn't shout at Ralph when the wind made him catch in the bridge. Maybe when Ralph's gone, he'll treat you better. Maybe it's having two bosses he can't handle.'

Suzy sniffed in disbelief.

'I don't know what we're going to do without you, Uncle Ralph.' Suzy hung from his neck while her Aunt Joan collected bags of dirty washing from the cabin and Jason washed down the boats with the mop. 'We'll never manage!'

'Come on, girl. None of that defeatist talk. You'll be fine with Jason and Julia.' He gave Julia a grin. 'You've got a good team there.'

'I've got two people who are good. But we're not a team, Ralph, not really.'

'That's where the skill comes in. Making a team out of individuals. Now, I've told you about the post?'

'Aunt Joan will bring it, or send someone. And the bed linen.'

Ralph nodded. 'And you know I'm going to hospital on Friday, but after I'm out, you can ask me if anything goes wrong.'

'No, you can't,' said Aunt Joan, emerging from the cabin laden with bags. 'You're to convalesce. And Suzy will never be able to take charge if she feels she has to refer to you all the time.'

'Oh very well. I suppose you're right.'

But while Ralph was twitching with impatience at the wheel of his car, Joan told Suzy not to worry. 'I can probably help you with most things, but I would appreciate it if Ralph thought it was all going well, even if it isn't. Which I'm sure it will.' After which helpful statement, Joan kissed both Suzy and Julia, and allowed herself to be driven away at top speed.

'Well, it's just us now,' said Suzy, covering her anxiety with a sunny smile. 'Shall we go to the pub for a meal? Jason? Would you like that?'

Both women tried to bring Jason out of himself. Julia asked leading questions about canals and boats, Suzy tried to get him to talk about his life. But Jason remained churlish. They conferred in the Ladies'.

'He's a prick,' said Suzy, curling her eyelashes with her

finger. 'I'm fed up. From now on, he's going to do what he's told, or else. No more Mrs Nice Guy.'

'Perhaps he'll respond to a firm hand.'

'Yes, and I know where,' said Suzy with her mouth open, putting on lipstick. 'The first thing is we get the crew cabin. He can live in his precious traditional back cabin with no bathroom. Agreed?'

Julia agreed. The two nights she had spent in the back cabin had been relatively cosy, but access to a bathroom was a necessity.

'And pumping out the loos is his job, no question. Even Ralph said it was his job. And he's to bloody well stop being so pooey about everything.'

'But, Suzy, if it's his job to empty –'

'You know what I mean. There's no need to be disgusting. Can you think of anything else he should be doing?'

Julia thought an occasional hand with the washing-up would be nice, but decided not to mention it. It would only make Suzy feel guilty because she didn't help either, and Suzy had enough on her plate at the moment.

Jason accepted Suzy's instruction that he should have the back cabin in silence. 'It'll give you more room,' Suzy explained, finding it hard to keep up the oppressive employer stance.

'OK,' he said. 'You girls want another drink?'

'The word,' said Julia, 'is "pre-women".'

'Ugh?'

'Yes, we will have another drink,' said Suzy, although they both knew that, while they still shared the looless back cabin, it was a very bad idea. But neither of them wanted to reject what could have been an olive branch.

They had arrived at the Stratford boatyard just a week before their first passengers were due to arrive. The yard was going to fit a new shower pump in one of the bathrooms, do something to the fuel injectors, steam clean the holding tanks and do other small, nameless tasks which involved men leaving trails of sawdust or engine oil as they whistled about their work.

Jason did mysteriously time-consuming things which included painting a strip of red paint between the brass bands on the butty chimney, which, they gathered, would make them more truly traditional.

After consultation, Julia agreed to add Jason's list of jobs to her own. She did this on a clipboard which had everybody's tasks in neat columns, some highlighted.

'If we're not careful we'll use up all the time making lists, and not be ready,' said Suzy, who considered Julia was getting a bit carried away with her 'Urgent', 'Not So Urgent' and 'Do Yesterday' lists.

'Sorry, it's the estate agent in me. But I think I've finished now. I've divided the jobs between us two, more or less.' She handed Suzy a list copied from the master sheet. 'And if we start now, and don't keep stopping for coffee, we should get done.'

Suzy regarded the bit of paper doubtfully. 'Well, I'll do my best, but actually, I've got quite a lot of office work to do, like making sure my passenger list is up to date, and that all the moorings we've got to book have actually been booked, and not just put on Ralph's "To Do" list.' She put her 'To Do' list on top of Julia's. 'The trouble is, seeing everything written down like this makes me panic.'

Suppressing a sigh, Julia picked up both lists. If she got up at six, and worked solidly until midnight, she might be finished before the week was out.

With the aid of a radio, Julia painted, brushed, repaired and cleaned, driven on by the knowledge that six passengers (luckily they were four short of their full complement for the first week) were going to arrive and wouldn't want paint pots, exposed floorboards and patches of mildew strewn about the place. She and Suzy didn't meet up often, but when they did, Julia realised Suzy was working just as hard with the administration.

55

When Julia had done all she could, she hunted down Suzy and waited for her to put down the phone.

'Bloody advertising people! Why do they always seem to get ads wrong? How are you getting on, Ju?'

'I think it's time we made up the beds.'

'Oh no. Far too early, it's only –'

'Friday. The passengers are coming tomorrow.'

Suzy went pale beneath her blusher, as if the mention of passengers made her realise exactly what she'd taken on. 'Oh God, is it? I thought it was about Tuesday. I'd better help you do the beds then. And I suppose the loos will need a good clean?'

'They certainly will.'

Julia could see reasons why Suzy shouldn't do this churning around in Suzy's mind. Fortunately for Julia, they weren't quite good enough for Suzy's conscience. 'Right. Let's get at it. Clean the loos.' Suzy hesitated. 'Er – how do you *do* that, exactly?'

Fortunately, Julia's spell as a barmaid had included having to make rooms ready for guests, and the landlady had passed on all sorts of tips and wrinkles. Aided by these, they eventually got the cabins looking clean and welcoming and the bathrooms gleaming as hygienically as possible.

'But we're going to have to do something about the bathrooms,' said Suzy. 'They smell clean, but they're not exactly fragrant. They need a good squirt of Crabtree and Evelyn. I'll put it on the list with little soaps and boxes of tissues.'

'I know Jason's going into town to get some countersunk screws. You could ask him.'

Suzy whinnied like an indignant pony. 'If you asked him to go into a chemist, he'd probably say he was allergic to them!'

Julia had worked out menus for the first week, having agreed to do all the cooking in the beginning to allow Suzy free rein to get Jason into line.

'But I should be able to be a galley slave quite often,' Suzy insisted. 'It's an easy run down the Avon, Ralph says, and, of course, Jason knows it like the back of his hand. We're breasted up or on cross-straps most of the time, so there's hardly any butty steering. With only six passengers, it should be really easy.'

'Don't tempt fate.' Julia was older than Suzy, and sometimes, she felt it.

Fate resisted temptation until lunchtime on Saturday, the first day of the season. The passengers were due to arrive at tea-time. As well as starting dinner, removing the detritus of refurbishing the boats, making a coffee cake and scones for tea, Julia had made bacon sandwiches for everyone. Suzy had broken out the passenger beer, newly acquired from the Cash and Carry where they had gone by taxi. They were waiting for Jason to come and join them.

When he appeared, he had his rucksack with him. 'Well, I'm off,' he said.

'Off where? We've done all the shopping.' Suzy pulled the ring off a can of lager and gave it to him.

Jason hesitated, came into the saloon and sat down, accepting the can.

Julia knew there was something wrong. She handed him the plate of sandwiches. 'Here, have one.'

Jason took a sandwich and ate it in three large bites. Then he drained the can. 'As I said, I'm off.' Julia felt her limbs go heavy as she began to understand. 'I can't work for a woman, two women. So I'm leaving.'

'Jason, you can't.' Suzy's voice shook with terror and indignation. 'The passengers'll be here in a couple of hours. We can't manage without you.'

''Fraid you'll have to. Can I have my money?'

'You can't leave. You're hired for the season. Uncle Ralph is depending on you – so are we!'

'I'm paid weekly, aren't I? And I want my money.'

Suzy saw he meant what he said and tried to be conciliatory. 'I haven't got enough cash,' she said. 'Just work the week out, please. Give us time to find someone else.'

Jason shook his head. 'Nah. You won't need me on the river. It's a doddle. There's only the Canyon when you really need a butty-steerer. Now, are you going to give me my money, or am I going to get nasty?'

Suzy stopped trying to appeal to his better nature. 'You've been nasty from the day you were born, Jason.' She scrabbled for her handbag which she kept hidden behind the bottles in the steps, and took out her wallet. 'Here's seventy quid.'

'You owe me a hundred.'

'You won't get a penny more unless you work out your notice.' Julia could see Suzy's hand shaking and hoped that Jason couldn't.

'Oh won't I? Don't be too sure about that!'

Then he took the money, picked up another sandwich, swung his rucksack on to his shoulder, and left.

Chapter Six

'Bastard!' said Suzy, her face buried in her hands. 'If I had time, I'd burst into tears. What are we going to do now?'

Julia also put her emotions on hold. 'We'll have to tell Ralph. He must have other people who could crew for us. What happened when Jason had a holiday?'

'Jason didn't have holidays. The old boatmen didn't, so he didn't.'

'Prat.'

'And I don't really think I can tell Uncle Ralph just now. Knowing him, he'll discharge himself from hospital and come back and help. Joan would never forgive me. He's put it off twice already.'

'You could ask Aunt Joan after he's had the operation and can't move.'

'I don't think that'll be until Monday. We've still got the first week to get through.'

Julia was mentally trawling her Christmas card list for people who might be a) remotely suitable, and b) fairly free, when someone knocked on the roof of the boat.

'Hello! Anyone at home?'

It was a male voice. Julia and Suzy exchanged agonised glances, but before they could speak, a large shape appeared at the double doors to the boat.

'Come in,' Suzy called weakly. 'It's probably a passenger come early,' she whispered. 'What are we going to do?'

The doors opened. 'Hi!' A man appeared, a little hunched in the doorway. 'I'm looking for Julia Fairfax.'

'Is that Oscar?' asked Suzy under her breath.

'I don't know who he is.' Julia got up. 'I'm Julia Fairfax. How can I help you?'

The man put his hand round hers and gently crushed it. 'I'm Fergus Grindley,' he said. 'Your mother sent me.'

This didn't help her identify him. Something about him was faintly familiar, but her mother could have sent anyone, from her friendly neighbourhood axe-murderer to a millionaire she came across while walking in the hills. Her brain free-wheeled uselessly for a few seconds and then stopped. All she could think was that her mother's timing was, as usual, spectacularly bad. 'I'm sorry . . .'

'You don't remember me? I suppose you were about ten when we last met. I was sixteen.'

Memory came flooding back and, with it, horror.

'I'm Lally Crossthwaite's son,' he went on. 'She married again after my father died. She still calls me Freddie.'

She remembered every detail now. He was the son of her mother's oldest friend, thrust down her and her siblings' throats since birth. And one hideous weekend she and Angela had been taken by their mother to stay with Freddie and his mother. Julia and her sister later decided that they had never been so miserable in their lives. Fergus (or Freddie, as he had been called then) had had a friend to stay and they had both been horrible to them.

There was a Christmas party in the local Big House and the two women were terribly excited about this visit to the local gentry. Julia's mother wouldn't listen to their pleas to be allowed to stay at home. The party had been the most miserable four hours they had ever spent. Freddie and his friend had been unutterably foul while the adults, safely tucked away in a drawing room somewhere, had had a whale of a time, drinking champagne and social climbing. They could hardly tear themselves away. The following day had been even worse. Freddie, under the pretence of moving it for the girls, actually dropped a spider on Julia's leg. It had taken her years to get over the phobia.

Afterwards their mother had gone on about how kind Freddie had been, ignoring their protests that he had bullied and abandoned them.

Ever since their mother had clung steadfastly to her version of his character. And this false impression was reinforced by *his* mother's blinkered view of her only son. According to her he worked extremely hard at school, was signed up for every extra-curricular activity, played cricket for his county and was a model of what a child should be. Later on, his academic prowess was tossed accusingly in their direction. Stunning exam results in dozens of subjects culminated in three As at A level and Oxbridge (Julia and her sister were convinced their mother thought there really was a university called Oxbridge) where he got a stunning degree. Little Freddie: they hated him from afar. And now little Freddie had turned into not so little Fergus.

'Oh yes,' Julia said, slightly dazed. 'I remember now. It's nice to see you, but not terribly convenient. I hope you haven't come from far?'

Suzy, seeing that Julia intended shepherding Fergus out of the door before he'd properly got in, took the matter in hand. She smiled, stunningly. 'Even if you haven't, have a beer or something. What about a bacon sandwich?'

Fergus, who couldn't quite straighten up, looked down at the two remaining sandwiches. 'Well, if you're sure. I drove down from the Lake District this morning.'

'Have them both.' Suzy thrust the plate at him. 'And here's a lager.' She opened it. 'Do you want a glass?'

'No thanks. This is fine as it is.' He sat down on the banquette.

'You look a bit tired,' said Suzy, having given him a thorough examination. 'You must have been up early.'

'Yes. I wanted to get through Manchester before the rush hour.'

'And you came all that way just to see Julia?' Suzy was unflatteringly surprised.

'Well . . .'

Julia helped him out. 'I expect my mother insisted you dropped in on me as you'd be passing. Which to my mother means within fifty miles.'

He took a gulp of beer and regarded Julia. 'She is a very charismatic person.'

'You mean bossy.'

Fergus smiled. The passing years had, Julia noted, been kind to him. They'd done away with the spots and the buck teeth, though the air of superiority was still faintly in evidence. His muddy hair had become darker and his nose and chin had become quite substantial. 'Not exactly,' he said. 'She gives you the impression that doing what she wants is what you *would* have wanted, if only you'd known about it.'

Julia was forced to acknowledge this was an accurate description of her mother. 'Out of the family, she's like that. In it, she's just bossy. And she sent you to see me?'

He nodded, his mouth full of sandwich. 'She gave me a cookery book she thought would be useful.' He burrowed in his rucksack. 'Here.'

She flicked through its glossy pages which were filled with photographs of woods. It was called *Food from Nature's Bounty* and was full of recipes for young nettle tops and obscure mushrooms. 'Oh my God!' Julia snapped it shut. 'It's got worms in it!'

'Has it?' Fergus was equally horrified. 'Thank goodness your mother's a vegetarian.'

'And you came all this way to give it to me?' said Julia.

Fergus hesitated for a second. 'I was at a loose end. Your mother wanted you to have it. The book I mean.' Somehow this hasty addition drew attention to his *double entendre*. Mentally, Julia ticked up another black mark against him.

Suzy was eyeing Fergus up and down speculatively. 'What sort of loose end? Long or short?'

'Sorry?' he asked pleasantly.

Julia remembered his ingratiating manners from fifteen-odd years ago. They had the same nauseating effect on her now.

'I mean,' went on Suzy, 'are you on holiday or something?'

'Sort of. I'm off to Italy to stay with a friend who's got a villa in Tuscany.'

Julia stored up this titbit for Angela. Fergus Grindley was just the sort of man who'd have friends with villas in Tuscany.

'And I suppose you're looking forward to it like mad?' went on Suzy.

'Well, yes.'

'It's just –'

'Suzy!' Julia interrupted her friend. 'I've just remembered something I simply must say to you. In private. Urgently. It really can't wait.'

Julia got up and almost dragged Suzy out with her to the galley. 'Don't do it,' she implored her boss. 'Don't ask Fergus to help us. He's a nerd and a bully. Trust me.' Suzy looked sceptical. 'Honestly!' Julia went on. 'There isn't time to tell you all the details, but believe me when I say we've got enough troubles without adding him to them.'

'I'm sorry. I won't believe you unless you tell me all the details.' Suzy's eyes gleamed at the hint of even such ancient gossip.

Julia grimaced. 'Years and years ago, when I was about ten, my sister and I had to go to a party with him and his friend –'

'Lucky you. I wasn't allowed to go to parties when I was ten.'

'Don't interrupt! It was awful. Me and Angela were made to wear dresses when everyone else was in jeans!

Freddie – Fergus, I mean – and his friend lured us into this cellar thing, telling us they were showing us the loo. We were desperate to go. Mum and Lally had promised us that Freddie and – what was his friend called? Anyway, never mind – they promised us that the boys'd look after us. But they abandoned us in this cellar and it took ages and ages to find the party again.'

'I expect they were embarrassed to be seen with you, if you were wearing, like, *totally* the wrong clothes.'

Julia scowled. 'And the next day they took us on a bicycle ride, on bikes that were miles too big for us. He made us go miles and miles. And when I got a puncture, Fergus got off his bike and walked beside me, mocking me every step of the way.'

'Jolly kind of him to walk with you.'

Seeing Suzy was not convinced, Julia threw in the card she thought must make Suzy see sense. 'Somehow my mother and his thought him walking with me indicated some childish crush – and don't ask me which of us had the crush – and have been trying to get us married off ever since. Now I've left Oscar and Fergus's marriage has broken up it will start up all over again. It will be the reason my mother sent him.'

'I wasn't going to ask him to help us,' said Suzy, untruthfully. 'I was going to invite him to come down the river with us for a few days. We've got spare cabin space.'

'The last thing we want to do is have more people to look after when we've got no crew!'

'And we could just ask him to help with the steering, a little bit. To give me a break. So I can help you in the kitchen.'

Julia instantly felt churlish, but also deeply suspicious. She was about to tell Suzy more about Fergus Grindley, when he appeared at the stable door. 'Have I come at a bad time?'

'Yes,' said Julia.

'Not at all,' said Suzy, at the same moment, only louder. 'We've just had rather a shock, that's all.'

'Too right,' muttered Julia.

'Our crew has just left us. Two hours before our passengers are due to arrive. I really don't know what we're going to do. My uncle, who owns the boats, is having open-heart surgery. We're in a terrible fix . . .' This was all accompanied with appealing upward glances and pathetic downward ones and ended with a direct look of supplication which Bambi could have learned from. 'Perhaps you might like to help?'

Julia couldn't tell if Suzy knew what she was doing when she moistened her lips and allowed the hint of a tear to gather at the corner of her lavishly lashed eyes, or whether she just went on to autopilot when she wanted something. But it was academic. Fergus melted. The thought that Suzy should have used that kind of charm on Jason did cross her mind, but she retracted it. Not even Bambi himself could have got round Jason.

Fergus harrumphed and blinked and looked down at Suzy. 'I have got a couple of days before I need to get back to my flat to pack, as it happens.'

'It would absolutely save our lives if you could stay and help until then. Wouldn't it, Julia?'

Julia couldn't bring herself to answer.

Julia shut herself in the galley and made chocolate mousse. If Suzy wanted to lumber them with Fergus, she could look after him. Julia put out pretty china mugs, plates, knives and little pots of butter and jam, so when the first guests arrived she could give them tea and the scones she had made earlier. Suzy and Fergus had disappeared, and Julia felt she, as the crew girl, shouldn't have to greet the passengers on her own, not on the first cruise. Her temper was not improved by Suzy coming into the galley saying, 'He's really not bad-looking, in a

65

rugged, old sort of way. Just right for you.'

'I have enough of that sort of thing from my mother,' she snapped. 'And if you told me he had spent every minute of his time since I last saw him working on narrow boats, I still wouldn't want a bar of him. Gift-wrapped!'

'Well, no, he said he's never been on a canal boat until now, but it doesn't make him completely useless.'

'Oh no? What about sailing? My mother's awfully keen on sailing types. It might mean he can catch a rope occasionally.'

'You sound like Jason. No, he hasn't had sailing experience, but you must admit, knowing how to sail three sheets to the wind or whatever it is wouldn't be a lot of use to us.'

'It would be better than nothing.'

'What have you got against him?'

'I did think I'd made it fairly clear.'

'I expect it was his friend's fault he was so awful. Boys are dreadful when they gang up.' This thought had occurred to Julia some time after that dreadful weekend, but she wasn't in the mood to give Fergus the benefit of the doubt. 'Anyway,' Suzy went on. 'He's just putting his stuff in his cabin.'

'Good thing we made up all the beds, then. He won't have to struggle with his duvet cover on his own. Now, shall I put the scones on the table, to look welcoming, or keep them in the kitchen, so I can warm them up in the oven?'

'Freshly baked scones! Julia, you're a miracle. I don't know how you do it.'

Suzy was shameless. 'If you really want to know, I'll tell you. They're so easy, I expect even horrible Fergus could do it.'

Fergus appeared in time to make Julia wonder if he'd heard this epithet. 'Can I wash my hands?'

'If you use that basin,' Julia snapped, not caring if he

had. 'It's against the law to use the same one for cooking and hand-washing.'

'Is it?'

'Yes.'

Julia was aware she should make more of an effort to be nice. Fergus was probably completely unaware that her mother had sent him to 'throw them together'. And even if Fergus was useless, he was giving up his time to help them. But a nagging little snippet her mother had told her about his marriage breaking up because his wife didn't want to give up her career and have children kept her angry with him. He was just another Oscar, and if her mother thought she'd even look in his direction she could just look in her crystal ball and think again. Torn between her personal feelings and her duty to the boats (for which he was better than nothing), she made an excuse to leave.

'I've just got to check on the cabins now,' she said, managing not to chide him for drying his hands on the clean towel she had just put out.

A few minutes later he found her removing the little vase of fresh flowers from his cabin. 'Ah, there you are. Suzy said, if you've got a minute, can you come and give us a hand? It's time to move down into the basin.'

'Oh?'

'She thought it might be better to take the motor down first, and then get the butty separately, so you don't have to breast up on your own.' He seemed puzzled. 'At least, I think it's what she said.'

'It's a technical term,' explained Julia. 'It means having the boats tied together side by side.' She felt suddenly nervous. The rehearsal period was over. Now it was nearly time for the performance. Perhaps having Fergus there wasn't all bad.

Suzy motored slowly and extremely carefully down the short stretch of canal which trickled along under and behind the hustle and bustle of England's number one tourist spot. No one noticed. Julia stood at the bow, with a rope in her hand and a boat hook at the ready, but she wasn't needed. Suzy was managing beautifully. Stuff Jason, Julia thought.

But the moment they slid under the bridge, what seemed like hundreds of flash bulbs went off. Suddenly they were on stage.

Julia, at the bow, ready to pole off if necessary, wanted to put a paper bag over her head. It seemed rude not to acknowledge the presence of several dozen people only yards away, but impossible to engage with so many of them when she had work to do. She must look pleasant, though, in case their future passengers were among the camera-snappers, so she put on a bland expression and stared into the middle distance. If she'd known how exposed the basin at Stratford was, she'd have brushed her hair.

Although more used to the attention of strangers, Suzy was concentrating too hard to be bothered by her public. There was space for them to get in, Uncle Ralph had arranged that long since. But could she get into it without touching the small, fragile, plastic boats on either side? Ralph had terrified them both with tales of litigation.

Julia watched from the bow, and as soon as she safely could, leaped ashore, mumbling apologies to the people she displaced, ready to stop the boat with a rope – or even her body, if Suzy looked like hitting anything. But Suzy manoeuvred the boat as if she'd been doing it for years. Julia grinned.

'Well done,' she said, hugging her as Suzy wrapped her stern-line a couple of times round the mooring bollard. Now the tourists had lost interest in them and drifted away, Julia looked about her. It really was a very pretty canal basin. Lawns and well-tended flower beds were interposed with statues. On the other side were trees. Her mind dragged itself to less appealing thoughts. 'Where's Fergus?'

'Oh, he's getting the butty. I've got to have a cup of tea before the passengers arrive. My mouth has gone completely dry, I was so nervous.'

Julia made tea but wouldn't let Suzy cut the cake or eat any more scones. She found a packet of digestives for her to fill up on. 'Fergus is being a long time,' said Julia after a while, feeling guilty in spite of herself. 'Should we go back and give him a hand?'

'He said he'd be fine, but we can go back and see if you like.'

But as Julia raised her head above the side-hatch, she became aware that everyone at the side of the basin had their attention directed towards the bridge. Turning round, she saw what they were staring at.

'Suzy, come and look!'

Suzy joined her and with several hundred tourists, looked on as a seventy-foot narrow-boat butty glided silently under the bridge and into the basin.

'It doesn't seem to have an engine,' said a man, clicking away with a camera.

'Then how come it's moving?' asked his wife.

'The guy on the roof with the pole,' said another man. 'See? He puts the pole in the water and pushes the boat along.'

Julia started to giggle. 'You said he had no boating experience whatsoever, but he lied. He can punt. I expect he learned that at Oxbridge,' she said, watching Fergus push the butty towards the motor.

'Which one did he go to, Oxford or Cambridge?' asked Suzy, not taking her eyes off Fergus.

'Dunno. According to my mother, it's one university.' Julia watched him choose the exact spot to plunge the pole into the water so the butty approached at the right angle. 'But knowing him, he probably went to both.'

'Well, it paid off. He's an ace punter.' Suzy admired Fergus for a few seconds longer. 'If I didn't like my men with the dew still on them, I'd fancy Fergus.' She shot Julia a speculative look. 'He's safely divorced, you know. Perfect for you.'

Julia did know and hid her surprise that Suzy should have found out all this already. 'Suzy, the reason women divorce men is because they are *not* perfect. The good ones they hang on to.'

'How good does he have to be, for goodness' sake? Heavens, you got engaged to Oscar because you liked his dog!'

'And his house!' she countered. 'But I've learned from my mistake and no way will I let myself be pushed into marriage with a man I've hated all my life!' Too late she remembered how well sound carried across water.

Suzy climbed on the roof of the motor boat and stood at the stern-end, prepared to catch a rope. Fergus threw her one, laid his pole carefully on the roof, then strolled down to the bow of the butty. There, he picked up the coil of rope and, keeping hold of the end, tossed it at the tee-stud on the motor. Either he had a Hoopla Blue from Oxbridge, or it was pure fluke, but it caught, and he pulled the butty to a graceful halt alongside the motor.

People on the bank started to clap and whistle. Julia, genuinely impressed, found herself smiling, and stopped struggling to think of something to say to prevent Fergus thinking she and Suzy had been talking about him. Suzy, more demonstrative by nature, flung herself at him. 'You're wonderful! A real hero.' She delivered a smacking kiss on the cheek, narrowly missing his mouth. 'Come and have some tea before the passengers come.'

Suzy and Fergus had disappeared on to the other boat on the pretence of doing something useful, leaving Julia to wash up the mugs, when the first of the passengers arrived.

'Hello, there! Is this *Pyramus* and *Thisbe*?'

Julia hesitated for a moment, in the vain hope that Suzy

70

would appear and greet her customers, and then went to the side doors.

'Yes, hello. You've found the boats. I'm Julia Fairfax. Let me help you aboard.'

Julia put out her hand and steadied the woman, who was dressed in nautical style, with white trousers and matching navy sweater and cardigan. 'Hi, honey, I'm Eileen Bernstein, and this is my husband Harvey. We're from Arkansas.'

Harvey followed his wife on to the boat and immediately hit his head on a beam. Julia winced, partly in sympathy, and partly out of embarrassment. How could Suzy leave her to welcome passengers on to boats without enough head room?

'Oh, I am sorry,' she said. 'Are you all right? Can I get you anything?'

'Oh don't worry about him. He's been hitting his head on everything since we came to Europe, haven't you, Harv?'

Harv rubbed his bald pate good-naturedly. 'Yup. I guess you get used to it.'

'Right,' said Julia, wishing she and Suzy had agreed on some sort of meeting procedure. 'Would you like me to help you get your luggage aboard, and show you to your cabin? Or would you like a cup of tea?'

'Harv'll get the bags aboard, but if you could make us a decent cup of coffee, we'd be so grateful.'

'It'll be a pleasure,' said Julia, feeling that, in fact, it would be an impossibility. Coffee was not normally a problem for her, but now, because it was important that she got it right, it would go hideously wrong. Where the hell was Suzy?

Right on cue, Suzy appeared, freshly made up and smiling. She descended on Eileen and Harvey in a cloud of charm and Arpège. Fergus followed more quietly, but no less effectively. The thought that Suzy might have been

71

rewarding Fergus in kind for his heroism flashed through Julia's mind, leaving a nasty little snail trail in its wake.

While Suzy was greeting Harvey, showing concern for his bruised head, and generally making the couple feel they were the only people in the world she wanted to be with right now, Julia retreated into the galley to wrestle with the coffee. Her welcome had been very low key in comparison.

'They want coffee,' she murmured to Fergus, who followed her, forgetting she had resolved to make no contact beyond what was absolutely necessary. 'And I'm not sure their idea of good coffee is the same as mine.'

'Make it strong enough, and I'm sure it'll be fine. Shall I take the tray through?'

Julia nodded. 'I'll be out in a minute with the scones. Should we have provided clotted cream, do you think?'

Fergus shook his head. 'Not when they've been travelling. It might make them sick.'

Julia glanced at him to see if he was joking but his expression was completely bland. She opened a jar of Aunt Joan's home-made jam, still trying to work it out. He had been a terrible tease when he was sixteen.

The Bernsteins drank the coffee without comment, but they enthused over the scones. 'These biscuits are so light!' Eileen called over the stable door.

'Thank you.' She paused for a moment before asking, 'Have you seen where you're sleeping?'

'Oh yeah. That nice young man showed us our state rooms. They're so darling. We're going to have such a good time.'

At that moment, the remaining four passengers arrived. When they had all shoehorned themselves and their luggage into their cabins and had the 'Introduction to the Plumbing' lecture, they filed back into the saloon. They had introduced themselves and, encouraged by the warmth and friendliness of the Bernsteins, had cut directly to given names.

All seemed to be going well, so Julia returned to the galley to check that her mousse was setting, but the Bernsteins had decided to fit in another few moments' shopping, and took their infectious enthusiasm with them. Suzy had gone off looking for somewhere to buy bottled gas, which left Julia in charge.

The remaining party fell into an awkward silence. Julia could almost see each couple deciding that the others weren't their type and resolving not to get on. There was a couple from Norfolk, Norman and something Julia couldn't remember, and two female Shakespeare buffs who taught English in a London comprehensive. They were called Mabel and Miriam, but Julia hadn't been able to catch which was which.

No one spoke. Julia, who desperately wanted to get on with the dinner, felt obliged to try and jolly them along.

All her conversational gambits had sunk like stones and she was wondering if anyone would crack a smile, or even raise an eyebrow, if she took off her clothes and danced on the table when Fergus came back.

He had been sent by Suzy to find out where the nearest water point was, and if there was anywhere on the river where they could tie up for the night. She sent him a silent, impassioned, plea for help.

'There's a lovely spot to tie up a little way down,' he said. 'Right opposite the theatre. But I was wondering if anyone would like a short tour of the town? Before dinner? I had a holiday job here when I was a student, so I know it quite well, and those official tours only show you the tourist places.'

Neither couple could resist the thought of seeing 'Secret Stratford'. Everyone brightened up, found their macs and their umbrellas, and prepared to enjoy themselves. The Bernsteins, who arrived back just as they were leaving, showed a little reluctance to go back into town when their feet were killing them, but Fergus made his tour sound so

73

enticing that they followed him like lambs. It was, Julia realised, being organised which they liked.

'What a hero,' said Suzy. 'You mean he just took them all away?'

Julia nodded. 'Like the Pied Piper. Did you get the gas okay?'

Suzy winced. 'Little problem, I'm afraid.'

Julia only had time to express her horror before there was a popping sound from the galley. The gas had run out completely.

'Dinner was almost cooked, wasn't it?'

Chapter Seven

Suzy had had a long day: Jason had walked out, Fergus had walked in, and the season had begun. Fully aware of all this, Julia tried to feel sympathetic but just felt infuriated. Dinner was not almost cooked. 'What was the problem?' she asked, trying to take deep, calming breaths.

'Daddy has put a stop on my credit card so I can't pay for it.'

'Couldn't you have paid with cash?'

Suzy shook her head. 'Jason took it all.'

'Can't you get cash out of a hole-in-the-wall?'

Suzy shook her head. 'Haven't got a card. Daddy says we live in a cashless society.'

If 'Daddy' had to cook a three-course dinner for nine people, thought Julia, grinding her teeth, without any means of doing it, he wouldn't say such silly things. 'That's ridiculous!'

'Well?' Suzy challenged. 'Have you got one?'

'Of course!'

Suzy instantly melted into contrition. 'Julia, I know it must be hell cooking without gas –'

'Not so much hell as plain impossible.'

'– but could you possibly lend me some money? Just until I get my finances sorted out?'

'I haven't got much on me.'

'But you've got some in your bank? That you could take out?'

'Well, yes.'

'So come along and get some money out then – quick, before the people at the gas place all go home!'

Julia glanced at the tower of washing-up which filled the sink, visible to anyone who happened to look over the stable door. 'I can't. I've too much to do here. I'll give you my card and tell you my number.'

Suzy was horrified. 'Julia! You mustn't tell anyone your number! I might steal all your money.'

'Then I'll steal your narrow boats.' Julia retrieved her bag from behind a stack of tinned tomatoes, and produced her card. 'We'll have to trust each other.'

Surprisingly, Suzy kissed her cheek. 'Thank you. No one's ever trusted me with money before. Everyone's always assumed I'd do something silly with it. Daddy always paid my bills and gave me the statutory lecture about how extravagant I am. But no one ever expected me to be any different.'

'Well, I'm sure you won't go mad and buy ten gas bottles instead of two, but how are you going to get them back here?'

'Not a problem. They've got an adorable lad on work experience who'd carry it here on his back, if they didn't have a van,' she said, and skipped off.

Suzy and the adorable lad came back reasonably quickly, which meant he hadn't recently gained any experience not connected with work, and between them, they exchanged two empty gas bottles for two full ones. Suzy gave the lad a couple of cans of beer and then announced that she wanted to move the boats.

'Down to the river where we can spend the night, to that spot Fergus found. Or do you think we should wait until he gets back, and can give us a hand?'

'We haven't got Fergus for long. We'd better get used to not having him.'

'What a pity he can't stay. We will really need someone next week, when we go up Tardebigge. You remember?

Forty-two single locks, that all have to be gone through twice, all in one day?'

Julia remembered. Ralph and Jason had made sure the word Tardebigge was engraved on her heart, let alone her memory. 'I'll give my mother a ring. She may know some-one. Suitable, I mean, not on their way to a glamorous holiday in Tuscany.'

They regarded each other wistfully, neither wanting to admit that the thought of a holiday in sun-drenched Italy seemed so much more appealing than a summer giving other people holidays, in the uncertain English climate.

Julia sighed. 'Shall we get these boats shifted?'

Fergus brought back his party to their new mooring on the river a united group, all eagerly looking forward to their holiday, determined to enjoy themselves.

'That was so kind of you, Fergus,' said either Mabel or Miriam. 'Would you like a glass of sherry?'

'That would be nice,' said Fergus. 'Shall I check with Julia to see if there's time before dinner?'

'Oh there's always time for a drink!' Suzy quickly intercepted the question. 'I make money on the bar. Not a lot, but it all helps,' she added, not quite quietly enough.

The guests all bought each other drinks, and Fergus brought Julia a glass of sherry. 'Oh, thank you! I could do with that.' He didn't instantly leave so she took the opportunity to make amends for her earlier churlishness. 'It was wonderful of you to take everyone off my hands this afternoon. They didn't seem to be getting on and I really didn't have time to look after them.'

'There's no need for you to thank me, Julia. I did it for Suzy, not for you.'

She had seen that mocking look before, while pushing a bicycle, and it still hurt. Denied a more audible form of self-expression – or even a decent four-letter word – by the public nature of the galley, she indulged in a secret, silent tantrum. By the time she had opened her eyes again, Fergus had gone. It was only later it dawned on her that he must have overheard some of her less pleasant remarks about him. But surely he should be relieved? According to her mother, Fergus's mother was just as keen as she was to pair them off. You'd think he'd be grateful that Margot's on-the-shelf daughter wasn't looking at him with wedding bells in her eyes.

In spite of Suzy's protests that she ought to come and eat with everyone else, Julia refused. She stayed in the galley, concentrating on getting everything hot at the same time. She had put a lot of thought into her menu, and had come up with one she hoped was neither too ambitious, nor boring. But although everything looked all right, she didn't want to be too near when people actually ate it, in case she'd made some disgusting mistake.

She swirled cream and sprinkled parsley on the soup, placed a hollowed-out tomato filled with peas by each pair of lamb cutlets, and put toasted almonds on top of the individual mousses. Everyone oohed and aahed satis-factorily. Except Fergus.

He came in with a pile of dirty plates. 'So how was it?' Julia asked, filling the sink with hot water, determined to be polite.

'OK.'

She looked over her shoulder. 'Only OK?'

'Well, I don't like hotel food much. I prefer home cooking.' Fergus was biting his lip. He could have been hiding a smile, but Julia's sense of humour was on a break.

She took her hands out of the hot water. 'What do you mean, hotel food? Who do you think produced that meal? A team of chefs from the Hilton?'

'Oh, I know you cooked it. I just can't stand all those fiddly bits, swirls of cream, little slivers of fruit and sprigs of mint. It just doesn't look like generous home cooking, like your mother's does.'

Julia's mother's cooking was usually brown, bran-filled and dished up on huge serving plates. They made you feel tired just to look at them. Fergus was undoubtedly teasing. But even while she knew this, she was too overwrought to produce the smallest, meanest smile. She had cooked a large meal under very difficult circumstances, she had applied all she had learned from every television cooking programme she had ever watched, from *Masterchef* to *Ready, Steady, Cook*, but he would have preferred food which could substitute as a third-world building material. Well, tough!

'You may not have spotted the difference, Fergus, but I am not my mother. Nor am I ever likely to be. Contrary to all *her* hopes and dreams it is not the height of *my* ambition to become a wife and mother, cooking homely meals for my bread-winning husband and my rosy-cheeked children! This is *professional* cooking!' Worked up as she was, Julia still crossed her fingers behind her back against the lie.

Fergus regarded her with that mixture of blandness and mockery which made her want to run her Sabatier through his vital organs (vital to a man, anyway) but he didn't comment. He just said, 'Shall I make the coffee?'

'If you think you can do it better than I can,' she hissed, and retreated into the bedroom.

Her sports bag protruded from behind the door. I want to go home, she thought. I want to pack that bag and go to where I'm wanted.

Except she wasn't wanted anywhere but here, really. Her house was let, her job had been hijacked from her, and even her current low spirits didn't make Oscar worth a train ride. So she brushed her hair, put on some lipstick and a large squirt of Suzy's perfume, and went back into the fray.

Norman, the male half of the couple from Norfolk, greeted her warmly as she appeared. 'Here's the cook.

Come and sit down and have a brandy. That was a wonderful meal.'

Julia found herself led to a seat and a glass put into her hand. When she next looked into the galley, Fergus was in it, doing the washing-up. Life was not all bad.

'So, what time's breakfast?' asked Norman. 'I'm an early riser, but I only need a cup of tea first thing. Can I help myself?'

Suzy and Julia exchanged shocked glances. 'Yes,' said Suzy, ignoring Julia's look of horror. 'We get up at seven.' Liar, thought Julia. 'But if you want tea before then, do help yourself. I think you'll find everything quite easily.'

'So what time is breakfast?' Norman asked again.

'Half past eight,' said Julia quickly, vowing to be in the galley, ready, by seven at the latest. Suzy might feel relaxed about passengers ferreting about for tea-bags behind her back, but Julia didn't.

They'd never actually talked about what time breakfast should be, or how they would find time to clean the cabins and the bathrooms before setting off. They had a belated, muted, conversation in the galley, while they boiled a kettle for Norman's wife's hot-water bottle.

'If we have breakfast at half past eight, what time shall we set off? Harvey Bernstein's already asked me. He likes to know the schedule.' Julia strained her wrist trying to undo the top of the hot-water bottle.

'Oh God, I don't know,' said Suzy. 'When we're ready, I suppose.'

'Not good enough. They want a time. It probably makes them feel safe.'

'OK. We'll have breakfast at half past eight, and set off at half past nine.'

'So when will we clean the cabins and stuff?'

'After breakfast?'

Julia shook her head. 'After breakfast is when they're in their cabins. Brushing their teeth. You'll have to do it while they're eating. Too bad if they have toothpaste in their washbasins all day.'

Suzy was not keen. 'What, and clean the loos and showers as well?' Julia nodded. 'But I'll have to check the engine, swab the dew off the boats, do all that sort of thing.'

'Do that afterwards. While I'm washing up.'

Suzy frowned. 'There must be a better way of doing it.'

Which meant one that didn't involve Suzy and a lavatory brush in combination. 'If you'd rather,' suggested Julia blandly, 'you could cook breakfast, and I'll do the cabins and get the boat ready.'

This wasn't the right answer either. 'Do you actually know how to start the engine?' Suzy asked acidly.

'Do you actually know how to crack an egg?' Julia glared back at her employer.

Suzy giggled. 'Sort of, but I can't get them into the pan unbroken.'

'Nor can I, actually,' Julia admitted. 'And you're right. I can't start the engine. I'll have to learn all that sort of thing, if we haven't got a crew. Oh, here's your hot-water bottle, Mrs . . . er.'

'So, how *are* we going to manage without a crew?' said Suzy a few long minutes later, massaging night cream into her face with light upward and outward movements. 'It's bad enough now, when we've got Fergus. Without him it's going to be hell. Apart from the cooking and the boat-handling, the passengers take so much looking after. Uncle Ralph should have warned me.'

'I expect it'll get better as the week goes on, and they know what to expect,' said Julia, who hadn't the energy to worry about fine lines in the tender tissues about her eyes. 'It's just because it's our first trip that it's such hard work.' She burrowed down deep into her sleeping bag. 'The other twenty-seven cruises shouldn't be so bad.'

*

81

With a supreme effort of will, Julia just managed to be in the galley, with the kettle on, before Norman appeared wanting tea. It was ten past seven. She could barely force her eyelids apart. Why did people who were on holiday want to get up so early?

'Good morning! It's going to be a nice one, I think,' he said brightly. 'I've just been for a walk. It's lovely here, isn't it? The willows growing by the river, and the meadows beyond?'

Julia nodded. She didn't like to tell him she'd seen nothing of Stratford except the Cash and Carry and what you could see from the boat when cooking or cleaning. She had only seen the theatre because they were moored right opposite it.

'Mmm, it is. Do you want a biscuit with the tea, Norman?'

'No thank you, dear. I'll just take this cup along to Florence and let you get on. I expect you've got lots to do.'

The rest of the passengers arrived in dribs and drabs, all wanting tea or coffee, or just a chat. Julia set the table and did what she could about preparing breakfast, cutting rind off bacon and, as a rash gesture to their American guests, making drop scones, which looked like American pancakes.

Suzy lurked on the roof, greeting the passengers as they appeared, and then ducking into their cabins while they passed the time of day with Julia. Whether she had time to do more than just wipe out the basins, empty the bins, and flap the duvets up and down, Julia doubted.

By the time all the guests had breakfasted, everyone on something slightly different to the offered menu, Julia decided that in future it would be much easier to cook for each person as they appeared. Then she wouldn't have to worry about getting eggs-easy-over all over the sunny-side-ups. But eventually everyone had had enough tea and coffee and conversation, and Julia could clear the table.

While the passengers offered left-over toast to the swans which rapped on the boat, demanding to be fed, Julia got on with the washing-up. Suzy had muttered something about coming back to do it in a minute, but Julia realised there were probably a dozen other things she had to do, and got on with it herself. She had dried every last cup and plate, and made pastry and chopped the onions for a quiche for lunch before Suzy reappeared. Fergus was nowhere about.

Suzy came into the galley scowling at the river guide as if trying to force it to give up more secrets than were on the printed page. 'If I knew how much of the route we can travel breasted up, it would be so much easier. If we have to single out – go one behind the other,' she added impatiently, 'they'll be stuck if they want anything from their cabins. And even if we're on cross-straps we'll have to fetch anything they want, 'cause we couldn't let them climb from one boat to another, not when we're moving.'

'Of course.' Julia wasn't too keen on doing this herself, but refused to admit it.

'I've just phoned ahead and got us somewhere to tie up at Bidford, so that's all right. But I know Bidford Bridge is tricky, because I remember Ralph and Jason talking about it. But they didn't bloody well mention what to do about it!' Suzy raised her eyes from the guide and took in the spotless saloon, the passengers feeding swans, and Julia, halfway through preparations for lunch. Her face crumpled. 'And I was going to wash up the breakfast.'

Julia flapped a dismissive hand. It was a lot of responsibility for anyone, let alone anyone as young and inexperienced as Suzy. 'You get on with the executive decisions. Let me take care of the simple things.'

'If only I had a clue what to do.'

'Could you ring Joan, get her to ask Ralph for some notes? You could say they're for Jason.'

'How likely is it that Jason would forget a single water-rat hole on any trip he's done more than once?'

'What else can you do? After all, the guide's not written for seventy-foot narrow boats. And you will have to tell Ralph and Joan about Jason leaving sooner or later.'

Suzy bit her lip. 'The trouble is, I can't help feeling that Jason leaving is my fault. If I was a better team-builder, he wouldn't have gone.'

'Nonsense! He's a toe-rag! That's why he walked out. No other reason. Go and phone. You'll feel better.'

Suzy disappeared into the back cabin with the mobile. When she reappeared, she looked even less happy. 'Well, I told Joan about Jason, and she's going to try and get some notes out of Ralph, without actually telling him why she wants them, and go through Ralph's address book for other likely crew. But she's had Dad on the phone. He's still furious with me for doing this and has threatened to set the Health and Safety people on to us. I thought he'd have seen sense, by now.'

Julia translated this as meaning: 'let me have my own way, by now'. 'Oh?'

'And Joan's worried sick because Ralph's never taken Health and Safety at all seriously. Somehow, he's managed never to be inspected, so there are bound to be loads of things wrong.'

'Well,' said Julia, trying to sound positive. 'You've got a separate basin for washing hands in, that's something. I know from my pub days you have to have that. It may not be too bad.'

'But they can close you down right away, so Joan says. They could leave our passengers homeless on the canal bank.'

'Couldn't we find out what the regulations are and comply with them?'

Suzy shook her head at this simple solution. 'No time. We'll just have to keep out of their way until the end of the season. It shouldn't be difficult. That's the advantage of being on boats, we're always moving.'

At slightly under walking pace, thought Julia. 'But they won't know where to start looking,' she said aloud, 'not having a schedule.'

Suzy looked pained. 'Unfortunately they might have. Joan sent a brochure to Dad, to make him feel better. The Health and Safety people could know as well as any of our passengers where we'll be on every Saturday of the season.'

'They probably don't work on Saturdays.' Julia's optimism was starting to sound a little forced.

'I bet they do. Anyway, Joan is going to try and find a crew for us.' Suzy's natural good spirits bounced back into evidence. 'And we've got Fergus!'

Julia shook her head. 'Not right at this minute, we haven't. I haven't seen him since breakfast. And even if he comes back now, we've only got him until he goes to Tuscany.'

'I was thinking of asking him to forgo Tuscany. Do you think he would? If I asked *very* nicely?'

In spite of disliking him intensely, Julia was forced to accept that Fergus was better than nothing, but she doubted even Suzy's powers of seduction. 'Why not? After all, what's Tuscany got that we haven't? Apart from sun, wine, olive groves and blue skies?'

'Hardly anything!' Suzy laughed. 'I'll go and grease the stern-gland. As soon as our sun-loving archaeologist, comes back let me know, and we'll set off.'

'How did you know he was an archaeologist?' Julia had forgotten this herself.

'Fergus and me,' said Suzy, ungrammatical and arch, 'have got to know each other quite well.'

Julia wanted to growl.

When Fergus finally arrived back, Suzy, who had been watching for him, instantly started the engine and set off. Julia kept herself out of the way so she wouldn't feel tempted to tell him what she thought of him bunking off for half the morning when he knew how busy they were.

But when he appeared in the galley her feelings got the better of her. She didn't actually turn on him like a fish-wife, but he got the message by the way she banged the kettle on the stove.

'So where were you? I know you don't have to be here, but seeing as you did agree to stay with us for a few days, it was a bit off disappearing like that, leaving us to deal with everything on our own.'

'You're still holding that weekend against me, aren't you? Well, just for the record, it was Clive, my friend, who got you lost in the cellars. I didn't know what he planned until later. I tried to come back and find you, but he wouldn't let me.'

'You should have ignored him. That's ridiculous.'

'Almost as ridiculous as bearing a grudge for all these years.' He leaned against the sink so she couldn't get to it and turn her back on him.

She sighed. 'I agree it does sound dreadfully petty. I suppose it's our mothers' fault. Yours kept telling mine how well you did at school and she told us. She even used to quote extracts of your school reports at us.' She didn't add that when Julia hit twenty-five and was still unmarried, her mother had also told her quite blatantly that Lally, Fergus's mother, didn't approve of his girl-friend (who subsequently became his wife) and that it would be nice if she and Fergus could get together. If they had actually obliged, it would have been an arranged marriage. 'No wonder I hated you. You were such a swot.'

Fergus had the tact to look embarrassed. 'Oh. I'm sorry. That must have been a pain. I worked hard at school because I didn't have any friends.'

For a moment, Julia's tender heart teetered in the direction of sympathy, but the expression in Fergus's eyes didn't quite bear out this pathetic statement.

'Didn't you? How sad. Perhaps if you hadn't been so horrible people would have liked you more.'

'Probably, but by the time I'd worked that out, I liked Latin and Greek.'

Julia extracted a tray from between the cooker and the sink. 'There's no hope for you, then.'

'Obviously not.' He lingered in the galley long enough to make Julia slightly regret her sarcasm. Then, 'I think I'll go and try my hand at steering,' he said, and went.

'I'm sure you'll be perfect at it,' Julia muttered, getting out the scales. And judging by how quickly Suzy appeared to savage the biscuit tin, he must have been pretty good.

'Fergus has been a complete hero, again,' said Suzy, through a mouthful crumbs.

'Oh? By taking hold of the tiller for you?'

Suzy regarded her strangely. 'No. Because he managed to get ace details on how to go down the river with a pair of narrow boats. Didn't he tell you?'

'No.'

'Oh, well, he did. He got talking to some people at the rowing club. One of them knew a man who used to run hotel boats down here years ago. The man at the club lent Fergus his bicycle, and Fergus cycled off to see him. He wrote it all down.' Suzy pulled a large brown envelope out of her back pocket. 'Look.'

Julia looked. Long detailed instructions about how to approach every bridge and lock on the river, all the way up to Worcester. So he was still a terrible swot. 'Terribly nerdy handwriting, don't you think?'

'Julia! I never thought you could be such a bitch! What have you got against him?'

She shrugged. 'I've told you. I just hated him as a child.'

'Well, he's not a child now and nor are you. Grow out of it!'

'OK,' conceded Julia. 'It was very clever and kind of him to get those details, but he has got nerdy handwriting.

It's hardly developed at all since he was a little boy.'

'How do you know?'

'He used to write my mother wonderful thank-you letters for Christmas presents. She used to show them to us. As examples. It's no wonder we hated him even before we met him.'

Suzy considered. 'Much as I hate to agree with you, that does sound a tad too good to be true.'

'Oh believe me, as a child, he was perfect.'

'And as I said before, he's not far off being perfect now.' Suzy left with a wet dishcloth slithering down her back.

Although Suzy's demand that Julia got over her dislike of Fergus was made more or less in jest, Julia did decide she must have a more positive approach to him. He was doing them a good turn. It wasn't his fault he was like he was, it was his mother's. And it was *her* mother's desperately unsubtle attempts at matchmaking which had brought him to them now. She mustn't take it out on him. So, when she had a few blissful moments before she had to worry about making a salad to go with the quiche, Julia climbed up through the engine room to join Suzy and Fergus. Suzy was steering, and Fergus was sitting with his arms over his knees, facing her.

'Hi!' Julia smiled as broadly as she could manage in the face of the brisk wind which was blowing. It was hard not to feel excluded by their mateyness, although she realised it was her own fault they had become a team she was not part of. 'I came for a breath of air. It's warm down in that kitchen.'

'Come and steer. You haven't done it while the boats are breasted up,' said Suzy.

Julia lowered herself from the roof to the counter. The river seemed more frightening than the canal, although it was hardly wider in some places. She held the tiller gingerly.

'It's really easy,' said Suzy. 'You'll soon get the hang of

it. It's like driving a car.'

'I haven't driven a car.'

'What, never?' Fergus seemed amazed. 'Why not?'

'I couldn't afford it when I was younger, and didn't need to do it when I was older. I should think I'm too old to learn, now.'

'Nonsense,' said Suzy and Fergus in chorus. 'You ought to be able to drive,' went on Suzy. 'It's a basic life skill. Like opening bottles of champagne.'

'What?' said Fergus.

'How is driving like opening champagne?' demanded Julia.

'They're both life skills. Ralph always used to go on about them when I was little. He said that everyone ought to know how to change a plug, drive a car, play the piano, ride a horse . . .'

'And make a decent béchamel sauce?' added Julia, so she could claim at least one life skill to her name.

'Well, yes, things like that.'

'And can you do all those things?' Fergus asked Suzy.

She nodded. 'The important ones, like driving, and opening bottles.'

'I suppose you can do everything,' said Julia to Fergus, feeling very inadequate.

'No. But I can iron, sew on buttons, drive and put on plugs.'

'And punt,' said Suzy.

He nodded. 'And Julia can cook if she can't drive.'

Rightly or wrongly, Julia felt patronised. 'And I can put on plugs, put up shelves, change light bulbs, unblock sinks, and put washers on taps. And run a damn good department, if I'm let!'

'Positively Renaissance woman,' said Fergus.

'Still not so hot on the steering though,' said Suzy, who had turned to see where they were going. 'If you go under those trees everything will be swept off . . . Too late.'

Chapter Eight

After an embarrassing half-hour fishing for everything from the roof which hadn't been attached, Julia hurried back to the kitchen, late for lunch. Judging by the passengers' cheery greeting, they had hugely enjoyed the little calamity, and were, in the nicest possible way, looking forward to the next one.

Julia, abashed at her dismal attempt at steering, resolved to have another go, and when she had washed up lunch and got dinner under way, she stuck her head out of the boat, to see if they were at a suitable place.

She was in time to see Suzy, with Fergus on the butty, on a short line, glide through Bidford Bridge like professionals. How had Fergus managed to pick up the knack of steering so quickly? Perhaps he was perfect at everything, as his mother claimed. She was chewing over this irritating thought when she became aware of someone on the bridge taking photographs. He seemed to have his camera pointed directly at her. Crosser than ever to have her bad temper captured on film, Julia retreated to the galley. If Fergus was so handy, he could help Suzy get the boats tied up on his own.

Later, she was washing aphids out of spring greens when Suzy came flying in, full of bad news. 'I've just heard, the river broke its banks during the winter, and now it's terribly narrow along one bit we go through tomorrow. We'll have to be singled out.'

'Well, let me know if you need me to help.'

'Er, no thanks,' said Suzy, as if asking Julia to do

anything to do with boat-handling was completely out of the question. Growling to herself, Julia resolved to become at least as good as Fergus at everything connected with the boat. She told Suzy of her ambition, and Suzy, duly impressed, said she would try and do more cooking. But although Suzy's expensive cooking course had taught her how to frost grapes and make chocolate rose leaves, it hadn't been so hot on peeling potatoes, or how to fill hungry people. The one day Suzy took over breakfast, so Julia could give the cabins a good go, she had to keep summoning Julia back every time anyone wanted a fried egg.

As the week went on the weather, which had kept some of the passengers inside, improved. It no longer seemed hard work looking after them, they looked after themselves. And although there weren't many locks, they all helped, pulling the boats about, fending off, opening and shutting the gates. Although the two women found time to tell each other how nice the passengers were when you got to know them, they neither of them cared to discuss what they would do after Fergus left them. He had been with them three days, and Julia had been expecting him to go any day, but she couldn't ask him about it, because she couldn't risk him misunderstanding her reasons for wanting to know.

After a gentle meander down the Avon, which included a night at Pershore, with Shakespeare's England on either bank, they reached Tewkesbury, where the Avon connected with the River Severn. Everyone, passengers and crew, fell in love with the town's many half-timbered buildings which threatened to topple over into the street, the series of alleys snaking through from the river bank to the town, and its golden abbey which looked over the town with calm benevolence.

Suzy, Julia and Fergus had decided that while their guests were exploring the town, they just about had time to visit the abbey themselves. Just before they got there, however, Suzy noticed a clothes shop and vanished, leaving Julia alone with Fergus.

'I won't be long,' she called.

'I'll believe that when I see it,' grunted Fergus, taking Julia's arm.

The minute they got through the doors of the abbey, Julia was entranced. A shaft of spring sunshine shone through the windows on to the golden stone floor. All the turmoil of the last couple of months fell away and Julia enjoyed a moment or two of perfect content. She wandered among the vast, golden pillars, awed by their size and majesty.

Just then, someone started to play one of Handel's organ concertos. The music took her soaring with it to the heights of the abbey. They both stood quite still for its duration and it was only after the unseen organist had finished playing, when they had been there some time, that Fergus led her away.

'Come on. I've got to have a word with you. Suzy too, if she ever reappears again.'

The sun seemed very warm after the coolness of the abbey. 'I'm sure she's only window-shopping. She hasn't got any money.' Julia lay down on the grass and shut her eyes. She didn't want to hear what Fergus was going to say.

Fergus sat beside her, pulling at the grass. 'I really must sort out my life before going abroad. I've spent far longer with you than I should have.'

Julia sat up. This was her chance to make up for all her churlishness. 'It was very kind of you to come with us at all. I'm sorry I've been so . . .'

'What?'

A gentleman, Julia thought, too late, wouldn't have asked that, but it was her own fault for giving him the opportunity. 'Grumpy,' she said eventually, in preference to: 'Thoroughly screwed up about my feelings for you'.

He seemed to read her thoughts. 'It must be such a change for you, working on the boats after your high-powered executive career.'

Hearing her mother's words in his, she laughed. 'It probably wasn't half as high-powered as my mother would have had you believe. She exaggerates terribly. But it is very different. I like it.'

'So it's just me that makes you so prickly?'

Julia's mouth opened and shut on her protestations. She decided the truth was probably her best bet. 'To be quite honest with you, Fergus, some part of me still thinks of you as Freddie. Who I hated.'

'But why?'

'I think it was the spider. It was years before I could deal with them myself after you put it on my leg.' She looked up and smiled, eager to distract him from the subject of her feelings. 'Dealing with spiders should be one of Suzy's life skills, don't you think?'

He looked down into her eyes, responding to her smile. 'It certainly should. But I didn't put it on your leg on purpose, you know. It started to wriggle and I dropped it. I don't like them very much myself.'

'Oh. I thought little boys were always fine with them. Rupert, my brother, just picks them up in his bare hand.'

'I couldn't possibly do that. I don't kill them, of course.'

'Of course not. I use a large plastic jug and put them outside. What do you do?'

'Julia, I don't know if you're deliberately dragging the subject out, but I think that's enough about spiders.'

Caught out, Julia blushed. 'Well, you started it.'

Fergus gave her a brief, reproving frown, which made her forget all about little Freddie. 'What I'm trying to get round to saying, if you'll give me the chance, is that I'm going to have to leave you.'

'Oh.' It was not unexpected at all, but it was still a shock.

'It's an easy run up from here, according to the notes.' From his back pocket he produced the much-thumbed, closely written envelope which had become Suzy's Bible. 'It's just a couple of hours from here to Upton-upon-Severn, and then on to Worcester, and lock up into Diglis Basin.'

Unjustly, Julia felt abandoned. She prised a circle of something which turned out to be bread dough from under a fingernail. 'Of course, you've got your own life. As I said, it was very kind of you to come with us at all.'

'But you for one will be pleased to see me go? Because of the spider?'

Julia swallowed, giving herself time to think of a yes or no answer which would be true, and yet not give him the impression that her feelings for him had changed. As she seemed destined to remain silent for ever, she was very glad that Suzy chose this moment to rejoin them.

'Fergus says he's got to go,' Julia said immediately, sounding horribly as if she were telling tales.

Suzy wailed. 'But then we've got the Worcester and Birmingham Canal! It's got hundreds of tiny little single locks. We'll never manage two-handed. Not with passengers. Couldn't you put off Italy and spend the summer with us?'

Julia was horrified. 'You've no right to ask Fergus to do that. He can't just put his life on hold because we've got no crew! It was very kind of him to help us for this long. He only said he could stay a couple of days in the first place!'

'I know.' Suzy flung herself next to him and took hold of his arm. 'And we've been so grateful. Haven't we, Julia?'

'Of course.' Julia turned her attention to a fine table-top tomb.

Fergus got to his feet and moved round so he stood in Julia's line of vision. 'But Julia would have been a lot more grateful if I'd been someone else. Isn't that right, Julia?'

Julia forced herself to meet his eyes. 'Fergus, I – I mean –'

'Don't struggle to think up a tactful lie, I don't care what you feel about me. It's just the bullshit I can't take.'

'I don't think you should use language like that in a sacred place, Fergus,' said Suzy primly. Grateful to have the tension broken, Julia chuckled.

Back on the boats, while Fergus disappeared into his cabin, presumably to pack, Julia would have retreated too, only Suzy needed her to help consider their extremely limited options.

'How are we going to manage?' demanded Suzy rhetorically as they sat in the sunshine on top of the boat. 'We can't depend on having helpful passengers. We've been lucky this week, having such lovely ones. We're not full next week, but if they all want waiting on hand, foot and finger, how are we to get by?'

Julia chewed her lip. 'I don't suppose you would get a whole boatful of people unwilling to lean on a lock-gate or open a paddle, but it is possible.'

'I wouldn't mind so much if it was a boatful, but it's only five. With five we just about break even, but I need to go into profit soon.'

Julia twiddled the end of a piece of rope coiled on the roof. 'Do the bookings get better later?'

Suzy nodded. 'Mmm. Leamington to Oxford is fully booked. If we ever get to Leamington, with all those locks and no one but us to work them.'

'We'll just have to go slower, not try to do so much in a day. Or would that put us behind schedule?'

'It would. And we don't want to be worrying about that as well as everything else.'

Julia sighed. Even if she became as adept as Suzy at the boats, with just two of them, the next week would be a very long haul. 'I'll ring my mother, and see if she knows anyone.'

'I thought you'd done that!'

Julia bit her lip apologetically. 'I sort of forgot.' Suzy's reproachful look made her go on. 'I didn't want to answer a whole lot of questions about what I thought of Fergus, didn't I *like* him, and stuff. I told you how she's been trying to marry us off for years. It would be much better if she just thinks he gave us the cookery book and left. What about Joan? Have you asked her?'

Suzy nodded. 'She and Uncle Ralph may come up with someone.' Her voice tailed away and Julia got the impression that Suzy's mind had wandered off the subject. 'Look!' she murmured. 'In that canoe, at twelve o'clock.'

Julia looked at her watch in panic.

'Not that sort of twelve o'clock, dimbo. I mean – oh, never mind. He's going right past us.'

'Who is?'

'The cutest little stud-muffin I've seen all week.'

The next twenty minutes gave Julia plenty of opportunity to watch Suzy's skill at putting out a line and hauling in her chosen catch. As they washed down the boats with the painted mop and river water, Suzy gave the stud-muffin a half-smile, and when he smiled back she tossed her head.

'Come on, Julia, let's go shopping,' Suzy said.

'What? You mean you've spotted another designer store? I thought you'd had your therapy for this morning.'

'Not that sort of shopping! Groceries!'

'Groceries?' Julia didn't know that this word was in Suzy's vocabulary.

'Yes! There must be something you need!'

'Well, of course there is. But should we both leave the boats at the same time?'

'Oh, Fergus is still around somewhere. He can repel boarders. Come on.'

Knowing there was a hidden agenda behind Suzy's sudden interest in food, Julia went happily. Her practical nature told her it was better to shop in Tewkesbury, when the passengers were all looking after themselves, than to

96

try and do it all on Saturday, which would be their first change-over day, and probably hell in a bucket.

Together they hit the supermarket and staggered back to the boats, arms stretched and fingers cut nearly in two by the plastic carrier bags. Julia got on board first, heaving her bags after her, cursing Fergus for not being around to help. When, a little while later, Suzy followed her, she was not alone.

'Where would you like these?' asked the young man from the canoe. He was, Julia was forced to acknowledge, even more stunning close up.

'Oh, just put them on the counter.' Suzy's voice was husky with admiration for his strength and chivalry. 'We'll put them away when we've finished. You are wonderful. My arms were practically dropping off.'

'It's all right. It wasn't heavy.' His voice had a sleepy Gloucestershire lilt which, Julia was fairly sure, must have lulled many an unwary girl into bed.

'It was to me,' said Suzy, dewy-eyed.

Amused and appalled at Suzy's shamelessness, Julia frantically tried to pack too much food into too little space.

'I've got to stock up on lager now,' Suzy said. 'Fancy giving me a hand?'

This was a blatant lie. The lockers in the fore-deck were full of it. Their first week's passengers had not been a beer-drinking crowd.

'We could do with some tinned tomatoes, too,' Julia said, thinking that she could learn from Suzy's un-scrupulous methods. After all, she'd spent most of her life being politically correct and sensible, and all it had got her was Oscar.

Suzy and the stud-muffin went off together, not exactly hand in hand, but certainly hip to hip in their faded denim and desert boots. They both looked extremely young, although Suzy could give her new friend five years, at least.

'Where's Suzy?' asked Fergus, when he appeared, too late to be useful, loaded rucksack at his feet.

'Gone shopping with a very young man, who, if he's not careful, will find himself going up Tardebigge.'

'So you won't need me to do it, then?'

Julia longed just to agree with him, but the thought of playing gooseberry between Suzy and her young man was not appealing. 'You can't do it,' she stalled.

'I could, possibly, if I abandoned my plans until the summer.'

'You wouldn't want to do that. I expect Italy is at its best in spring. Not too hot.'

'That's right.'

'Off you go then.' Julia tried to smile, to overcome her ungenerous thoughts, but only one half of her mouth would work. She felt Fergus looking at her and examined her deck-shoes, noting as she did so that they were already showing signs of wear.

'You don't want me to come back then?'

'Not if you'd rather be in Italy, no.' That, surely, was sufficiently ambiguous.

'OK. Well, I'd better be off. I've got to catch a bus to Stratford.'

'Why Stratford?'

'My car's there.'

Julia suddenly felt extremely stupid. Of course it was. How else had he travelled all the way from her mother in the Lake District? But he hadn't mentioned it when there had been several occasions at Stratford when having the use of a car would have made the whole difference. 'If you had a car,' she said carefully, omitting references to gas bottles and heavy loads of shopping, 'why did you spend all morning cycling off to find that person who used to run hotel boats?'

'Because it was in a garage, being mended.'

'So you broke down in Stratford? You didn't make a

special journey to see me at all?'

Facing the light, Julia couldn't see his expression. 'Not entirely. I had the book from your mother, but I had no real intention of doing more than posting it, until the car started overheating and I thought I might not make it back to Oxford. Then I remembered the book, deviated to Stratford, which I know well, and found a garage. They said they couldn't fix it for a few days.'

'So you didn't come with us to help us out? You needed a bed for a while!'

'Not really. I could have stayed anywhere.'

'At vast expense!'

He shrugged. 'That wouldn't have mattered. I could have got on with some research while I was in the area.'

'So it was . . .' The word teetered on the tip of her tongue as if reluctant to leave it. '. . . altruism which made you stay and give us a hand?'

He sighed, shrugged and shook his head slightly. 'It was whatever you like. I can't work out if you want me to be a nice guy who gave you a hand when you were in a spot, or a wicked adventurer who took advantage of two vulnerable women.'

Julia looked at him, thinking hard. But she couldn't work it out either.

'Anyway,' he went on. 'I can't wait for Suzy, so will you say goodbye and thank you to her for me?'

'She ought to be thanking you.'

He laughed. 'I'm sure she would, very warmly, if she was here. But she's not so I shall have to do without gratitude.'

Julia took a deep breath. 'As her deputy, I can thank you on her behalf.'

His eyebrow shot up. 'Sure you're not taking too much on yourself?'

She had been, until then. 'Of course not.'

'Good, then come here.' Next, Fergus, Mr Respectable,

the A-Grade Student with the Double First, pulled Julia to her feet and into his arms and kissed her, long, hard and thoroughly. She was still staggering slightly as he jumped off the roof on to the pontoon. It vibrated with every footstep as he strode away.

'Just as well he made such a quick escape,' said Julia to a passing swan, some minutes later. 'Or I would have slapped his face.'

As she predicted, by the time Suzy and her swain, who was called Wayne, returned from the supermarket, Wayne had become Jason's replacement. In spite of lacking his qualifications.

'Isn't it wonderful?' said Suzy. 'Wayne's unemployed at the moment.'

'Wonderful,' echoed Julia, wondering if Wayne found it wonderful too.

'So he's going to be our crew.'

Julia smiled. 'That's great. Have you much narrow-boat experience?'

'He canoes,' answered Suzy. 'And no one else we're likely to get is going to have narrow-boat experience, either.'

'True,' acknowledged Julia, who felt they shouldn't be having this conversation in front of Wayne. 'And canoes are narrow. Have you done much cooking?' As she asked him, she felt Suzy's indignation boring into her, but she ignored it. 'The thing is,' she explained to them both, 'until you get a bit of experience, I'm going to have to help out with the boats a lot. Which means I'll need help in the kitchen.'

Wayne grinned. He had white, even teeth under an attractively crooked smile. His hair was very short and very fair, and his pectorals were trying to escape from the T-shirt he wore under his suede jacket. A good-looking lad by anyone's standards. 'My uncle runs a burger stall which goes round the shows. I've helped him out often enough.'

Julia brightened up considerably. He should at least know how to chop an onion. 'That is handy.'

'How much are you paying him?' Julia demanded, as soon as Wayne had gone home to tell his mother and to get his things. 'He looks as if he's got potential.'

Suzy giggled. 'As what, exactly?'

'As a replacement for Jason, that's what.'

'Oh. Well, I'm paying him the same.' Suzy wrinkled her brow and fell silent.

'That sounds fair enough,' said Julia. 'He probably wouldn't have come for less.'

'No. But I should pay you more than him. I mean, you're more like a partner than an employee.'

'It's all right. We agreed a hundred a week.'

'I think I should pay you a salary. Monthly. More than Wayne.'

'Suzy, that's really kind, but can you afford it?'

Suzy flushed. 'It might be easier like that. My cash-flow situation is fairly bad. In fact' – Suzy had the air of someone eager to get a load off her shapely chest – 'it would be a whole lot easier if I could pay you in a lump at the end of the season. Pay you more. Than I would have done.'

Julia thought for a moment. 'Well, I don't suppose it makes much difference to me really. But what shall I do about spending money? For my bits and pieces?'

'Do what I do, use the petty cash. Oh Julia, you're such a doll. How can I ever thank you? And don't worry, I haven't forgotten I owe you for the gas.'

The passengers were sorry not to have the opportunity to say goodbye to Fergus.

'He was such a nice man,' said one of the lady English teachers. 'Finishing a book, you know.'

Julia didn't know, but nodded anyway.

'Yes. He had a term's sabbatical to do it in. Very

considerate, those universities. Do you think school would give me time off to finish reading *War and Peace*?'

'What is his book about?' asked the second lady teacher.

'Something to do with fourth-century mosaics,' answered her friend. 'Can't remember exactly what.'

'Oh yes. I knew it was something Roman. It should be very interesting. Archaeology is something of a hobby of mine. I always watch *Timeteam*. So how did you come to meet Fergus?'

Julia flushed, as if she'd picked Fergus up off the side of the river, like Suzy had Wayne. 'He's an old friend of the family.'

'So you'll know what happened to his wife?'

'Um – not really.' She may not particularly like Fergus, but she didn't want to gossip about him.

'So what does young Wayne do exactly?' asked the archaeology fan, disappointed.

'He's unemployed. It's a great stroke of luck for us, actually,' went on Julia, on solid ground once more. 'Our proper crew just walked out on us, two hours before you were all due to arrive.'

'Oh. So Fergus wasn't your crew then?'

'No. He was just helping out. In a friendly way.' Now he was gone, Julia wished she'd been more friendly herself.

'*Such* a nice man,' the lady teacher said again.

'Wayne's very nice too,' said Julia.

'I'm sure. Have you known him long?'

Julia busked her way through a maze of half-truths. 'Er – not personally, but I think Suzy knows him quite well.' Well, she would do by now, even if she hadn't when she employed him.

The two ladies regarded her as if they knew perfectly well what Julia meant, but fortunately the Bernsteins came through with their souvenirs which had to be admired, so they didn't comment.

On the short journey from Tewkesbury to Upton-upon-

Severn, Wayne turned out to be quick on the uptake as they went through the lock. Later, he steered perfectly up the river, the two boats side by side.

Julia saw a kingfisher, a flash of blue like a streak of artificial silk, it was so bright. A good omen, she told herself firmly.

But although Wayne came into the galley and offered to help wash up the lunch, and chatted matily with the passengers while he cleared the table, she didn't find him as stunningly attractive as Suzy did.

'He's got such super genes,' said Suzy, when Julia went up with a cup of coffee and Wayne tidied up the ropes at the fore-end.

Julia peered at them, but from seventy feet away, couldn't see they were anything special. 'They look like ordinary 501s to me.'

'Not that sort of jeans!' Suzy shouted with laughter. 'I meant genes with a G.'

'Oh.' Julia wasn't as confident as Suzy that their conversation couldn't be heard. Just because Suzy couldn't a hear a word that was shouted to her from the bow while she was steering, it didn't mean sound couldn't carry the other way. 'How do you know?' she added.

'You just need to look at him! He's a hunk! Just what you need to make the perfect baby.'

'Suzy, you're not thinking of having a baby, are you?' Suzy had a lot of qualities that Julia greatly admired, but she was given to wild flights of fancy.

'No, no, of course not. But if I were your age . . .'

Why did everyone think of her age in terms of making babies? First Oscar and now Suzy. 'Suzy, I am not approaching the end of my child-bearing years, and even if I was, Wayne is about twenty years too young for me. And however beautiful he is, I don't want his child!'

As Julia ducked down into the engine room, she became aware of Wayne's somewhat startled expression as he looked towards the steering end of the boat. The fact that her suspicions about sound travel had been proved correct didn't help Julia's temper.

They passed a peaceful night at Upton, and in the morning they set off early for Worcester, to give the passengers a chance to see the cathedral and porcelain factory. They found a place on the river to moor, and the passengers streamed off, giving Julia and Suzy a chance to do some necessary chores. Diglis Basin, which they knew would be crowded and difficult to find space in, could wait until after this week's passengers had left, and before the next lot arrived.

Their last dinner together was both celebratory and sad. It seemed to Julia and Suzy that their dearest friends were leaving them, and they weren't looking forward to having them replaced by a lot of strangers.

'I can't believe it was your first week in operation,' said Florence. 'You did so well. And Fergus, of course.'

'Yes.' The English teachers allowed themselves to become a little misty-eyed at the thought of Fergus.

Julia and Suzy were also quietly proud at how well they'd managed, but knew that the river was easy compared with what they had to tackle the following week. Just going up from the river to the canal basin was going to be challenging enough.

Next morning the passengers all kissed Julia and Suzy goodbye, and promised to send their friends and to come again. They thanked Wayne less profusely, got into their waiting taxis and went away.

Julia felt quite tearful. 'They were *so* nice. Do you think we'll ever like another lot as much?'

Suzy sounded choked too. 'Remember what Ralph said? You get to like them all in the end.'

'They gave me a tip,' said Wayne. 'Shall we share it?'

'Oh no, you keep it,' said Suzy. 'Unless Julia . . .?'

'Oh no,' Julia declared, as if she had no need of such charity. 'You've earned it.'

That little matter settled, Suzy became business-like. 'Right, let's do the cabins. Come on, Wayne, I'll show you the way to change a duvet cover.'

A new variation on an old theme, thought Julia, and followed them more slowly.

Chapter Nine

꧁✤꧂

'God! I'm glad we've got Wayne!' said Suzy soon after their passengers had left.

'Why particularly? Because of all those locks we've got ahead of us?' Julia asked.

'Locks, schmocks. No, it's the pump-out. I know this is going to be my business and the boss ought to be able to do everything so he can tell the workers how to do it, but the thought of the pump-out makes me gag. Wayne did it without turning a hair.'

'He hasn't much hair to turn,' said Julia, but she saw Suzy's point.

The cabins and less savoury tasks done, they decided they could afford to stop lurking out of sight on the river, and move up the deep river lock into the yacht basin, where their next set of passengers would eventually meet them. Fortunately there were lots of people around eager to help, but it was a baptism of fire for Wayne, and a real test of their boatmen's skills for the two women. But they managed it, without shouting, without mishap, and, cleverer still, without banging into anything that dented.

They had finally squeezed alongside and tied up, and were collapsed in the saloon, recovering from the narrowness of their last encounter with a plastic boat, when the man sent by Aunt Joan arrived.

He was in his early sixties, cheerful and called Fred. He had worked with Ralph years ago, and although he had left long since, he still thought of hotel boats with affection. Suzy had, she told Julia later, asked Joan if he might like to come back to the boats and be a crew. But apparently he was now heavily into showing chrysanthemums, and wouldn't leave them. He brought with him clean laundry and mail. He handed Suzy a typed letter in a very expensive white envelope.

She opened it immediately. 'My bloody father,' she muttered, and then read it, clicking her teeth and ranting softly about the unfairness of some people.

Julia had a similar envelope with Oscar's assertive handwriting on it, and another one, typed, which had been redirected from her home. She decided to wait until she was alone to open her letters in case Oscar's made her react like Suzy. She didn't want Fred thinking they were both completely mad.

'Can I get you something to drink?' she asked him, covering for Suzy.

'Cup of tea, love. I won't stay long. I know what Saturdays are like. In the old days we always had to turn the fridge upside down on Saturdays.'

This caught Suzy's attention. 'Did you? Why?'

'It was a gas fridge, and it was getting old. The pilot light kept going out. The only way to get the air out of the system was to turn it upside down. Bloody nuisance. Had to take everything out, of course. And someone always came to see you while you were doing it. But in a lot of ways life was simpler back then. There weren't so many rules and regulations. Joan was telling me you have to worry about Health and Safety people now.' He shook his head pessimistically. 'Terrible. I don't know how you'd get old boats like these hygienic.'

Julia and Suzy exchanged anxious glances.

'Oh well.' Fred drained his mug. 'I'll let you get on, then. Good luck, and see you next week at Leamington.' Wayne came into the saloon at that moment. 'I hope you're feeling fit, young man,' said Fred. 'Forty-two locks in front of you. And that's just Tardebigge and the Stoke flight.' Wayne smiled beatifically. 'Pity about Jason,' Fred went on. 'You need experience on that canal.'

Everyone tried not to feel anxious about the lack of Jason or the arrival of the new passengers – and it wasn't just their personalities they were concerned about. 'We need healthy, helpful people,' Julia explained to Wayne.

'Particularly as we've only got five passengers this week,' added Suzy.

'And what if you don't get them?' enquired Wayne. 'Leave them on the tow-path? Or shall I go down the pub and round up the local tug-of-war team?'

Fortunately, the first guest arrived at this moment, so they weren't obliged to answer.

'Hi! Have I got the right boats?'

The owner of this aristocratic, husky female voice turned out to be Delphine, a pleasant, attractive advertising executive, who announced she was going to do nothing except drink gin and tonic and watch the scenery.

If Delphine had arrived on any of their other scheduled routes, this information would have cheered Suzy enormously. But now she handed Delphine a cup of tea. 'I'm sure you'll feel much more energetic after a good night's sleep.'

'I don't think so, darling. I'm so stressed out. Do you mind if I smoke?'

'In the well-deck, please,' said Julia. 'Shall I bring you some cake?'

Delphine, who was extremely thin, regarded the cake. 'Mmm, chocolate. I really shouldn't, but then . . .'

'You are on holiday,' Julia finished for her, putting a large piece on a plate.

Delphine bit into it. 'Yummy. What time does the bar open?'

Each new arrival was assessed and tactfully interrogated for heart conditions, bad backs and recent operations. They ended up with Delphine, delightful but idle, a couple whose male half was a steam enthusiast, who looked fairly promising, and a couple of women from New Zealand, who could turn out to be really helpful, but might not.

'One of them's got knitting with her,' said Suzy while Julia was peeling potatoes. 'I saw it peeping out of her bag. Not a good sign.'

'I don't know. She does come from New Zealand. You probably have to support the local industry.'

As soon as everyone was established on board, they processed slowly up the canal to find a quiet spot for the night. Julia stared out of the window as the hidden face of Worcester slipped past: the porcelain factory, the allotments and little terraces of houses. The rapid change from urban to rural scenery was one of the things Julia loved about canals.

They had to go through six locks before they could reasonably expect to find a bit of canal wide enough for them to tie up alongside.

'This'll sort the men from the boys,' murmured Suzy to Julia at the first of these as together they heaved the bottom gate shut on the motor.

But fortunately for everyone, there were a fair number of people hanging about the tow-path, willing to help and give advice. They had to endure the usual comments about seventy feet being too long for boats these days, and people tended to think that their steam enthusiast, John, was in charge, not Suzy. But Julia felt able to go and attend to her sizzling chops and bubbling potatoes and not feel she was leaving Suzy short-handed.

Eventually, the engine noise ceasing, rapidly followed by the sound of mooring spikes being hammered in, told Julia it was time for dinner. She clattered a pile of plates into the oven and washed the saucepans.

'Sorry to go on so long.' Suzy thrust her dirty hands under the tap, narrowly missing the draining potatoes.

'It's hard to find somewhere we can tie up breasted. The canal seems so narrow after the river.'

Julia thought she looked tired and a bit depressed. The letter from her father had probably affected her more than she would have liked to admit. But when she went into the saloon, Julia saw some of her natural bounce return. The saloon looked pretty and welcoming, the table was set and all the passengers had started drinking. And one of the women from New Zealand was poring over the canal guide.

'All those locks! They look like little legs crawling up the page, don't they?'

'And we have to go through each one twice,' said her friend. 'I might have a go at helping tomorrow. I just wanted to learn how they worked tonight.'

'You're all so energetic,' complained Delphine. 'I'm on holiday to rest.'

'The important thing is,' said Suzy, pouring herself a large vodka, 'that you enjoy yourselves. How you do it is up to you.'

'Oh good,' said John's wife, who'd kept her tapestry hidden in her luggage until now. 'John gets bored on holiday unless he's allowed to get dirty.'

'Oh?' said Delphine. 'How come?'

'He likes shovelling coal best. But as long as he can wear his boiler suit, he's happy as Larry. Me,' she went on philosophically, 'I do bargello.'

Suzy gave her a sideways look. 'Just as long as that doesn't encourage our New Zealand friend to do her knitting instead of working locks,' she muttered to Julia. 'A sewing circle is no good to us.'

It was not until Julia and Suzy had at last packed their passengers off to bed that Julia remembered her letters, stuffed unopened in her jeans pocket. She ripped into Oscar's first, anxious to get to bed herself.

'Oh no!' She lay down and screwed up her eyes. 'I don't

believe it!'

'What?' demanded Suzy.

'It's Oscar. He's booked a holiday with us.'

'Ohmygod. How awful for you.'

'That's not the worst.' Julia wanted to howl. 'He's bringing his mother with him!'

Suzy watched Julia have mild hysterics while she creamed her face. 'Open your other letter. It might be good news.'

Julia took a while to grasp the meaning of the other letter. It was from a solicitor. It seemed that Strange's were pursuing her for theft. According to the letter they alleged she had taken valuable papers with her when she left, and these had been used to set up a rival organisation. A specialised lettings agency had set up in the town, and it was all her fault. Allegedly.

'Not good news?' enquired Suzy, when Julia hadn't spoken for some minutes.

'Confusing news. I'm being accused of stealing some papers from where I worked and giving them to a competitor. I have no idea what they're talking about. I swear I didn't take anything with me except pictures of my sister's children and my spider plant.'

'Then why are they accusing you of taking them?'

'Probably because Darren's lost the papers and is blaming it on me. And they're paranoid about competition. How did I manage to work there so long?'

This was a rhetorical question but Suzy wanted it answered. 'So, how did you?'

'Well, I really liked most of the other women who worked there, and when I first started setting up the lettings department, Peter Strange gave me a pretty free hand. Then I was out of the country a lot, arranging a deal with a big Finnish company.' Julia became aware that her boss was staring at her anxiously. When applying for the job, she'd described herself as a glorified secretary.

111

'I had no idea you were so high-powered. You didn't tell me any of this at the interview.'

'Would you have employed me if I had?'

Suzy exhaled slowly. 'No way! I'd have been far too terrified.'

'I didn't mean to mislead you. And all the stuff I did at Strange's wasn't at all relevant to hotel-boating. I would have been terribly disappointed if I hadn't even got an interview.'

'And I'd've been up shit creek without a paddle if I hadn't given you the job.' Suzy giggled. 'But what will you do about being accused of stealing, then?'

Julia shrugged. 'Tell my brother about it, I suppose. He's a solicitor. He mostly does boring things like conveyancing and boundary disputes, but he could probably come up with something. He told my sister he'd help if I wanted to sue for constructive dismissal.'

'Instead they're suing you.'

'I know. Ironic, isn't it?'

Suzy, who had been looking doleful, brightened up. 'Tell you what! Let's have a brandy! We can celebrate you being here and having the right sort of brother, and it'll help us sleep. I'll go and fetch the bottle.'

The following morning, too early for her sister, who had had another broken night with Petal, Julia rang. 'Ange. Sorry to be a pain, but could you get on to Rupert for me? I haven't time to listen to the lectures.'

'Why?' Angela, for her part, had no time for pleasantries.

'Bloody Strange's is suing me for taking papers out of the office.'

'What? How odd. You didn't, did you?'

'Of course not! I expect Darren's lost them, that's all. But I could do with a little legal back-up from Rupe.'

Angela yawned loudly. 'I'll get on to him as soon as I can find a minute to phone. Oh, how I yearn for a good night's sleep!'

Julia was sympathetic. 'Those babies do take it out of you. Just as well I didn't marry Oscar, I would never have coped.'

This made Angela wake up. 'I'm really glad you didn't marry Oscar too, but not because of the babies. My babies are my life's blood.' She yawned again. 'You'd love yours just as much if you ever had any.'

'Yeah, yeah, I'm sure I would, if ever I was unwise enough – but enough of that. You'll speak to Rupert?'

'The moment I have a chance.'

'It's all going to be absolutely fine!' said Suzy confidently as Julia laid a tray for coffee. 'Wayne's steering like a dream. The passengers have all got the hang of it – except Delphine – and are going like stink! I don't know why everyone makes such a fuss about this canal!'

Suddenly there was a bang which sent the tray of coffee mugs crashing into the sink and Suzy charging out of the boat. Julia, having caught a cake just before it landed on the floor, followed her out.

'What the *fuck* do you think you're doing?' It was a fierce-looking girl in dungarees standing on the roof of a seventy-foot narrow boat. She was hurling abuse at Wayne with a vehemence Julia hadn't often encountered. 'Now you've got the bloody motor stemmed up. What a game of soldiers!'

Suzy glared back at the girl, and took a breath to defend her golden boy. But after taking in the situation, she changed her mind, pushed Wayne out of the way, and reversed *Pyramus* so it was no longer sticking into the bow of the first pair of hotel boats they had come across.

'Sorry about that,' said Suzy. 'It's our first season, and our first time up this bit of canal.'

The girl in the dungarees had the wind taken out of her invective by Suzy's apology. 'Oh. Where's Jason?'

Suzy had by this time thrown a line to Wayne, who had

jumped ashore, and was now pulling *Pyramus* gently into the side. 'He left us before the first passengers came.'

'Holy shit! The bastard! Why'd he do that?'

Suzy shrugged. 'Couldn't work for a woman.'

This statement melted any residual annoyance. 'Typical bloody man. But where's Ralph?'

But before Suzy could answer, a very tall, lean young man appeared on the scene. 'Would you mind getting the motor out of the fucking way, so we can get the fucking butty out of the lock?' he demanded, although his tone was less aggressive than his language.

Julia, who had got off the boat at the first opportunity, wondered if he spoke like that in front of the passengers, and hoped that none of theirs was in earshot. Not that she didn't have a specialised vocabulary of her own for moments of stress, but she tended to keep it for when she was alone.

Somehow, the boats got disentangled and, despite such an unpromising beginning, both crews were keen to have a good gossip with others of their kind, and agreed that a coffee stop was in order. By the time Julia had fished out broken shards from the sink, found new mugs and served coffee and biscuits to the passengers and brought up a tray for the others, Suzy, Wayne, and the four members of *Otter* and *Beaver*'s crew were chatting away to each other like old friends.

'Come and meet *Otter* and *Beaver*'s crowd,' said Suzy. 'They've been telling us how to use those little hooks at the side of the canal for pulling the butty out of the lock. This is Jed' – this was the man who had sworn at the girl – 'and Jade.' This was the girl who had sworn at Wayne. 'And Nellie and Annie.' She indicated two long-legged lovelies who made Julia's thirty-plus years and size fourteen jeans seem ancient and fat.

'Hi!' She held out a packet of Hobnobs reserved for emergencies. 'Biscuit?'

'I can't believe you guys manage with only three crew,' said Nellie, as the packet of biscuits shrank away in Julia's hand. 'We find it hard enough with four. Who else cooks but you, Julia?'

'No one,' said Suzy. 'Julia's a saint.'

'Mug more like,' said Nellie.

'So,' said Jade, 'what happened to Ralph?'

'I told you he was my uncle? Well he's had to give up hotel-boating. I was going to run the boats this year with Jason, only he buggered off. He's such a pig.'

'He hasn't gone with this new pair, then?' asked Jed.

'What new pair?' asked Julia.

'We don't know they're a new pair,' said Annie. 'We just supposed there must have been one being built because someone was hanging round the boatyard a while ago looking for crew. It could have been for an existing pair.'

'And that lock-keeper up near Birmingham was pretty grumpy when we passed,' agreed Jade. 'Didn't he say his girlfriend had gone back to the bastard he'd saved her from? He was really bitter about it.'

'So do you think she left him to go back to Jason, then?' asked Annie.

Jed shrugged. 'Sounds like it. And I can't imagine him staying away from canals for long.'

'So how do you know Jason and Ralph?' asked Julia, who didn't want to think about Jason's love-life.

'Oh, we've been working this pair as a team for two years now,' said Jed. 'You get to know the other pairs quite well if you tie up near each other, and have a good session at the pub. Which is why,' Jed continued, 'I was surprised when this guy came round looking for crew. We would have heard if there were any new pairs being built at any of the boatyards.'

'Well, I really ought to be doing something about lunch,' said Julia.

'If there's only one of you, you'd better,' agreed Nellie.

115

Suzy also got to her feet. 'Thank you so much for telling us about the hook. I've been cursing that block on the roof of the butty, and now I know what it's for.'

'That's perfectly all right,' said Jed, mimicking Suzy's Sloaney accent. 'It was fun running into you. See you again, in Chelsea.'

Suzy gave him a snarl which ignited Jed's smouldering interest in her. 'Next time we meet up, sunshine, it'll be at a pub, and we'll see who's first under the table.'

Jed's female crew all laughed.

But Suzy didn't waste time crowing over her most recent conquest. 'I've just had the most dreadful thought! Supposing that man looking for crew is also looking for a pair of boats to buy? If Jason and his girlfriend have got back together, they'd be perfect. She was a cook, remember.' Julia nodded. 'And what pair could quite easily be for sale? If we don't make a go of it? Ralph needs the money for the boats quite badly. Joan told me she thought he ought to sell them outright, and not let me have them on easy terms. After his operation he'll be feeling weak. He could easily be tempted to sell if someone offered him ready cash. Jason might have known that. It may be why he left.'

It did make sense. 'You mean the new buyer would put Jason and his girlfriend on as crew?'

'They'd be ideal. They know the boats, he knows the cut, and she's an ace cook.'

'But she'd have to be very good with people to make up for him. And as a couple, they're unstable. They split up before, they might easily do again.'

'But they're not going to tell the buyers that, are they?'

With difficulty, Julia searched for something positive to say. 'Well, they're not likely to buy the boats mid-season, are they? I mean, who would want to do that?'

Suzy shrugged. 'We're only two weeks into it. Even if it took a while to arrange, they've still got half the summer and the autumn left. Or' – Suzy was well into pessimism now – 'it could be someone who just doesn't want us to operate.'

'Well, they wouldn't bother to find crew, would they? And Ralph wouldn't sell to anyone but you, especially not mid-season.' Julia sounded as reassuring as she could, having suddenly remembered the man taking photographs at Bidford. Supposing he wasn't just a happy snapper, but a scout for a rival hotel-boat firm? She dismissed this as paranoia, caught from her old firm's reaction to a bit of mislaid paperwork.

'Ralph wouldn't.' Gloomily, Suzy picked a piece of broken mug out of the plug-hole. 'But Joan might, while he's in a weakened state.'

'I'm sure she wouldn't do any such thing. Now, are we going to stay here for lunch?'

They did, and so, apparently, did *Otter* and *Beaver*, for while Julia was frantically trying to wash everything up, to get it safely stowed before they moved off again, Suzy clattered in.

'Good news! John's been talking to them on *Otter* and has got this block and tackle thing cracked. So he's going to take charge of the butty with the other passengers.'

'Oh.' Julia slowed up a little. John, their steam enthusiast, had temporarily become a canalaholic.

'Which means you and I can forge ahead with the motor.'

'Oh.' Six plates got shoved into a box rather rapidly.

'I'll work the locks, so I can keep an eye on the passengers. You steer.'

Julia stopped altogether. 'But what about Wayne?'

'I'll have to leave him with the butty, bow-hauling. We can't let the passengers do it all until I get there to help.' Suzy sounded shocked.

'No, I suppose not. But you know my steering's not all that hot.'

'It will be by the time we get up to the top of Tardebigge, sweetie. We'll set off in ten minutes?' Suzy clattered out again without waiting for a reply.

Chapter Ten

'I told you it was just practice, didn't I?' said Suzy when, much later, she came into the galley to drink a couple of mugs of water in one go. 'We'll make a boatwoman of you yet.'

They had left Wayne and the passengers to pull the butty with the aid of a rope and a pole, and had taken the motor boat on their own. With *Pyramus* safely tied up, Suzy was now on her way back to help with the butty while Julia got on with the cooking.

They had got into rhythm. Julia had put the motor's engine gently ahead which wedged it in the entrance of the lock while Suzy worked the paddles. While waiting for the water levels to equalise, Julia dashed back down to the galley and chopped onions, made scones, or prepared marinated chicken breasts. When she became aware of the motor boat nosing its way into the lock, she dashed up in time to bring it gently to a halt at the other end. While the lock filled, it was back down to the galley, sometimes coming up to find that the boat had taken itself out of the lock and was now halfway to the next. Just as well, thought Julia, that the locks were so close together.

By the time the motor had reached the top of the flight, as Suzy had foretold, Julia's steering was first rate. She could steer into a lock and bring the boat to a halt without even thinking about it.

'I must say,' said Julia. 'I do feel a lot more confident about it.'

Suzy wiped her mouth on the back of her hand, Julia

having snatched away the clean tea-towel. 'I'm so glad. Because it means you won't mind steering through the tunnels tomorrow. Wayne told me it does his head in.'

Julia had had a long day, which had included an extremely irritating telephone call from her brother.

'It's just like you, Julia,' he had complained, 'to go and lose something really important.' This followed a long harangue about the folly of this latest enterprise and of ridding herself of 'a decent guy like Oscar'.

Aware that by this time the lock was full and the boat was halfway along to the next, Julia tucked the mobile under her chin and ran out to take the tiller so they wouldn't bump into anything, but missed the last section of diatribe. 'Sorry, Rupert, I missed most of that. I'm steering the boat and trying to mash potatoes.'

'For God's sake, Julia! What do you know about boats?'

'A lot more than I used to. Now if you don't mind, I really haven't time to chat.'

Rupert never chatted and resented this implication. 'I am trying to help you, Julia. Are you sure you didn't take the papers by mistake?'

'Rupert! I swear I took nothing but the children's baby photos and a pot plant!'

'Are you absolutely sure?'

Julia swallowed her irritation. 'I think I'd notice if I'd had a bundle of files under my arm. Now if you don't mind, we're climbing a flight of forty-two locks, and I'm in sole charge of the motor boat.'

'And can you really trust someone who'd leave you in charge of a boat?'

She could hear her brother puffing with disbelief and disapproval long after they had disconnected.

Now, several hours and several thousand (or so it felt) locks later, she was in no mood to be sympathetic to perfectly healthy young men who suffered from claustrophobia. 'Suppose I told you it does *my* head in?'

'But you can't!' wailed Suzy, who didn't know about the phone call. 'Wayne's being so good about everything else. I really don't want to upset him.'

'You don't mind upsetting me, though.' Then she saw the look of concern develop on Suzy's face and added, 'Only joking.' She smiled reassuringly. 'I'll steer the butty through the bloody tunnels. What will Wayne do though? Walk over the top?'

Suzy nodded. 'But he promises he'll wash up after dinner for the rest of the week. As a penance for being so pathetic.'

While steering through long, dark, dripping tunnels, stuck a hundred and forty feet away from the headlight and the cheerful passengers, was not a lot of fun, Julia discovered that singing helped. It was only afterwards, when they applauded as the boat emerged into the sunlight, that she discovered they had heard every wrong note.

She had given a cursory thought to the missing papers, but the solicitor's letter had been maddeningly unspecific. She couldn't offer suggestions as to where they might be without knowing which papers they were.

She said as much to Rupert when she rang him later in the week, when she wasn't steering. 'You'll just have to get them to tell me which papers.'

'It must include some sort of client list,' said her brother. 'Or they wouldn't be suggesting you passed them on to a rival firm.'

'I never had a client list as such. I just had files, which are all still there, as far as I know.'

Before her brother could reply the phone lost the signal. There were distinct advantages, Julia decided, to mobile phones.

The week seemed to flash by and, as everyone got jolly on Friday night, their second week of cruising was pronounced as successful as their first. All the passengers declared they wanted to come back. Even Delphine had discovered she wanted to do more than just drink and smoke on holiday, and although she never quite got the hang of how locks worked, or which way she should push a balance beam, she had walked along making encouraging comments, and once, with Wayne standing behind her with his hands on the windlass, managed to open a paddle. 'Never taken so much exercise in my life,' she wrote in the visitors' book.

John and his wife Betty said they'd definitely return, possibly that season. 'I much prefer canals to those dirty steam engines he's so partial to,' said Betty. 'It won't take me weeks to get the coal out of his boiler suit when I get home.'

Julia, Suzy and Wayne were all tired, but satisfied. Wayne was now a fully integrated member of the team, filling the tanks with water and emptying the pump-out with equal aplomb. 'It's only tunnels I don't like,' he explained to the passengers.

'Well, I think Julia does that really well,' said John. 'And *I* like her singing.'

After the ordeal of the Worcester and Birmingham and the Northern Stratford canals, they had an easy third week while they meandered on down the Grand Union Canal to Oxford. The weather vastly improved and they had nice, athletic passengers, eager to join in. There were plenty of pubs to visit and the anxieties raised by the meeting with *Otter* and *Beaver* seemed to have faded.

One evening they tied up early, and the passengers all disappeared, either to walk and bird watch, shower, or have naps, thus giving Julia and Suzy time to look at the bookings.

Joan regularly sent them a list of who was coming when, and more to the point, which weeks were worryingly sparse. There were no weeks actually empty, but some only had four passengers. And although this took the strain off Julia a bit, it added to Suzy's anxieties. The one week which was full was when Oscar and his mother were coming. Julia couldn't decide if this would make it better or worse. Would their irritating habits become less noticeable, or drive a whole boatload of people mad?

'And the week after that it's the school party,' said Suzy, 'which is eight. Six children and two teachers. That should be fun. And while we're on the subject of fun, how would you feel if I moved in with Wayne?'

Julia's mind went into overdrive. 'What do you mean?' she screeched, as she had a vision of herself in sole charge of a party of schoolchildren, their minders and the boats while Suzy and Wayne went to live in a starter home on a housing estate.

'I mean, would you mind if I moved into the butty with him? I mean – would you be embarrassed?'

'Never mind me, what about the passengers? Oscar's mother is frightfully proper, she'd have a fit! And some of our other passengers are quite elderly too. They might not like it.'

'I've thought about that, but I don't think they need to know. After all, if we get up before them, they won't know where we've been sleeping.'

'Honey, I don't want to rain on your parade, but do you really think that you and Wayne could be up before the passengers? You know only larks come on holidays like these. They're all up before dawn.'

'Delphine wasn't!'

'Delphine was the only passenger not likely to be shocked.'

Suzy started to pout. It was a reflex action, something which happened automatically whenever her will looked like being crossed.

'But it's nothing to do with me,' Julia went on. 'If you think you can keep it from the passengers . . .'

Suzy hugged her. 'I knew you wouldn't be stuffy about it. It was just Wayne being ultrasensitive.'

Suzy and Wayne sharing a bed didn't seem to affect their working relationship and as they gained experience the increase in their efficiency was staggering. Wayne even got over his fear of tunnels, forced to confront it by Julia being in the middle of a phone call with her brother and insisting on getting off the boat and walking so she wouldn't be cut off.

But as spring turned into early summer, edging the canal with frills of cow parsley, hawthorn blossom, and, in the surrounding woodlands, bluebells, Julia felt the beauty of her surroundings almost made up for her increasing fatigue. What they needed to make her perfectly happy was another pair of hands, to help with everything, not just working the boats.

They were back at Leamington Spa when Ralph and Joan appeared with the clean linen just after the last passenger had left. Suzy flung herself at her uncle, causing him to stagger back and sit down suddenly.

'Ralph! Joan! How lovely to see you! You look great!'

This wasn't quite true. Ralph looked decidedly frailer than he had done before his operation, but declared himself to be 'fighting fit'.

'So how are you girls getting on? And who's this?' he added, as Wayne came in laden with plastic bags from the supermarket.

'This is Wayne, we found him on the river at Tewkesbury. He's been such a hero, taking over from Jason just like that.' She snapped her fingers.

Ralph growled. 'If ever I see that young rascal again –'

'You'll look the other way,' said Joan. 'It was very wrong of him to leave the girls in the lurch like that, but there's no point in you risking your health to tell him so. I'm sorry I haven't managed to find a replacement, Suzy dear, but I've been very busy.' She gestured towards Ralph in explanation.

'Oh don't worry, Aunt Joan. And we've got Wayne now. So, how are the bookings? Have you got another twenty people to fit in the empty cabins?'

Joan and Ralph looked anxiously at each other. 'I'm afraid not,' said Joan. 'In fact, they're quite a bit down on last year.'

Suzy crumpled into a chair. 'People have heard you're not running them. It was bound to happen.'

'I suppose that may be true,' agreed Joan after a moment. 'And what Ralph's –'

'No need to mention that,' Ralph interrupted.

'Mention what?' said Suzy, uncrumpling so she could concentrate.

Ralph started to speak but Joan overrode him. 'It's no good trying to pretend, Ralph. They might as well know.'

'Know what?' demanded Suzy. 'The suspense is killing me!'

'That we've had an offer for the boats,' said Joan. 'A very good offer.'

'Who from?' asked Julia, to fill the sudden silence.

'We don't really know,' said Joan. 'We've been approached by an agent. But they're offering a lot of money. More than they're worth, really.'

'Providing we sell them immediately,' said Ralph. 'With what bookings we have got.'

Julia watched as Suzy held back from protesting that of course, Ralph couldn't, wouldn't do such an awful thing, and admired her for her restraint. Suzy seemed to have grown up a lot recently.

'What do you want to do?' Suzy asked quietly.

'We don't want to sell up,' said Ralph instantly.

'We need the money, dear, you must admit,' said Joan. 'Ralph never made proper provision for a pension –'

'Never thought I'd retire, that's why,' he growled.

'So you'd like to sell the boats?' Suzy asked.

'Like isn't the word,' said Joan. 'Really, selling *Pyramus* and *Thisbe* is the last thing Ralph wants, but we do need the money.'

'I wish you wouldn't talk about me as if I weren't here.' Ralph sat up straighter. 'We need the money, yes, but I'm not convinced young Suzy and Julia and, er, Wayne couldn't make a go of it.'

'I'd really, really, like to try,' said Suzy. 'I'm sure I could raise the money somehow to pay you all in one lump if you gave me a bit of time at the end of the season.'

'The interest rates would be crippling,' said Joan. 'Unless you asked your father.'

Suzy inspected her fingernails, obviously fighting back tears. Asking her father would be admitting defeat; she'd be more likely to go to a back-street money-lender with a rate of interest high enough to pay the debts of the entire Third World.

'But remember Sy Cline, our American agent?' Ralph went on, more optimistically. 'He said if ever we sent him a promotional video, he'd be able to fill us for the whole season. I just never got round to doing it.'

'It would cost a fortune,' said Joan dismissively. 'And what do we know about making videos? We can't even programme them.'

'Perhaps Suzy knows someone in the film industry?' said Julia, trying to be positive.

Suzy shook her head. 'Sorry.'

'How much would it cost?' Julia asked. 'I've got some savings. If it would guarantee bookings, it would be an investment. Suzy could pay me back.'

Ralph shook his head. 'We'd need several thousand pounds to do it professionally, and it would be a very long-term investment. You'd never see your money again.' He looked at Suzy seriously. 'Would it break your heart if we sold up?'

Suzy took a deep breath. 'I would really appreciate it if you could wait till the end of the season, just to give me a chance to raise the money, even if it's a tiny one. But when it comes down to it, your health is more important than my happiness just now. I could go back to Daddy, and I expect I'd think of something I felt as committed to as the cut. I might even get a job on one of the other hotel-boat pairs.' She clasped her hands over his. 'You do what you need to do, Uncle Ralph. Don't worry about me.'

Ralph's mouth opened as he tried to think of the right thing to say. Joan said, 'There, there,' to no one in particular. Julia felt close to tears, partly because she was so tired and worried, but mostly because to have come so far, without a trained crew, to have made all those passengers happy, and then to have it all taken away by some unknown suits in an office far away, was devastating.

'Er – excuse me,' said Wayne. 'It needn't cost thousands to make a video. If that would stop you having to sell up, I'd make you one for a few hundred.'

All eyes turned to Wayne, who was sitting on the step looking sheepish, as if he was admitting to a weakness and not coming up with a business-saving plan.

'What?' said Suzy.

'How?' said Ralph.

'All I need is a decent camcorder,' said the stud-muffin, beautiful, biddable, but until this moment, not apparently a potential rival to Quentin Tarantino. 'I'm going to film school in October, and I've been making videos since I was a kid. I've got a mate with access to an editing suite. If you want me to do it.'

It took everyone a moment to take this in. Then Suzy stepped over several pairs of legs so she could fling herself at Wayne, reminding Julia of an Afghan hound, long-legged, long-lashed and affectionate. 'Of course we want you to do it! Don't we, Uncle Ralph? You could hold out until we've given it a try?'

'The last thing I want to do is sell the boats to someone

else. It would be a real shame when you're obviously doing so well. The trouble is getting the money for the camcorder . . .'

Julia put her hand up. 'I did offer my savings. Five hundred would be nearer what I've got than five thousand.'

'That's settled then,' said Suzy. 'Wayne will make us a video and the Americans will come flocking in.'

'Not quite as simple as that, I think,' said Ralph, 'but it gives us a fighting chance. We owe her that much, dear,' he said to Joan.

She sighed. 'In which case, I suppose I've got some good news. You know we had a couple of spaces on the week with the school trip? Well, I've managed to fill them.'

'Oh, jolly good,' said Suzy, non-committally.

'Yes. Most people are put off by the thought of sharing with schoolchildren, but it seemed to be no problem with these people. Which is handy, because Ralph always gives the school far too big a discount, so to have a couple of paying customers will just make us break even.'

'Well that is good,' said Julia, who felt that Joan wasn't getting enough credit for this coup. 'Who are they?'

'People who are coming the week before – next week – who've decided to book for two weeks. Shows great confidence, don't you think? Before they've even got here?'

'It certainly does,' agreed Julia.

'But then,' Joan went on, 'they're friends of yours, so it's not surprising.'

'Friends of mine?' Julia was flummoxed.

'You know, Mrs Anstruther and her son. Oscar, isn't it?'

Julia gave a strangled gasp of horror. Suzy frowned at her.

'That might be a tad awkward for Julia,' she said. 'She and Oscar were engaged and they didn't part on the best of terms. He's so miffed that she gave him the push that he wants her back.'

'Oh dear,' said Joan. 'That would explain why he asked the names of the crew before he booked the second week.'

Julia's strangled sounds became more tortured.

'We really need more crew, Uncle Ralph,' said Suzy. 'Julia does all the cooking at the moment. If we could have someone else, they could give her a hand.'

Ralph shook his head. 'And pay them with what? We can't afford another crew member, not at the moment.'

'What about that nice man who helped you the first week?' asked Joan.

Julia fled.

Chapter Eleven

Julia turned and smiled a little stiffly as she poured tea into
Oscar's mother's cup. Oscar's mother stretched her lips
towards the edge of her face, but as a smile, it was a worse
attempt than Julia's. Suzy picked up a plate of scones and
held it out to Oscar, who took one, and laughed heartily,
as if it had made a joke. Suzy, charming for England,
passed the plate to the other passengers, who all took one
and put it on their plates. No one said much. Julia edged
her way down the boat with the teapot and filled the
remaining empty cups. She was just sighing with relief
that she had managed not to spill scalding tea on anyone's
thinning hair, when a black Labrador, soaking wet,
bounded up the middle of the boat and shook himself,
showering scones, tea and passengers alike.

'Cut!' shouted Wayne.

'Oh Oscar! Can't you keep that dog under control?' said
his mother. Julia, terrifyingly, found herself agreeing with
her.

'If you don't allow dogs to come,' explained Wayne,
doing something technical to his camcorder, 'we can't
have him in shot.'

'But Sooty's so *sweet*,' said Suzy.

'People aren't going to bring their dogs all the way from
America,' said one woman, who had left hers with her
sister, and was glad to have something furry to stroke.

'Yes, but if they think we let dogs come and they don't
like them, it might put them off,' said Julia. 'And heaven
knows what would happen if the Health and Safety

people arrived now.' She wiped at an empty plate with her apron. 'I'm sure you're not allowed animals where people eat.'

'Unless they're Guide Dogs,' said the woman deprived of her pet. She was now dabbing at Sooty with her silk scarf.

'The Health and Safety people?' asked Mrs Anstruther, Oscar's mother. 'Haven't you been checked by them yet? I did rather wonder.'

Julia could just see her inventing illnesses and blaming the lack of hygiene. She resolved to blame Sooty for anything which went wrong with Mrs Anstruther, from legionnaire's disease to warts.

When he and his mother had arrived, and Oscar had broken it to Julia that he hadn't been able to get Sooty into kennels, Julia's instant reaction was to say, sorry, but Sooty couldn't come too. Not because she was any more resistant to Sooty's brown eyes than anyone else, but in the hope that Oscar might be forced to take his pilot-case-on-wheels, his mother and his dog back home.

Unfortunately, just as Julia was making her little speech about consideration for the other passengers, Suzy had appeared, and said that of course Sooty could stay, as long as he behaved himself. But although Sooty had not behaved himself, he had ingratiated himself into the hearts of all the passengers, and so neither he nor his owners had been banished.

Only Julia and Wayne were less than thrilled to share the boat with an animal who regarded food not just as a means to support life, but rather as life itself. To Sooty, stealing food off the table was a mission to be accomplished even if it made him sick. Julia, who had to replace the breakfasts, the plates of cakes and pots of butter that he helped himself to, found this added burden to her already heavy cooking load trying. Wayne objected to Sooty because he regularly leaped into the canal and brought

131

most of it back into the boat with him before shaking himself vigorously and splattering it over everything, including the lens of the camcorder. Sooty also hogged the camera, in spite of being told he wasn't in the film, and managed to get some part of himself into almost every shot, even if it was just a tail or a stray ear. They were now undergoing a final attempt at the 'Welcoming English tea on arrival' sequence, and everyone was getting bored.

'Miss Boyd,' said Mrs Anstruther. 'Might I trouble you for another cup of tea?'

Julia winced. It was Monday, all the other passengers knew each other's life histories, and Oscar's mother was still calling Suzy 'Miss Boyd'.

Suzy, who had Wayne to help relieve her tension, gave a jolly smile. 'Oh, do call me Suzy, or I won't know who you're talking to.'

Oscar's mother winced and narrowed her eyes. She would not have ended a sentence with a preposition, even in her thoughts. 'I prefer to use Christian names only among my friends.'

Suzy wasn't used to being snubbed any more than Sooty was, and although she tried to hide it, Julia could tell she was hurt. 'You win some, you lose some,' she said, and picked her way through the passengers and out of the front of the boat – away from the teapot.

Not for the first time, Julia wanted to kill the monster in a Jaeger suit. Alone of all the passengers Oscar's mother refused to make the smallest concession to boat life. She was patronising when she wasn't downright rude; she insisted on wearing quite unsuitable clothes and court shoes, and then complained because her soles slipped on the gangway. She changed for dinner, into even more unsuitable clothes, making all the other guests and Julia feel scruffy. She had to have tea in bed at seven, but didn't appear for breakfast until nine, spending the intervening period in the shower, so that all the other passengers had to share the other bathroom, and they had to fill up with water every day because she used so much. Wayne tried to keep her out of range of his video camera as much as possible, because, he explained to Julia, she would put people off coming more than the dog would.

Julia started to clear the table. It would be time to set it for dinner soon.

'Julia, dear,' Mrs Anstruther caught Julia's elbow, causing a jammy, half-eaten scone to slide off the pile of plates she was holding into Sooty's waiting jaws. 'I did ask Miss Boyd for more tea but she chose to ignore me. Might I trouble you for a fresh pot?'

Julia was not at all flattered that hers was the only Christian name Mrs Anstruther used apart from Oscar's. She had overheard her explaining this lapse of protocol to the other passengers.

'She was engaged to my son, you know. Such a narrow escape! Practically on the shelf, well past her child-bearing years, and no one could call her a beauty. Frankly, I don't know what the poor boy saw in her.'

Now, Julia inclined her head in Oscar's mother's direction. 'Of course I'll make you more tea, *Violet*. I know you like it fresh.'

Oscar joined her in the galley as she was putting on the kettle. 'Mother doesn't like you using her Christian name. She asked me to tell you.'

'Oh, doesn't she? Well, that's just too bad.' Julia slammed the kettle on to the stove and lit the gas.

'Julia! You never used to be like this when we were engaged.'

'When we were engaged, we didn't spend much time together, and only one day with your mother. And I think you'll remember, if you cast your mind back, that I was exactly like this. You know your mother and I hate each other. I don't know why you had to inflict us on each other.'

Oscar harrumphed. 'You know why I came, Julia. I

133

wanted you to know I'm not a man to be put off if I fall at the first fence. I still want to marry you. In spite of what Peter Strange told me about you stealing –'

'Stealing, Oscar?' Julia's wrath was terrible to behold. 'I'll have you know that I didn't steal anything! Strange's have obviously lost some papers and are blaming it on me. And as they won't tell me what they've lost I can't tell them where to look!'

'Sorry, old girl. I didn't want to upset you. I never believed you'd do anything wrong anyway. It's just with this new business starting up, Peter's a bit strung up about it. I'm not the sort of man to listen to gossip.'

Julia washed cups furiously, decrying the fact that Oscar so often felt obliged to tell people what sort of man he was, when most men seemed able to let people make up their own minds. Fergus flashed into her thoughts. He was a man she had technically known since childhood, yet really, she knew nothing more about him than could be discovered from a decent c.v.

'Even if I had a change of heart,' she said, managing to catch him with her elbow as she wielded a tea-towel, 'your mother wouldn't hear of it. She thinks my "child-bearing years" are over, apart from all my other faults.'

Oscar drew breath to tell Julia that he was not the sort of man to be told whom to marry by his mother, but didn't. They both knew it wasn't true.

'Now,' she went on firmly, 'if you wouldn't mind taking this tea to your mother? I've got to make another meringue case for dinner, since Sooty ate the first one.'

Suitably chastened, Oscar left Julia to it.

Although she acknowledged to Julia that Oscar was definitely not husband material, Suzy was far better disposed to him than Julia. He wasn't bad-looking, he was polite, and, more, he was very keen to help.

Anxious to keep Sooty out of the way of Wayne and Julia, Oscar kept off the boats during the day. He set the locks, and worked the boats through. He also steered the butty, and although Sooty couldn't be persuaded to steer with him, preferring to swim alongside, or bound along the tow-path, it did ensure his absence. Oscar had come genuinely to like canals.

'I wish I'd never asked Wayne to make that video,' moaned Suzy to Julia, the following morning, while they waited for a lock to fill. 'With that camcorder permanently welded to his eye, he never has time to do anything else.'

This was true. Julia had had several miles of film taken of her steering the butty, staring into the sun, trying not to let her eyes water. And more miles of her bending over to look into the oven, or emerging red-faced from having done so. There was more footage of guests with their mouths open, having noticed the camera and stopped mid-sentence, than anyone could ever want, and the boats had been washed down with the painted mop so often by Suzy in her shorts that the paint was wearing thin.

'He says he's nearly finished, and you did want him to do it.' Julia leaned back against the balance beam, enjoying a spell of enforced idleness.

'But not all the time. I didn't realise it meant he wouldn't be able to work the boats. If it wasn't for Oscar, we'd be sunk.'

Julia didn't reply. Her sense of fair play acknowledged that Oscar was being very useful, but her feelings for him made it impossible to acknowledge it openly.

By Banbury, the passengers had shaken down into a homogenous group – apart from Mrs Anstruther – but the crew were all on edge, with the passengers and with each other. Because of this, they arranged for the passengers to spend the morning exploring the town, and to have their lunch at what they hoped was a suitably sedate hostelry. It would probably be the first time in her life that Mrs Anstruther had been in a pub.

This was designed to give Julia time to find out from her

brother if Strange's had found their lost papers. They hadn't, and Rupert was full of foreboding about what Strange's would do. But Julia was in no mood to be lectured and cut her brother short so she could sort out the galley, something she had meant to do for ages. Suzy and Wayne were busy filling up with water, pumping out the toilets, and doing something which took them into the depths of the butty's back cabin which Julia didn't care to know about. Not, she tried to persuade herself, because she was jealous. Sex, she had read in a Sunday paper over someone's shoulder while she cleared the table, was not a primal need. But she did think they might have been doing something more useful while they waited for the tanks to fill.

Julia was on her knees, the entire contents of the fridge surrounding her, while she sorted through vegetables which were no longer recognisable, little dishes of sauce which never got turned into soup, and other detritus which was three-quarters compost, when she heard a knock which said, 'Trouble' even louder than it said, 'You Will Never Now Complete This Task'.

Reluctantly, Julia got up and went to the side doors of the saloon. 'Yes? Can I help you?'

A youngish, fair-haired man of medium build, wearing a linen jacket, showed her an identification card. 'Tracked you down at last! Ron Jones, Health and Safety.'

Julia let out a little squeak which would have been a full-blown scream if her self-control wasn't so well honed.

'Can I come in?' asked Ron Jones.

'Can I say no?' asked Julia.

Rather to her surprise, he laughed. 'Yes, but why would you want to?' He climbed down into the boat.

'Because I've got the fridge all over the floor and you might close us down.' Julia stood with her back to the door, trying to block his view of the galley.

He looked past her into it without difficulty. It probably

hadn't looked so untidy and disorganised since it was built. 'Hmm. I can see why you might think that.'

Where was bloody Suzy? This man was made of flesh and blood! One of Suzy's 'I'm Suzy, aren't I cute' glances would have him on his knees, same as any other male. But in the circumstances, she didn't think it was worth trying an 'I'm Julia, I'm highly organised and efficient' look, because although it was usually true, having so much clutter about her would make it lose credibility.

'However,' the Health and Safety Inspector went on, turning his gaze back to Julia, 'closing you down is not why I'm here.'

'Isn't it?'

'No. I'm more interested in making it so I don't have to close you down. Prevention is better than cure, you know.'

Julia was still not sure. He was younger than she was, quite good-looking and didn't seem quite as terrifying as his title, but she was reluctant to face an Ordeal by Health and Safety Inspector without Suzy or Wayne. Despite the gentle but rhythmic rocking of the boats, she would have gone for reinforcements if that wouldn't have given him the opportunity to peer into every grimy crevice. God knows what he might find.

'I suppose I'd better let you do your thing.'

'It's hard for me to give advice without having a look round.'

'And I suppose you do have to see the galley?' Julia backed into it protectively.

'It is rather essential. If you're feeding people on board.'

'It would be much better if you started in the saloon.'

Ron Jones surveyed the myriad little pots, jars, and, on a newspaper, a pile of green slime which had once been edible. 'Presumably you don't always keep those things there?'

'No.' Julia began to shovel them up into the newspaper, tossing the ramekin dishes into the sink so he could actually get into the room. 'I'm sorting out the fridge.'

'And are you the proprietor?'

'No. The proprietor's – not here.'

'Well, I can either leave you some leaflets and come back and give you a full inspection another time, or have a look round now.'

'When might you be coming back?'

Ron Jones looked vague; whether deliberately or not, Julia couldn't tell. 'Could be any time this week, or next.'

'Then it might be better' – Julia had done some quick thinking – 'if you had a look round now, while all the passengers are out, and it isn't a meal time.' And while Sooty was safely out of the way.

'If you prefer. But I should talk to the proprietor, really.'

'I'm afraid that's not possible.' Suzy could be a bit of a liability; it might after all be easier to handle this on her own.

'Very well. I'll have a quick look, give you a few pointers and the guides, and come back to see if you've complied with all the regulations. Now, let's see . . . separate hand-washing facilities. Good.' He ignored Julia while she removed the filthy hand towel and stuffed it into a cupboard. 'Is the water drinkable?'

'Oh yes.'

'Then could I drink some?'

'Of course! Would you like tea, or coffee, or anything? I didn't offer before because I thought it might look like a bribe.'

'Water will be fine.'

She watched intently while he drank it. 'Can you tell if it's got germs in, just by drinking it?'

Ron Jones laughed. 'Of course not! I was just really thirsty.'

All in all, Julia and Ron Jones got on like a house on fire. Far from being the jobsworth bureaucrat, nit-picky and officious, that Julia had imagined he would be, he was pleasant, helpful and seemed to go out of his way to find ways whereby they could comply with the regulations with minimum upset or expense.

'These wooden work surfaces are fine if they've got a few good coats of waterproof varnish on them,' he said. 'You will need to have a thermometer on the fridge, and it would be a good idea to have antibacterial hand-wash liquid freely available. I'll just jot down a few points that need further attention . . .'

Julia had sat Ron Jones at the table in the saloon so he could write in comfort when Oscar and Sooty appeared.

'Damn pub wouldn't let the dog in,' he said. 'So I brought him back here. He'll be happy enough with you.'

Julia made wild gestures with her arms and rolled her eyes, trying to indicate to Oscar the vital importance of removing Sooty immediately. Unsurprisingly, Oscar failed to understand.

'Oh, hello,' he said, when he saw the saloon wasn't empty.

'This is Ron Jones, the Health and Safety Inspector,' said Julia, hoping this might make Oscar march Sooty briskly out of the way.

This didn't work either. Oscar's hunched stance took on a belligerence which made Julia nervous.

'Oh, are you?' said Oscar. 'You like sticking your nose into other people's businesses and making it impossible to function, do you?'

'Oscar! It's not like that –'

'Give a man a title and a funny hat,' he went on, glaring at Ron Jones's unencumbered head, 'and they think they can boss the rest of the world around. Damn fool regulations! No one on the continent takes a blind bit of notice about them! It's only this bloody country where people give a damn about hygiene anyway. In France they do what they like. Well, you needn't think you can throw your weight around here!'

'Oscar! Please!'

Ron Jones had risen from his seat. He and Oscar were of a size. Sooty, sensing a potential rough-house, frisked about encouragingly.

'Just because you've got a clipboard doesn't give you the right to go round harassing young women.' Oscar's fist clenched, though he kept it well down.

'Sir.' Ron Jones had been in similar situations and wasn't going to be bullied by the likes of Oscar. 'I feel I should advise you –'

'What's going on?' Suzy and Wayne appeared, looking flushed. 'We heard voices.'

'This is the Health and Safety man,' said Julia quickly. 'Oscar seems to think he's been harassing me.'

'Health and Safety?' Suzy squeaked. 'Oscar's blind, you know.' She turned to Ron Jones. 'Sooty's his guide dog.'

'Suzy, I don't think –'

'I am not blind!' Oscar took this as an insult.

'And this is not a guide dog,' said Ron Jones, removing Sooty's paws from his chest.

'He is,' persisted Suzy, 'but he's on holiday.'

Ron Jones's face underwent some sort of upheaval, almost as if he were trying not to laugh. 'Sir!' he addressed Oscar only when he had himself under control. 'If you are the proprietor, I should advise you that keeping animals anywhere near food preparation areas is strictly illegal! Make proper provision for this animal, or I shall be forced to bring against you the full force of the law.'

'But he's not the proprietor! I am,' said Suzy, still squeaking. 'Oscar's just a passenger. And Sooty really is on holiday.'

Ron regarded Suzy with the same indulgent disbelief that most men regarded her when they realised she was the boss. 'In which case, madam, I shall leave all the guides you need to bring you up to the required standards, and come back at a later date to inspect you.'

Suzy put her hand on his arm. 'You are a sweetie.'

Oscar made a noise which caused Sooty to sit down and put his head on one side, inspecting his master with interest. 'He's nothing of the kind! If you were a little better acquainted with the ways of the world, you'd know that!' he snapped.

'And if you were a little better acquainted with the ways of animals, you wouldn't let that creature jump up!' said Ron Jones. 'Good afternoon!'

Julia ran after him down the tow-path. 'Please, Mr Jones! Don't take any notice of Oscar. He's just a passenger. He only brought Sooty because he couldn't get him into kennels. We won't ever let another passenger bring their dog, I promise.'

Ron Jones turned and looked at Julia. 'It's all right. I know the type. He seemed very protective of you, though.'

'We used to be engaged. For some reason he still wants us to be, although we drive each other mad.'

'You poor girl! Can I buy you a drink to make up for it?'

Reluctantly, Julia shook her head. She felt entitled to bunk off for a bit, and leave Suzy and Oscar to sort out the mess on the galley floor, but knowing it was more likely that they would kindly leave it for her, she decided against it. 'I'd better go back before Sooty eats everything. We'll have to set off again when the passengers get back.'

'Well, you have my sympathy if they're all like that oaf.'

Julia smiled. 'Oh, Oscar's a happy dream compared to his mother!'

Oscar's mother didn't approve of pubs. Nor did she think Banbury sufficiently historical to be worth the pain caused by her tight, medium-heel leather shoes. Oscar was sulking after the fiasco with the Health and Safety Inspector, and was not amused when Suzy and Wayne retold the tale to the other passengers, who all were.

At last they were ready to set off. Julia, whose nerves had stood up to the day's alarms and excursions surprisingly well, found Oscar's large, immobile presence reading in the saloon oppressive. He was there because Wayne, ordered by Suzy to put the damn camera away and get his act together with the boats, had taken over the steering of the butty. All the passengers had got off the boat rather than risk being left with Mrs Anstruther, and Wayne wanted Oscar to supervise them working the locks. But Oscar had enjoyed steering the butty, and even the chance to tell a lot of other people what to do did not make up for this privilege being removed. It was also impossible for him to take orders, even if presented as a tentative request, from the likes of Wayne. Thus he had decided to stay in the saloon and read, leaving Wayne and Suzy to manage without him.

His mother, finding there was no one to talk to, came to the stable doors to have another go at Julia.

'I dare say the Health and Safety man wanted you to change all the work-tops. Wood is terribly unhygienic,' she said.

'No, actually.' Julia smiled, pretending Mrs Anstruther would think this good news. 'Wood is fine if it has enough coats of waterproof varnish on it.'

'Stainless steel is better.'

'Possibly.'

'And I think you'd find it easier if you used a balloon whisk for those egg whites. When I was taught to cook at my finishing school in Switzerland, we used a fork on a plate to make meringues.'

'That must have taken a long time.'

'It was considered important for a lady to know everything about running a house so she could direct the servants.'

'Not much call for that sort of thing nowadays. Most people don't have servants.'

Mrs Anstruther inclined her head to indicate she was conceding a point. 'Not called servants, I grant you, but lots of people have people in to clean, or do the ironing. I do myself.'

I bet you do, thought Julia.

'And while I would never dream of letting dear Mrs Ruddles feel she was not valued, the servant classes remain the same, whatever they like to call themselves.'

'Really? I'm afraid I don't feel qualified to comment.'

Mrs Anstruther nodded. 'It's one of the reasons, if I may say so, that I felt you and dear Oscar were not really suited.' She made it sound as if she had ended the relationship, not Julia.

Julia got out the baking parchment while she thought of something appropriate to say.

'So it is left to those of us who are thus privileged to inform those less fortunate as to the correct way of doing things.'

Julia struggled for the words which would crush this woman and her impossible snobbery and realised that words alone would not do it. A ten-ton truck might have a struggle.

'And I know you won't take it amiss if I point out a few little things which I have noticed are not done correctly.'

Julia didn't try not to take it amiss, she just tried to keep her hands off the Sabatiers when she was within knife-throwing range of Oscar's mother. Eventually, unable to trust herself for another minute, having been told to add bicarbonate of soda to vegetables to make them green, to wash salads in at least three changes of water, and to put soup through the sieve rather than use the liquidiser, she excused herself, and stepped off the back of the boat, when the canal narrowed at a bridge, to get some time on her own.

Unfortunately, Oscar saw her go, and took it as the ideal opportunity to do a little courting. He leaped off at a corner, and bore down on her, Sooty thundering at his heels.

'Glad of a chance to speak to you alone,' he boomed, marching along beside her.

'Likewise!' said Julia. 'If you don't do something about your mother, I won't be answerable for the consequences. She has spent the entire afternoon in my galley telling me how to do things!'

'She's only trying to be helpful.'

'She is not! She is trying to make me do things the way she was taught to do them at her precious finishing school, a hundred and fifty years ago!'

'The old ways are the best.'

'The old bags certainly aren't! Call her off, Oscar. Make her go for a walk - anything.'

'You know she can't walk in those shoes.'

'I'll lend her a pair of trainers! Just get her out of my way. I can't work with her there, telling me I'm doing it wrong. I've tried being rude, but she's too thick-skinned to notice!'

'I think you're being very unreasonable.'

'I think I'm being a saint! But I can't guarantee being one for much longer. Why did you bring her? Why did you come?'

'I told you. I wanted you to see me. You seemed pretty damned determined to avoid me. This way, you can't.'

The truth of this was too obvious to argue with. 'But why bring your mother? She can't be enjoying herself one bit.'

'I thought if you two got to know each other better, you'd overcome your differences.'

'Oscar, you are such a wanker!' said Julia, and pushed him into the canal.

'Mmm,' said Fergus, appearing from nowhere. 'Are you sure he can swim?'

Chapter Twelve

Julia screamed. The insanity she had been driven steadily towards by Oscar, his mother, the Health and Safety Inspector and several weeks' hard work with no time off, had now overtaken her. She was seeing things.

'Sorry,' said Fergus. 'Did I give you a fright? I was just walking up from the station. I saw you push him in just as I got on to the tow-path. Do you think we should give him a hand?'

Julia looked at Oscar, floundering about in the water. He had been joined by Sooty, who was thoroughly enjoying himself: every time Oscar got to his feet, Sooty managed to knock him off them.

Julia's emotional turmoil was making her feel sick. For a moment she wanted so badly to push Fergus in to join Oscar, she felt it safer to remove herself from temptation. It was only the thought of having two wet men and a dog in the boat instead of only one which stopped her.

She deliberately walked away from the canal into the fields because a sudden vision of herself as Ophelia lying in the water, garlanded with flowers, was also rather appealing. But what she knew, and Ophelia didn't, was that people didn't really float like that, and the canal stank.

Not that she really wanted to end it all. Not for a second. But she badly needed to put some space between herself and the cause of all her tension. And she never wanted to cook again.

She knew all hell would have broken loose back at the boats. Oscar would be ranting and raving, his mother

145

would be telling everyone that she'd always known Julia was unstable, and Suzy would be looking faintly bemused that steady old Julia had suddenly flipped, pushed a passenger into the cut, and then just gone off, without cleaning up the mess or anything. Wayne would be cursing because he didn't get the whole lot on video. And Fergus? Nothing came to mind. He had probably just been a vision, called up by her deranged mind.

Sunshine broke through from behind the clouds, surprisingly hot. She found a patch of grass free from thistles and cow pats and flung herself down on it. If she walked too much further she might get lost, and then what would happen? She imagined a search party, led by Oscar, quartering the ground, looking for traces of her. She chuckled.

Lying there was bliss. No one knew where she was, no one could ask her for more hot water or for more toast. Or, just as she was stirring something which would turn to glue if she left it, for ice. The hot sunshine on her eyelids was soothing away her stress. Her mind started to wander, and she slept.

She could only have dozed off for a few minutes, but she felt as if she'd been asleep for hours when she awoke, aware that someone was with her. She half opened an eye. Fergus seemed to be sitting beside her, watching her. She shut the eye. Either she was still asleep and was dreaming, or she had been so maddened by stress that figures kept manifesting themselves, a low-alcohol version of d.t.s. If she'd had the energy she would have got herself to a doctor for some nice Prozac. But she didn't have the energy, and so decided to go back to sleep instead, to make him go away.

But in her half-waking, half-sleeping state, the question of Fergus intruded in a way she was sure it never would have done had she been fully conscious. There was no doubt that since he left, he had slid into her thoughts far more often than he any right to. He was an old enemy. He had been with them barely a week. So why did her mind keep slipping out of gear leaving her dreaming about Fergus, when there were so many real, immediate problems? Why did she wish so much that she hadn't been so churlish when he'd really been there? If she'd behaved better he might have forgotten Tuscany and his book, and stayed, at least a bit longer. Perhaps if she'd been nicer, he wouldn't keep coming back to haunt her in spectral form. He might come along in real life, and give Julia another chance to have a good look at him and find out if she'd glamorised him in her mind.

She slept again until she was woken by a fly landing on her nose. She brushed it off and found it wasn't a fly, but a tuft of her own hair; Fergus, real or imaginary, was tickling her.

He was lying on his elbow looking at her. 'Sorry. I couldn't go on watching you sleep for another second.' Then he leaned forward and kissed her.

Julia thought she might as well go along with it. It was, after all, probably only some particularly realistic erotic dream and she was unlikely to have sex in any more concrete way. She would wake up in a minute anyway, and it was not at all unpleasant to lie on her back being kissed by someone who knew what he was doing. In fact, quite the reverse. This dream person seemed to know exactly how to go about enflaming her whole body while only their mouths connected. Even when this altered, and the weight of his body began to slump on to hers, it was pleasant. It made her feel secure; loved, somehow. All an illusion, she told herself, but kept her eyes shut. Illusions were perfectly valid sometimes.

Her fingers burrowed into his hair. It was silky, springy and had obviously just been washed in pleasant-smelling shampoo. What a good thing I didn't push him into the canal, she thought idly.

His fingers started to probe around the neck of her shirt with delicate little movements. Extremely sensitive of him, she thought, but why didn't he just undo the buttons and get on with it? Otherwise the dream would go away before he'd really got anywhere. She shifted a little to allow him better access. Her breasts really did crave more attention than they were getting at present.

She resisted the temptation to open her eyes. All the glorious sensations which were washing over her would go away if she opened her eyes. So she undid his shirt buttons by feel only. Her fingers felt the modest amount of hair on his chest, and traced his surprisingly developed pectoral muscles. Perhaps his interest in archaeology wasn't purely academic, perhaps he did some digging as well. His nipples hardened satisfyingly under her finger-tips. It gave her a sense of power. It was nice to be proactive in a dream. Usually her attempts at control failed.

All her shirt buttons were undone now and her bra seemed unusually tight. She wondered vaguely if she could undo it without sitting up, waking up, and making the whole thing vanish. She moved a hand round to her back to fiddle with the fastener and found herself helped. The bra came undone quite easily and a second later was pulled away from her breasts. That felt better. The bra was still up round her neck somewhere, but her breasts could breathe. Then it was her nipples which were springing to life and her breasts were getting all the attention they'd wanted and a whole lot that hadn't even occurred to them.

'Shift over here a bit.'

Fergus's voice was husky and his breathing was a little short as he half lifted, half rolled her to one side, landing her on something soft and dry.

In spite of her reluctance to break the dream, Julia opened her eyes. Nothing changed, her feelings of arousal didn't fade away. And it was the real-life Fergus who was making love to her, with such academic concentration. And the real, academic Fergus had brought something to lie on. Dimly she remembered her mother telling them about his achievements in the Scout movement. Even as quite small children she and Angela had thought scouting was sad. Little did they know how useful all that preparedness could be. But, she recalled, as he undid her jeans and slid them down with great efficiency, archaeology had that practical side to it too.

She was naked, and she had got his shirt off before either of them spoke.

'Julia, are you sure?'

Julia nodded. Nothing happened. Fergus was waiting for a proper answer, on one side of the paper only. 'I'm quite sure.'

Julia rolled Fergus on to his back, nearly pushing him off the sleeping bag into a patch of stinging nettles, and trailed her breasts over his chest until he groaned. No further attempts at conversation were made for what seemed like a long time.

'Don't you think we should talk about this?' Fergus asked later. 'I know I've wanted you since I first saw you again. But you didn't seem too keen on me.'

'Hardly surprising.' Julia had just discovered what nice ears he had. 'You talk too much.'

Fergus sighed and allowed Julia to lead him where he was only too willing to go.

Afterwards, as she lay with her head on his chest with his arm round her, reality began to creep back, slowly at first, and then with terrifying speed.

'What's the time?' she asked him.

'A little after six.'

'Agh! Dinner! I must go back.'

He tightened his grip. 'Let Suzy cook dinner. After all, I imagine they won't have moved the boats without you on them.'

149

'They might have. Oh God, I've been so irresponsible!' She drew herself up on to her elbow and looked down at him. 'I can't believe I just ran away from the boats and then' – she forced her mouth to say what her brain was so reluctant to accept – 'had sex with you. I'm no better than Suzy!'

'Not having slept with Suzy, I can't compare, but I promise you, I was more than satisfied.'

He stroked her shoulder with his finger, but she pulled away, reached for her scattered clothes and started dragging them on.

'I don't know what got into me. I'm sorry, Fergus. I've never done anything like this in my life! It's practically a zipless fuck!'

He frowned. 'Run that by me again?'

She was hunting for her other sock. 'Oh you know. It's when you have sex without talking to each other first.'

Fergus started to put on his clothes, but in a more leisurely fashion. 'I don't want to make too much of it, but we're not exactly strangers. You've known me since you were a little girl. It was only when I was a teenager we fell out. There are pictures of us together as children, on a beach.'

'Are there? I didn't know that.' Momentarily, she was diverted. 'But it doesn't make any difference. When you appeared on the boat I didn't recognise you. Even your name had changed. Our mothers may be old friends, but we aren't. It's no more morally acceptable for me to . . .' She paused. '. . . to make love to you, than it would be if we'd met in a singles' bar.'

'I've never been to a singles' bar. But surely, we did practically share a roof for nearly a week.'

'But we didn't speak to each other. I'd forgotten you were an archaeologist until one of the passengers reminded me.'

'Well, whose fault was that?'

150

There were new blond highlights in Fergus's hair, caused by Tuscan sun, no doubt. 'I know it was my fault, which is what makes this whole thing so dreadful.'

'I didn't think it was dreadful. Did you?'

Julia was scrupulously honest. She was suffering the tortures of the damned now, but at the time she had enjoyed herself thoroughly. 'No. Doing it was wonderful, but the thing itself, us, making love, when we don't know each other, don't care about each other, was completely wrong and immoral. I'm not the sort of person who does things like that, and I don't expect you are either.'

'Not usually, no.'

'Well, we'd better just accept that we both behaved completely out of character, it was a one-night –'

'Afternoon, actually.'

'– afternoon stand, and it should never have happened.'

'I agree it was unorthodox.'

'Unorthodox! Only you could use a word like that at a time like this!'

'But we could do the getting to know each other thing afterwards. And when we have, we could make love again with a clear conscience.'

Julia's eyes widened in horror. 'No. Never again. I'm sorry, but I couldn't! I'm planning to go travelling after the season and I . . .' She faltered. She didn't want to say she wanted to travel with a whole heart, and that for her, sex was entwined with love. She couldn't have sex with him again without it, and if she loved him, how could she be properly independent? 'Please, don't mention this again to me or to anyone else, ever. It was just an aberration.' Fergus had shifted so that the sun was behind him and she couldn't see his expression, so she couldn't tell if she'd mortally offended him or not. She chewed her lip for a moment. 'Now, I must get back to the boat and have a shower.' She cleared the gathering sob from her throat. 'If that bitch has left me any water!'

It took enormous courage for Julia to go back and face everyone, and would have done even if she hadn't made love to Fergus while she'd been away. Her behaviour had been appalling. She'd lost her temper with a passenger, pushed him in the canal, and then disappeared for hours.

She found the boats unusually quiet. There were no hysterical screams issuing from the saloon as she approached, nor was there smoke issuing from the galley windows. Julia felt a little cheered, and wondered if she could slip in secretly and have a shower before she announced her return. Otherwise, she was convinced that everyone would take one look at her and know what she'd been up to. But it was not to be. Suzy appeared the moment she put her foot on the gunwale.

'Julia!' she said warmly. 'How are you?'

Julia was confused. 'Suzy, I'm so sorry . . .'

'Julia, *I'm* so sorry! It's all my fault. I put far too much on you. No wonder you flipped.'

'Is Oscar all right?' Julia blushed with shame just thinking about what she had done to Oscar.

'Fine. He's taken his mother to Oxford in a taxi.'

Julia's spirits rose. Good could come out of evil if Oscar and his mother had decided to leave. 'What? Have they gone home?'

Suzy shook her head. 'Gone shopping, and then out to dinner at the Randolph. She did want to leave, but Oscar persuaded her not to.'

'Why? He can't want to stay, not after what I did to him!'

'Well, I'm glad he did! We can't afford to just throw passengers away, you know. Even if they do ask for it.'

'Oh Suzy! I'm so sorry.'

'Don't be. It's working out fine. They're not leaving, so I don't have to give them their money back. And it gives us all a night off from them.'

'You being so nice about it is making me feel guiltier than ever. Let me have a quick shower, and I'll get on with dinner.' Frantically, she tried to think what she had planned to cook, but couldn't.

'Have a long shower. We've got plenty of water and Peggy's cooking dinner.'

Peggy was the one who particularly loved Sooty. 'Suzy! You can't let a passenger cook dinner just because I –' What had she done that she could possibly admit to?

Julia tried to insist but found herself forcibly frog-marched to the bathroom by Suzy. 'You're covered in grass, and is that cow muck on your shoulder?'

She slunk away, sure that everyone could tell she must have done more than just have a nap in a field to warrant all that grass.

She emerged feeling cleaner and less guilty about the Oscar incident, but worse about what had happened afterwards, particularly as Fergus was sitting in the saloon with Suzy.

'Today's getting better and better,' announced Suzy, pouring whisky into a glass for Julia. 'First Oscar and his mother burger off, and then Fergus arrives to be extra crew for a while. Isn't it great?'

'Oh,' she said blankly. 'Hi, Fergus!'

Fergus got to his feet and kissed her cheek. 'It's good to see you again, Julia.'

Julia realised he had said nothing about meeting her earlier on. 'It's good of you to come back. Was it just a whim? Or what?'

'I wrote and asked him,' said Suzy. 'I knew we just couldn't cope with only three of us any more. You were having to do far too much cooking, and with Wayne spending all day welded to a video camera, we were going crazy. He left me a contact address.' Suzy looked thoroughly pleased with herself. 'He's going to stay as long as he can.'

Julia wished she could join in the general rejoicing, but just felt that having a nervous breakdown was preferable

153

to having to share such a small space with Fergus. In the circumstances. 'I suppose overwork would explain why I pushed Oscar into the cut. I am so sorry, Suzy.'

'So what was it that pushed you over the edge, so to speak?' said Fergus, disingenuously.

'Well, the Health and Safety man had come, and –' Julia stopped mid-sentence. Fergus must have helped Oscar out of the water. How had he explained his subsequent disappearance? And how could she find out without accidentally telling the world that she and Fergus had spent the missing hours making love in a field?

'So what time did you arrive, Fergus?' she went on, looking at him a lot more intently than such a casual enquiry usually warranted.

'Oh – Actually, it was rather odd,' he replied. 'I happened to turn up moments after you must have pushed Oscar in. He couldn't get out because the dog kept knocking him over.'

'Sooty! Where is he?'

'Gone shopping too,' said Suzy. 'I don't know how the Randolph will cope with him.'

'And then,' Fergus persisted. 'I realised I'd forgotten my sleeping bag. I'd put it down to look at the map and forgotten it. I had to walk all the way back to the station. It took me ages.'

Was it his years as a boy scout or his university education that had made him such a good liar? 'Oh,' said Julia. 'It was very kind of you to rescue Oscar.'

'By the sounds of it, you'd have all preferred it if I'd left him there to drown.'

'He wouldn't have drowned,' said Suzy. 'The canal is only about four feet deep and that's only right in the middle. But it might have taken him a while to get out.'

'What did his mother do when she found out about it?' Julia asked.

'Had hysterics,' said Suzy glibly. 'Slandered you dreadfully. Unfortunately, all the passengers were on your side and wouldn't agree when she said you'd behaved appallingly and should be dismissed, instantly.'

Julia buried her head in her hands. 'She's right you know. You should sack me.'

'No chance, sunshine. You're not getting out of it that easily. Anyway, if you hadn't pushed Oscar in, I might well have pushed in his mother. That would have been far worse.'

Julia raised her head. 'I suppose they cancelled the second week?'

'No such luck. Oscar seems determined to stick it out, and she won't leave him in the hands of that harpy. Meaning you.'

'He must be so penny-pinching he can't bear to lose his deposit. It's the only explanation. How did I manage to go out with him so long without noticing he was mean?' Julia was astounded.

'It's not that,' explained Suzy. 'I actually offered him the full amount back, although God knows, we can't afford it. But he wants to stay' – Suzy started to giggle – 'because he thinks you're a hell of a girl!' The giggles got worse. 'Talk about "Treat 'em mean and keep 'em keen"! You've got him just where you want him now!' She curled up into a ball and shook with laughter.

'Actually, he was where I wanted him when he was in the canal! And you had to go and pull him out!' She glared accusingly at Fergus and at the same moment realised that she had the most almighty crush on him.

'I knew it would be my fault somehow,' said Fergus mildly. 'It always is.'

Julia felt weak suddenly. How was she going to keep her cool with Fergus, who turned her on just by looking at her, and who probably thought she was the easiest lay in the history of seduction, and Oscar, whom she actively disliked but who had some sort of weird crush on her? She put her head in her hands. 'Oh God!'

'Have another drink,' said Suzy, pouring her one.

Chapter Thirteen

Dinner was a delightful, light-hearted meal. It was also the first meal Julia had eaten at a table since the beginning of the season.

'I'm not sure I can digest things sitting down any more,' she said. 'Although it is really lovely for a change. This is delicious,' she added to Peggy, who had cooked it. 'You must write down the recipe for me.'

'Pleasure, dear. It's ever so easy.'

What wasn't going to be easy was seeing Oscar again, so she made sure she was safely tucked up in bed before he and his mother got back. A night's sleep would help. She couldn't stop herself wondering how Fergus was getting on in his tent on the canal bank, though.

Things were not a lot better in the morning, but she made tea for Oscar's mother as usual and when he came to collect it, grasped the nettle.

'Oscar, I really am so sorry for pushing you in. It was unforgivable. I don't know what came over me.'

'I expect you've been overdoing it lately. Got overtired. Women do that, I know.'

'But I shouldn't have done it, no matter how tired I was.' Julia fought hard to keep herself apologetic. Any minute now he would blame her behaviour on her period. Not that he'd actually use the word.

'And perhaps it's getting to that "time of the month"?' he said.

Julia made an effort to unclench her teeth. 'It was nothing to do with being tired, or my hormones. I can't

157

make any excuses, Oscar. It was just bad temper. I'm very sorry, and I hope your mother wasn't too upset about it.' At this moment Sooty came bustling up. 'I see Sooty seems to have recovered,' she added.

'Well, Sooty was in his element. Got covered in mud. We both did. Just as well that chap was there to pull me out. What happened to him, by the way? Didn't see him again until we came back last night.'

'I think he said something about leaving his luggage at the station, and having to go back for it.'

Oscar scratched his head. 'That's funny. I could have sworn he had bags with him. They were on the tow-path as I landed.'

Julia felt herself blush and was sure Oscar would notice. 'Well, I don't really know as I wasn't there.'

'Where did you go, by the way?'

'For a very long walk. It made me feel much better.'

She reflected that in some ways it was true. She did feel a great deal better. Perhaps that Sunday paper was wrong. Perhaps sex was a primal need. If only it didn't come booby-trapped with emotional side effects.

She dreaded seeing Fergus again. He would be a lot harder to cope with than Oscar because her feelings were involved. And not only involved with him, but so convoluted in themselves that Julia couldn't work out how she felt. All she knew for certain was that she couldn't deal with anything like that happening again. Sex with him had been lovely, but sex for her meant emotions and some sort of commitment and that wasn't what she wanted right now. She was too tired and too busy. And at the end of the season, she wanted to go travelling, with no baggage other than that which could be put in a rucksack.

For a moment she thought wistfully of Suzy and her casual attitude to sex. She gave Julia the impression that she'd have no problem escaping with Fergus for a few luscious afternoon romps in the hay, and then kissing him goodbye when he left with no regrets and a lot of lustful memories. It was a lot more complicated for her. Even if it wasn't, the boats really didn't need them all disappearing in the middle of the afternoon for a *siesta amorosa*.

No, it must never happen again, she would explain to Fergus. It would have been a lot easier if that pastoral scene really had been an erotic dream. There had been a moment, before she had properly woken up that morning, when she had wondered if it had all been a figment of her sex-starved imagination. But then reality woke her fully and she was forced to accept that yes, she had made love to Fergus, whom she had hated since childhood, and whom her mother wanted her to marry, in a field, within a mile of Oscar and all Julia's responsibilities.

Fergus kissing her was unexpected enough. That alone would have caused some hours of wondering speculation. But for her to have let him – no, to have actually *encouraged* him to touch her, undress her and eventually make love to her, caused enough bewilderment to send her into therapy for years. How could she have been so foolish? He would have stopped at any time. In fact she dimly remembered him wanting to talk more and kiss less, but she had silenced him. The more she thought about it the worse it got. Meeting Fergus now would be like dreaming she was walking down the High Street naked, and then waking up to find that was what she was doing.

Possibly, she thought, ferociously chopping apricots to beef up the muesli, because that was more or less what had happened. Really, the girls who never had to face their one-night stands again were saved an awful lot of embarrassment.

It was unfortunate that Fergus, no doubt trying to be discreet, came upon her when she was burrowing under the bunk for another box of cornflakes. She screamed and banged her head when he said her name.

'Ow – ooh! Why did you have to creep up on me like that?'

'I'm sorry. I didn't know you'd have your head under the bed when I came in. Put some arnica on it.'

'I haven't got any arnica. You sound just like my mother.'

'Julia, I do realise I haven't behaved like the perfect gentleman, but do you think you could possibly stop making me apologise for things that aren't my fault?'

Julia clutched the cornflakes protectively to her. 'Sorry. I'm feeling a bit . . .' She attempted to find a way to describe the hurricane of confusion which was whirling round inside her and came up with: 'Ratty.'

They apologised their way through the narrow corridor and got to the galley. 'Have you seen Oscar?' said Fergus.

She nodded. 'Have you?'

'Just now. He was taking Sooty for a walk.'

'When I saw him he seemed to not quite believe that you'd left something at the station. He said you had lots of stuff on the bank.'

'I know. I think I managed to suppress any ideas he might have had.'

Julia snorted disdainfully. 'Oscar hasn't enough imagination to have ideas.'

'Don't you believe it. Oscar would suspect any single male under seventy who came within yards of his chosen woman. And you are she.'

A terrible fatigue seemed to swamp her. A few hours off yesterday had not been sufficient. She needed three weeks away from it all. 'I can't believe that Oscar has any real feelings for me.'

'No.' Annoyingly, Fergus agreed with her. 'It's more a territory thing with him. He saw you first, therefore you're his.'

'Are you implying that he suspects there's something going on between us?'

'I'm afraid so.'

A horrible thought dawned on Julia. 'You didn't encourage him, did you? I mean, you told him he was wrong?'

'But there was something going on. You can't have forgotten.'

Julia found herself beginning to tremble. 'Fergus, you didn't tell him what happened between us yesterday?'

He hesitated just long enough to turn faint doubt into screaming certainty. 'Of course not.'

She wiped away the mist of sweat which had gathered on her forehead. 'Then what did you say?'

'Not very much. I just said I was an old family friend. He didn't like that. And I have to tell you that I don't think he believed me when I tried to imply there was nothing else.'

Now she felt sick. 'Oh God. It's not bad enough that I behaved like a complete slut and slept with someone who's practically a stranger. But now Oscar knows about it.'

'He knows nothing of the kind. Don't overreact. He only suspects we may have – feelings – for each other.'

'That's almost as bad. And we've got him and his mother for another week!' She ended on a squeak as the knife she was using to slice tomatoes went into her finger.

Fergus took hold of her bleeding finger and held it under the tap. 'Then why don't we tell him? Come out and admit that we are having an affair?'

'But we're not! And don't waste water!' She tried to pull her hand away but couldn't.

'I'm not wasting it, I'm using it. And why aren't we having an affair? We slept together, didn't we?'

'We made love in a field! That does not mean we're having an affair!' She reached across with her other hand and turned off the tap.

'One shag does not an affair make?' Fergus took the towel she had only just put out and wrapped her hand in it.

'You don't have to be so crude about it. And that's a clean towel.' Again she tried to regain possession of her hand.

'That's why I used it, and I thought I was being poetic.'

'Well you were wrong. And I can carry my hand myself, now.' He ignored this and kept hold of it. 'How long are you staying?' she asked.

'How long do you want me to stay?'

She wrenched her hand out of his grasp, dropping the towel on the floor. 'That's a loaded question. I have no idea how long you planned to come for, or how long Suzy asked you, so don't try to bring my feelings into it.'

'Fair enough. Have you got a plaster?'

'In that drawer by the cooker. How long?'

He regained his hold on her hand and tenderly wrapped a strip of blue plaster round her finger. She admired his careful technique, not convinced the cut warranted so much fuss, but finding his concern irresistible.

'Well, I told Suzy I could manage a fortnight, and would then ask around if any of my students could help out.'

'I know she can't afford to pay anyone.'

'It would be cheaper to pay someone than have you carried off with nervous exhaustion.'

'It won't be nervous exhaustion that gets me. It'll be total insanity.'

Fergus frowned, but just then Sooty bounded in, covering the galley floor with mud.

'Oscar'll be here in a minute,' she hissed. 'Will you please let go of my hand?'

Fergus looked down at it, as if he had forgotten he was holding it. He released it only when he had checked that the plaster was well stuck down. 'We've got to have a proper talk about this, Julia. I don't want to make life harder for you, but you can't just run away from the situation.'

'Just convince Oscar that there is nothing going on, now

or ever!' she hissed, hoping that somehow she'd manage never to be alone with Fergus again.

'But that wouldn't be true.'

'*Please!*' she pleaded, although a small, mad, part of her wanted him to fight it out with Oscar on the tow-path, man to man.

'Morning!' boomed Oscar from the other end of the saloon.

'Very well,' agreed Fergus. 'If you insist.'

Julia felt weak with relief and disappointment. 'Hello, Oscar,' she called back, 'yes, the bacon's on,' picking up the unopened packet.

Oscar came down towards the galley, thus ensuring that his muddy footprints, as well as his dog's, went the entire length of the carpet. As he got near enough to see Fergus standing next to Julia, his early morning bonhomie faded like early morning mist does, quickly and silently. 'I hope it won't be long,' he snapped. 'My mother fancied some with her toast. And she wants another cup of tea.'

Julia tipped most of the water out of the kettle and put it back on, the second water-wasting offence within ten minutes. She slashed open the packet of bacon with a knife, wishing it was Oscar she was slashing. 'It won't be more than a minute or two. Would she like a tomato with it?'

'Would you like me to set the table for breakfast?' asked Fergus.

'Yes,' said Oscar. 'That galley is a little cramped for two.'

'You're so right, Oscar,' said Julia and, having tossed the rashers haphazardly on to the grill pan, immediately removed herself to her cabin. There she indulged in a small tantrum. Could she stand another twelve days of this? Wouldn't it be better to ask Fergus to leave? But then, she realised with horror, she'd have to explain to Suzy why, which would mean confessing. No, better to suffer another ten days of Oscar's jealousy than tell Suzy what she'd really been doing when she ran away. It wasn't that

Suzy would disapprove, but Julia would never hear the end of it.

While for Julia, the situation was hell on earth, Suzy was delighted by the rivalry between Fergus and Oscar.

'They're bending over themselves to be helpful,' she told Julia. 'Fergus has undertaken to plough through all those Health and Safety leaflets and do what he can to make us comply. And when Oscar overheard him telling me, he was so desperate to compete, he said he'd fix the shelf which fell down.'

'Only because it was in his mother's cabin,' said Julia.

'Yes, but it saves me or Wayne having to do it.' Suzy saw Julia's scepticism. 'Don't look at me like that. I'm sure I could put up a shelf if I had to.'

'I'm sure you could.'

'And Oscar has volunteered to take you in a taxi to the Cash and Carry, when we get to Oxford. To stock up for the school party next week.'

'Oh Suzy!'

'I tried suggesting he took me instead, on Friday afternoon, but he came up with a hundred reasons why that wouldn't be possible. He obviously prefers the more mature woman.'

Not for the first time, Julia threw a wet dishcloth at her boss.

The trip round the Cash and Carry was a nightmare. Julia had written a list, but didn't know her way around, and had to keep going back for things she had missed. And because it was far bigger than an ordinary supermarket, a mistake cost her miles of walking past walls of breakfast cereal, tinned salmon and brown sauce as high as cliffs.

Oscar, trotting at her heels, was not helpful, for, while she was trying to concentrate, he tried to pump her for information about Fergus.

'So what does an archaeologist earn these days?' he demanded, as if he would have known what one earned in the sixties.

'I haven't a clue.'

'Do they get a house, these lecturers?'

'Oscar, I don't know. I never went to university, and I don't know any lecturers.'

'Fergus lectures.'

'So do you, Oscar. It doesn't mean a thing.' She ducked round a pile of pallets about thirty feet high looking for soap-filled pads and narrowly missed being run down by a fork-lift truck.

'Considering he's such an old family friend, you don't know much about him.' Oscar nearly trod on her heels as he followed her.

'Could you possibly reach me down a case of tuna fish?' she asked, thinking of all the things she knew about Fergus that she couldn't possibly tell Oscar. 'Oh, and we'd better have one of baked beans for the kids.'

'My mother doesn't like baked beans.'

'Doesn't she? You do surprise me.'

'As I was saying, you don't seem to know much about him.'

'For the millionth time, Oscar, Fergus is not an old family friend! Our mothers are friends, but he bullied me and my sister. We hated him and I don't think he liked us much.'

'So why did he turn up on the boats?'

'Because my mother asked him to give me a cookery book and because his car broke down!'

Oscar humphed. Julia reflected how often the truth sounded like lies and lies sounded like the truth. 'I know you don't believe me, but it's true.'

And it disguised a raft of dishonesty.

Up until now, all the new passengers had settled in

sufficiently to feel part of the family by Sunday night. But the schoolchildren were different. For a start, none of them wanted to be there. They ranged in age from thirteen to sixteen and they wanted fast food, loud music and alcopops. Orange juice, home-cooked vegetables and scenery were no substitute for disco lights and alcohol. There were six of them, and they had two teachers, one of which, Sylvia, trapped Julia in the galley as she was peeling potatoes.

'Our head is a great believer in outward-bound courses and things. She thinks they're character forming. She can't understand why children don't want to get freezing cold and wet and why teachers don't want to make them. She thought this was the next best thing.'

'Some people,' said Julia sternly, 'would compare staying on a hotel boat with staying at a jolly good hotel, not camping on a Scottish hillside in the middle of winter.'

Sylvia giggled. 'Not that woman in the knitted suit, though.'

Ruefully Julia acknowledged this was true. 'No, well, she's the exception who proves the rule. Now, I can't serve chips, or Mrs Anstruther, in the suit, will moan. But if I made sauté potatoes, would the kids like that?'

'They'd love it. But I don't know why you should put yourself out for them. Ungrateful brats. Their parents have spent all that money sending them here, and they don't even want to walk along the tow-path.'

Julia had wondered the same thing to Suzy, the first evening, when the whole party had gone into a mass sulk because their teachers told them that no, they couldn't have lager. Suzy had sighed.

'I expect their parents wanted them out of the way for a bit. Lots of parents don't know what to do with their kids.'

Julia had instantly felt guilty for allowing herself to be annoyed by the constant buzz of six sets of headphones and their lack of appreciation of the meal she had cooked.

Now, she said to Sylvia, who seemed barely older than her charges, 'Perhaps they didn't want to come.'

'Probably not. They're supposed to be doing a project on Industrial Archaeology. Bill, my colleague, thinks that hands-on learning is far more valuable than just doing it out of books. But it does mean –'

Just then a scream sent Sylvia rushing out of the galley to see who had fallen in, leaving Julia to set about peeling five pounds of carrots.

But after the first two days, they settled down. They understood that spending hours in the shower was not socially acceptable, although Mrs Anstruther, who thought she was the only person who had been properly brought up, did it. They learned that joining in was less boring than opting out, and that teachers could be remarkably tactful about people who smoked as long as they did it well out of the way of everyone who didn't. After all, Bill told Sylvia, and Sylvia told Julia, making a big deal about it wouldn't actually turn them into non-smokers, just more secretive ones.

'I think Mrs Anstruther actually preferred it when they were careering all over the place threatening to fall in. She could complain more easily. Now she has to think harder,' said Fergus.

Julia growled her disagreement. 'She'd find something to complain about at a five-star hotel. "Not really the clientele you'd expect at a place like this,"' she mimicked.

Fergus laughed. 'Well at least the kids are happier.'

The three girls inevitably fell in love with Wayne, which meant Suzy had to have a little talk with him after lunch, while the young people and their minders were all examining a quarry. Julia, who had taken her mountain of vegetables on to the roof of the butty to peel, so she would be out of reach of Oscar's mother, listened in with amusement.

'It's not that I mind them fainting every time you smile

at them,' said Suzy, not quite truthfully, 'but could you try not to let yourself get distracted? Hitting the bridge yesterday meant Mrs A's cosmetics all fell off the shelf and on to her bed. She was very annoyed.'

Wayne gave a grin which made even Julia's heart beat faster. 'I can't see to steer properly with those girls draped all over the butty roof. Sorry.' Suzy instantly forgave him. 'I got some good shots of them sunbathing, though,' Wayne continued, unaware that this might put his forgiveness in jeopardy.

'Well I don't want them on film,' said Suzy.

Wayne put a protective hand on the camcorder. 'I thought they made a nice change from all those . . .'

'Women of a certain age,' Julia supplied for him.

'That's it.'

'They may cheer up your life,' said Suzy firmly, 'but we don't want our American friends thinking that you have to have blue nails and a pierced navel to fit in, or that school parties are a regular feature. I think it's high time you stopped filming and sent it off to your friend to edit.'

'That film could launch my career,' Wayne protested. 'I could take it to college with me as a sample of my work.'

'You can do that far better if the film has actually been edited.' Firm but kind, Suzy prised the camcorder out of his hand. 'Pass it over, there's a good boy. Otherwise we won't be in time for it to be of any use. The American agent has got to see it before the end of the season. I'll put it in the post for Ralph now. He's got the address of your friend?'

Wayne nodded, his pout almost as devastating as his smile. 'Don't know how it's going to turn out,' he said sulkily. 'My mate's into experimental film techniques.'

'Tell him he won't get a penny unless it's usable,' said Julia, whose pennies they were.

The boys in the party, who had been hoping for a bit of uninterrupted posing for the girls, turned their testosterone in Suzy's direction, who knew exactly how to keep them in her thrall. She knew when to flirt, when to chide and when to allow them a glimpse up the leg of her shorts. Once upon a time Julia would have been shocked by this blatant manipulation. After two months of uninterrupted hotel-boating, anything that made life easier was morally acceptable. And it did: Suzy's fan club fought to open the lock-gates before the lock was empty so Suzy could steer in without having to stop first. They struggled to open the paddles before Wayne, older, stronger and practised, could. They tied up the boats far too tightly, they hammered in the mooring stakes far too deeply, but they were so eager for a smile, or even a kiss, that they kept out of Mrs Anstruther's way. The smell of Lynx reached toxic levels.

Mrs Anstruther should have been pleased that 'that oik with the earring' was no longer videoing every little incident, and that the boat was child-free except at meal times. But being pleased was not part of her make-up and she took advantage of Fergus's apparently sympathetic ear and educated accent to moan continually about 'young people nowadays', which included the people who looked after them. She reserved her most cutting remarks for Sylvia, who least deserved them.

But Sylvia, completely unknowingly, got her revenge by falling in love with Oscar. Not even Mrs Anstruther could fail to notice her drinking in every pompous remark her son made, and looking at him with big, adoring eyes. Only too aware that Oscar might easily tire of courting the unresponsive Julia and become flattered by Sylvia's devotion, she was anxious.

Julia, who happened to be out of sight sweeping the corridor in the butty, could hear Mrs Anstruther, on the motor boat, unburdening herself on the subject to Fergus.

'Of course she is much younger than Julia, so she could bear Oscar as many children as he liked, though one would hope that a boy and a girl would satisfy him. And she's biddable, too. We wouldn't have to put up with those temper tantrums that Julia has treated us to.'

Fergus interrupted. 'She sounds ideal. Why don't you encourage the match?'

Julia had to imagine the expression of horror on Mrs Anstruther's face, but as she had seen it often, this was not difficult. 'My dear Fergus, have you gone mad? I couldn't let Oscar marry a girl like that!'

'But why not? What's wrong with her?'

'Her vowel sounds! I dare say you haven't noticed, but unfortunately I'm cursed with a perfect ear. I just could not live with a girl who has even the smallest hint of an accent.'

'But what kind of an accent does she have?'

'Estuary English. I expect you've become accustomed to it, but I can't and won't tolerate it in my drawing room.'

Julia had to disguise her giggles with a sneeze.

Chapter Fourteen

In spite of pleading with them not to, Bill and Sylvia had insisted on ceremonial thanks and speeches of farewell on their last night, before dinner. Julia stood in the galley doorway suffering silently. She had – foolishly, it turned out – decided to make cheese soufflés as a last-night treat and didn't know if they'd survive better with the oven on or off. Mrs Anstruther would make some acid comment whatever happened, and was now listening to praises being sung to people she despised in a way which reminded Julia of a stuffed polecat she had once seen in a museum: static but vicious.

It had been a long and tiring fortnight, and Julia was keen to get this last dinner over before she lost what remnants of sanity she still had and committed grievous bodily harm on an elderly widow, having failed to drown her son. But she had to watch, agonising about her soufflés, as first Wayne, then Suzy, then she herself were presented with wildly unsuitable gifts.

Oscar cleared his throat, unable to miss out on any ceremony going, and produced a plastic carrier. 'A small gesture of gratitude for the splendid time you've given m'mother and myself.'

He handed Julia and Suzy boxes wrapped in chemist's bags which turned out to be embarrassingly expensive scent. Suzy thanked him with her usual lusty enthusiasm and Julia was forced to kiss his cheek. Both girls avoided Mrs Anstruther, lest they be turned into pigs.

'Can I serve dinner now?' Julia asked, when she'd

judged everyone had oohed and aahed enough. It was hard not to sound churlish when everyone had been so kind.

'Not quite, it's Fergus's turn,' said Suzy. 'He's been so good to us when we were short-handed.'

'Gave me a hand out of the cut when I needed it,' put in Oscar, with a guffaw, forgetting for a moment that Fergus was his supposed rival.

'And as you all know, he's leaving us tomorrow . . .' Suzy went on.

Julia, who hadn't realised it was so soon, suffered a pang of anguish which made her hiccup.

'And so I've got him a present too.' She handed him a box which he duly unpacked. 'Your very own windlass,' Suzy announced, 'to make sure you don't forget the canals.'

'That's really very kind of you, Suzy.' Fergus kissed Suzy firmly. 'Just being on the canals with you all was reward enough.'

Julia blushed, sure there was a *double entendre* there intended for her. 'I really do think we should eat now,' she said. To their enormous credit, the soufflés were still inflated.

The following morning, possibly because of the hyperbole written by the school party and Oscar, Mrs Anstruther declined to write in the visitors' book. Considering she had hated the canals from the moment she had set foot on the boats this was just as well. It was only, according to Fergus, in whom she had confided, her devotion to her 'beloved son', and her determination to keep him out of the hands of 'that harpy', which made her come at all.

'If only she'd told me,' Julia murmured to Fergus while she washed up cornflake bowls. 'I could have sent her an affidavit promising not to lay a finger on him.'

'Just as well you didn't. She'd have sued. You pushed

him in,' Fergus reminded her.

'But I wouldn't have if I hadn't been so maddened by her. I'd have been my usual pleasant self the entire time.'

'Oh really? That I would like to see.'

Remembering how unpleasant she had been to Fergus during his first trip, Julia blushed and scoured the frying pan.

At last everyone had collected most of their belongings, the school party had been carried away by their mini-bus, and it was only Oscar and his mother who were holding up the business of the day.

But eventually, not even Oscar could think up any more excuses to hang around and handed his mother on to the tow-path where the crew were all waiting to say goodbye. ('Making sure the old bag really leaves more likely,' muttered Suzy.)

Mrs Anstruther shook hands with Julia and Suzy but ignored Wayne, although he carried her suitcases to the car and generally behaved in the pleasant, self-effacing manner of someone hoping for a tip. Fergus was rewarded with gracious thanks for his civilised company, 'making the whole thing a little more bearable'.

Oscar crushed Julia to his manly chest. 'I've not given up hope with you, my dear. Still want to marry you. I like a girl with plenty of pluck.'

He embraced Suzy only a little less warmly, and handed Wayne a ten-pound note. He drew Fergus a little apart so Julia couldn't hear what he said to him, but she had a horrible feeling it was something like: 'Don't think because I'm off the scene I'm out of the picture.'

After they had all gone, the entire crew slumped in the saloon, drained of every drop of good nature, energy and enthusiasm.

'What are we going to do without you, Fergus?' wailed Suzy. 'I'm so tired I could sleep for a week. I'll have to work the locks now you're not here.'

'I've got a student who might be willing to come,' he said, 'but you'd have to pay her.'

'I'll pay her. I'll sell the pearls Daddy gave me for my twenty-first.'

'Suzy!' said Julia, shocked in spite of herself. 'You didn't bring them with you, did you?'

'Well, not on purpose. I found them in one of the pockets in my sports bag. They'd probably been there for ages. They're supposed to be quite valuable. Daddy made a big fuss about insuring them.' Suzy suddenly brightened up. 'Hey! Why don't I say they've been stolen and claim the insurance?'

'Because it would be dishonest,' said Julia.

'Well, we'll sell them then,' said Suzy. 'They're mine, after all,' she added, becoming aware of Julia's unspoken disapproval.

'Selling things is never easy. Especially when you're only in a town on Saturdays, and are always running round like a mad thing. And you never get the real value.' Julia didn't feel that Suzy bouncing into a jewellers wearing shorts, work boots and a tight T-shirt would gain more than a visit from the police, which Suzy might thoroughly enjoy, but would not get them any money.

'Why don't you let me have the pearls?' suggested Fergus. 'I could arrange to sell them in Oxford to someone reputable, and let you have some money on account. If I don't get as much for them as I lend you, we can settle up at the end of the season.'

'Brilliant idea. I knew you were clever, Fergus, no matter what Julia said.'

Fergus regarded Julia with a sternness she hadn't encountered before. 'Mmm. I'd like to take Julia for a short walk, if nobody minds.'

'Oh, go ahead,' said Suzy.

'Excuse me!' said Julia. 'I mind. I've got far too much to do and no energy to go walking for pleasure.'

'I don't think this qualifies as "pleasure", and I won't keep you long. I really need to talk to you in private.'

Julia got to her feet, seething with resentment and anxiety. To announce in a loud voice that you need to talk to someone in private is almost as bad as blurting out whatever you wanted to say in a room full of people. In fact probably worse, because of the speculation it would cause.

'Really, Fergus, I haven't time for this,' she said, as he dragged her along the tow-path and up a track. 'You know how hectic Saturdays are.'

'I need to know where I stand with you.' With his hands on her shoulders, several inches taller than her, he seemed to Julia to be standing in rather an advantageous position. 'Are we having a relationship, or not?'

'Not,' said Julia.

'So us making love was just some sort of – aberration?'

'Yes. I was overwrought. I didn't know what I was doing.'

He snorted in disbelief. 'You could hardly have been doing anything else!'

'I know it seems a bit odd . . .'

'Just a bit.'

'But I really didn't know what I was doing. I mean, I was half asleep. It's so unlike me, making love when I'm not in a steady relationship. Usually . . .'

He cut through her rambling apologia. 'And you don't want to do it again?'

'No.' Although it was not his love-making she didn't want to repeat, it was all the emotion which went with it, on her part anyway. And explaining this would not only be complicated, it would be too revealing. It was easier to just send him away.

Fergus looked down at her, frowning slightly. 'That's all? No explanations – excuses, even?'

She shook her head, wishing this whole conversation

was taking place in entirely different circumstances, when she wasn't dotty with tiredness. 'I really don't want any sort of relationship.' Was a relationship what he had in mind? 'It was just a . . .'

'Holiday romance?'

'Not a holiday, and not a romance, though it was . . .' She paused. She didn't want what had been truly enjoyable, and intensely romantic, to be downgraded to a mere pastoral romp. '. . . pleasant,' she finished weakly.

Fergus made an irritated noise. 'Oh for God's sake! There's no getting any sense out of you. I wish I – Oh, let's go back.'

As she had known would happen, Suzy gave her a knowing glance when they joined the others but fortunately there was no opportunity for any intimate chat.

When he said goodbye to her, a couple of hours later, it was all Julia could do not to burst into tears. He was so cold.

'Well, Julia, thank you for a lovely time. It's a shame I couldn't stay longer. But duty calls, you know.'

'Oh yes,' said Julia, impressed by her ability to hide her turmoil. 'Of course it does. Have you got a lot of work to do?'

'Only a book to finish. It was due at my publisher's last week.'

'Oh dear. So if Suzy hadn't summoned you, you'd have got it done by now?'

'Probably.'

'That Suzy, she's so thoughtless.'

'She's not the only one.' Then he kissed her, hard and roughly, but without hugging her.

Saturday flew by, as it usually did, in a flurry of shopping, cooking, cleaning and bed-making. They were not full for the next week, so Julia cleaned the double cabin at the end, but didn't make up the bed. Suzy and she had agreed earlier always to make up all the beds, so if anyone looked through the windows (as people frequently did), they would think they were full. When Suzy reminded Julia of this she got a sharp reply.

'Well, you do it then. I just can't do anything extra. It's either make up that cabin, or make a cake for tea, and I really don't think we can offer new passengers old cake, do you?'

Suzy crept away, surprised at Julia's vehemence.

As Julia tipped ground almonds into her cake mixture, she tried to convince herself that life would be easier now that Fergus had gone. But however hard she thought about it, she couldn't think of a single way in which it would be. It was like *Brief Encounter* all over again – a case of completely crap timing. If she'd met Fergus a year ago, before she'd met Oscar, and subsequently decided that marriage and children were not for her, or at least not yet, it would have been different. But because she'd met him at the beginning of her new life, when she was totally taken up with the boats and cooking, she couldn't cope. Especially as Fergus was recently divorced and probably only looking for a quick fling. And although in theory this should fit in with her own feelings, in practice she didn't want Fergus for just a brief affair.

Julia was licking out the cake bowl when she heard the rumpus accompanying the arrival of a passenger. Hastily, she washed her hands and checked her mouth for traces of chocolate.

'How dare anyone come so early? Well, they're not getting tea until the cake's cooked. Where the hell is Suzy? As if I didn't know!' Muttering crossly, she went out.

There on the tow-path, surrounded by carpet bags made of real carpet, draped with shawls, her long hair piled on her head, held up with Native American silver clips and combs, was Julia's mother.

This time Julia did burst into tears. She clambered out of

the boat and into her mother's arms and was fervently embraced. Her mother smelled of sandalwood and patchouli, and her dangly earrings dug into Julia's cheek, but love flowed from her.

'Mummy! Darling! What a surprise! Have you come for a holiday?'

'Well, yes, but I've really come to give you a hand. I rang the office and explained who I was. I spoke to a very nice woman called Joan, and she told me you had spaces free and could really do with some help, so I just piled into the car and came. Let me look at you. You do look well. Have you put on weight? Or is it just that you've got a tan?'

Suzy and Wayne, hearing the commotion, emerged from the back cabin. 'It's wonderful of you to come, Mrs . . .' said Suzy.

'It's Fairfax, same as Julia, but you must call me Margot, darling.' Suzy was then embraced. 'You must be Suzy. I'd like to say I've heard a lot about you, except that Julia hardly ever rings me.' Julia started to protest. 'Oh I know how busy you've been, darling. Now, can I get on? I don't care where I sleep. I've brought a tent, in case.'

'The double cabin at the front is free,' said Suzy. 'I'll just run and put bedding on it.'

'Don't bother, dear,' said Margot. 'Just give me the things and I'll do it myself.'

'Shall I take your bags?' Wayne was blinking at this woman, obviously wondering how someone who was the same sex and much the same age as Mrs Anstruther could be so completely different.

He said as much to Julia as she rummaged in the linen cupboard. 'Chalk and cheese isn't in it. She's lovely, your mum.'

Julia sighed. She *was* lovely, but like clotted cream fudge, a little went a long way.

Julia's mother insisted on taking over in the galley. She washed everything in sight, even things which were clean, and set about making wholemeal scones. Julia indicated the cake, having long since decided that cake or scones should constitute tea, not both, or the passengers could never manage to eat dinner.

'Nonsense, darling. Brown flour doesn't clog you up like white flour does. Anyway, the milk was sour, I had to use it up.'

'She's lovely, your mum,' said Suzy. 'She's just taken over in the kitchen like she's always been there.'

Julia, who, unusually for a Saturday, had found time to wash her hair, was forced to agree. What she didn't tell Suzy was that her mother had declared the menu Julia had decided on was far too full of protein and had devised a vegetarian meal which used three days' supply of vegetables and would undoubtedly give passengers unused to a high-fibre diet an uncomfortable time.

The passengers, when they came, all adored her on sight, although they did think she was the owner, and had to be convinced that Suzy was.

'It's stunning, isn't it?' said Margot. 'What young women today can do? Here's Suzy, running her own business, at, what? Twenty?'

'Twenty-four, actually.'

'But still practically a child. Have a drink, Winifred, do.'

Unfortunately Winifred hadn't yet had the bar explained to her, which meant that her dry sherry was on the house. Suzy might still think that having Margot to stay was wonderful, but Julia was already beginning to have her doubts.

Wayne was totally won over. Julia's mother did have a special way with young men and he trotted off back to town to buy more vegetables without a word of complaint. And he told her all about his video, the film-speak sounding a little strange in his leisurely West Country accent.

Margot was enchanted. 'It sounds thrilling. Very arthouse. I am sorry I won't be able to see it just yet. You must send me a copy.'

Julia and Suzy had been exchanging dubious looks. They wanted the video to show hotel-boating and canals to Americans, not to make a statement about man's inhumanity to man.

'But, Mum,' Julia now protested. 'You haven't even got a television, let alone a video.'

'But I've got lots of friends who have. They might like a canal holiday too. In fact, I could probably get you lots of new business.'

'She can sell ice to Eskimos,' said Julia to Suzy. 'As long as it's not for her.'

'I'll see you get a copy as soon as they're available, Margot,' said Suzy. 'We need all the help we can get.'

Ron Jones, the Health and Safety man, came back that week. Unsurprisingly he too fell under Margot's spell.

'It does make a change from my last visit,' he told her, drinking a cup of tea and eating a date slice so full of fibre it could have clothed the world. 'There was a very irate chap who seemed to think I did nothing but make trouble.'

'When, of course, all you are doing is your job. Some people just can't take criticism. If the kitchen is unhygienic, something must be done about it. I've done a lot of cleaning since I've been here.'

This was true, but not a lot of it had been necessary, and Julia didn't feel it did their case much good to tell him about it. 'I think you'll find we've addressed all the points you raised,' she said.

'You mean Fergus did,' said Suzy. 'He was great.'

'Fergus? Fergus was here?'

Julia was mentally kicking herself for not warning Suzy not to mention Fergus. 'You know he was, Mum, you sent him.'

'Was Fergus the one who I thought was going to attack me?' asked Ron Jones. 'With the dog?'

180

'Oh no, that was Oscar,' said Suzy. 'Julia pushed him in the canal.'

'Julia!' Margot was shocked. 'You didn't!'

'He really deserved it, Margot. Just because he was engaged to Julia, he thought it gave him the right to attack poor Mr Jones, who had been terribly helpful and not at all difficult,' Suzy went on, obviously in the hope that Ron would continue to be helpful, and pass all the alterations Fergus had made. 'But poor old Oscar wouldn't have been able to get out of the canal if Fergus hadn't rescued him.'

'So Fergus came back, then?'

'Sooty kept pushing him over,' said Julia, in a vain attempt to distract her mother from Fergus. 'He's Oscar's dog, a black Lab. Absolutely adorable, but such a handful. And he really shouldn't have brought him on the boats.'

'Just tell me, darling,' Margot took hold of Julia's hand. 'Did Fergus actually come to visit you?'

'Oh yes,' said Suzy, unaware of the trouble she was causing for her friend. 'Twice. The first week he helped us out when we had no crew. A real star. And then he came back. You've only just missed him, in fact.'

'Why didn't you tell me, darling? I was only on the telephone to his mother the other day and she never said a word about it.'

'Sorry, Mummy, it just went clean out of my head. You can see how busy we are.' Though actually, with only seven passengers and her mother to help, they were not as busy as usual.

Mollified, Margot offered Ron Jones more tea.

'Actually I think I ought to have a look at what you've done to comply with regulations,' he said. 'Pleasant though it is sitting here and eating these delicious date slices.'

Suzy got up. 'I'll take you on a tour. But Fergus was very thorough.'

'It was kind of Fergus to come back,' said Margot, as she

and Julia walked along the tow-path so as to be out of the way. 'He's such a nice man, don't you think? I mean, I know it has always been a little joke between me and Lally' – it had never felt like a joke to Julia – 'about how lovely it would be if you two got together. I know you never took any notice, and Fergus went off and married that dreadful woman . . .'

'Did you ever meet her?'

'No, but –'

'How do you know she was dreadful? She might have been charming.'

'Well, Lally said . . .'

'Mummy, darling, you must admit that no woman would be good enough for Lally's darling son. She could have been a saint and Lally would have hated her. Thank goodness you're not like that.'

Margot was silenced, but only for an instant. This subject was too close to her heart for her to allow it to be closed. 'Well, I suppose you're right about Lally, although I do think if Fergus met the right girl, she'd be perfectly OK as a mother-in-law.'

Julia concealed her scepticism behind a small cough.

'But considering how Lally has always doted on him, Fergus has turned out very well, don't you think?'

Julia did think, very hard indeed. The wrong thing said now would set both mothers into a frenzy of match-making. The last few years would be as nothing to the pressure they would now put on to get their respective children up the aisle. She owed it to Fergus as well as herself to put a stop to any romantic ideas her mother might be nursing. 'He really was very helpful. But not exactly the sort of man one could fancy, is he?'

'Well, I thought he was very attractive. Manly, you know.'

Julia did, but she wasn't letting on. 'I suppose he was all right. The passengers all thought he was gorgeous. But of course, they were all much older than me.'

Margot didn't reply for a few moments. She hated to think of herself classed with women who were much older than Julia. She was a mother and a grandmother, and very maternal, but part of her wanted to be thought of as a young woman in her prime. She set off on a slightly different tack. 'Of course, I know Lally can be a bit bossy, but apparently his first wife really *was* dreadful. Didn't look after him, didn't want children, was only interested in her career. Lally told me she knew straight away it would end in tears.'

'I've heard olive is very good for grief – you know, the Bach Flower Remedy?' With luck, this would get her mother off Fergus and on to alternative therapies.

'I've got a chart in my cabin if you want to make sure, but going back to Lally, she told me all Fergus wants to do is to settle down and have children.'

Julia shuddered. Lally would probably insist on potty-training and boarding school, just like Oscar's mother. But she took care not to react too violently or her mother would think she was faking all her lack of interest. Which of course, she was. She gave a small yawn. 'That makes him seem rather dull, doesn't it?'

Margot was torn. The core of her being was deeply conventional, and for years her exterior had been too. But her new persona, acquired after she was widowed and had gone on a formative courses in radionics, colour therapy and the benefits of colonic irrigation, was far more of a free spirit. Settling down with a wife and two point four children was a notion she should despise. Where, in domesticity, was the room for self-discovery, or for getting in touch with the spiritual side of oneself?

After a brief internal tussle, Margot came down on the side of convention. After all, she had been involved in the New Age for a comparatively short time. Thirty-odd years of marriage had left a deeper scar.

'Not dull, dear. Just responsible. And, of course, Lally said to me just the other day –'

'You seem to be in very close touch with Lally, these days.'

'Our lives have more meeting points than ever, yes, but what I was trying to tell you' – and what Julia was trying so hard not to hear – 'is that she really wished Fergus would find a nice girl like you.' Margot paused. 'Actually, she said "you".'

'I know. You and she have wanted me and Fergus to get married since I was born.'

'Oh not really, darling! But now you've broken off your engagement –'

'You didn't tell Lally that I'd broken off my engagement, did you?'

'I just might have mentioned it.'

'Oh that's all right. That'll stop her thinking I'm suitable for Fergus. After all, according to what you said, I ditched Oscar for exactly the same reasons Fergus's wife left him. Lally wouldn't want him involved with another woman like that, would she?'

'But you're not like that really.'

'Yes I am! I want freedom, to be able to travel, to have whatever job I like. To have a career, or just have fun! Just like you've been doing since Daddy died. Only I'm not getting married so I don't have to wait to be widowed before I can.'

Her mother didn't reply for some time. 'I will just say, darling, that much as I loved Daddy, still do love him, having children was the most wonderful and fulfilling part of my life, and I wouldn't have missed it for all the freedom in the world.'

Julia felt tearful again. 'Oh, Mummy, that's a lovely thing to say.'

'So I do think you should get married and have children before it's too late . . .'

Chapter Fifteen

A couple of months after Julia's mother descended on them for a week, Julia and Suzy were sitting on the roof of the butty, enjoying the hot August sunshine.

Suzy yawned and stretched a naked sun-tanned leg, admiring its shape and colour and the painted toenails of the attached foot. 'Things do seem to have settled into some sort of rhythm,' she said dreamily. 'Think how hard things used to be. Since Mel came, it's been a happy dream. My tan's come on a treat.'

'We certainly never had time to lie around chatting before she came.' Julia was peeling potatoes. The passengers – only four of them, but a hardy lot in spite of being in their seventies – had come together so they could play bridge. Now they had gone off on a walk, taking Wayne and their afternoon tea with them. Suzy was supposed to be doing paperwork.

Suzy sat up and picked up her Biro. 'I'm not really lying around. I'm just working things out with my eyes shut. But Mel is fab. She's so keen and eager to learn. Cooks jolly well too. Fergus was clever to send her.'

'I don't expect he knew how good she'd turn out to be,' said Julia. 'He wouldn't have tested her cooking.'

'Why are you so reluctant to give Fergus any credit for anything? He's saved our lives lots of times but you can hardly bring yourself to say thank you.'

Julia contemplated the potato peel which was curling out from her peeler. 'It's probably because Mum has always gone on about how marvellous he is. But it is churlish of me.' She sighed. 'We would have been really stuck without Mel as my cooking seems to have gone right off lately.'

'Has it? I hadn't noticed. Are you worried about your old firm suing you, or something?'

Julia shook her head. 'I've hardly given it a thought, actually. The whole thing is so ridiculous, I can't seem to take it seriously. Especially when we've been so busy. So you don't think my cooking's gone off?'

'It seems just as good as ever to me. But Mel is good with the boats too. In fact, she's a dream crew member. Do you think I should ask her if she'd like to come back next year?'

'Absolutely. She's made all the difference to my life.'

'Having your mother here that week made things easier too, didn't it?' went on Suzy. 'She was ace. You are lucky to have a mother like that. She really participates in your life, instead of just disapproving of it all the time. So unlike most mothers.'

'She can take over, rather.'

'Well, yes, but in a good way.'

'I suppose so.' Although at the time she had had mixed feelings about being shooed out of her own galley, she felt obliged to agree. She'd been ungracious enough about Fergus.

Suzy didn't notice Julia's mixed feelings. 'In fact, I think we've got this hotel-boat thing cracked. If Wayne's video turns out all right, and we get the people from America, we'll be laughing. And even if it's crap, we should get more bookings than this year. Almost everyone except Oscar's mother said they wanted to come again and bring their friends.'

Julia, who, in spite of Mel, was still feeling tired, couldn't quite share Suzy's undiluted optimism. She was remembering all the difficulties they had had at the beginning of the season, when Jason had abandoned them hours before their first group of passengers. But it was too nice a day to spoil, so she kept her negative thoughts to herself.

Mel was indeed a jewel. She had arrived by taxi with a rucksack saying that Fergus had got loads for the pearls and that she'd been paid by him until the end of the season. She had bags of energy, was cheerful at all times, and had an endless supply of recipes for pineapple upside down cake, lamingtons, and similar homely delights. The passengers all loved her, and tipped her lavishly.

'You're worth every penny,' Julia and Suzy said a little enviously the first time they saw this. Passengers didn't tip Suzy because she was the owner, and presumably making a fortune, and they didn't tip Julia because she seemed more like a partner than an employee. 'That's *so* unfair!' Suzy said to her. 'You *deserve* tips.'

Julia shrugged. 'That's the downside of being so friendly with the boss.'

Suzy hugged her and later on, gave her a charming pair of earrings she'd bought in a canalside shop. 'There have to be upsides too,' she had explained.

Now, having delivered the peeled spuds, and been reassured by Mel that she didn't need or want any interference in the galley, Julia decided against sunbathing in favour of a walk. The sun, which had been pleasant for a while, was making her feel a bit sick.

'I'm going to see if I can find some early blackberries,' she told Suzy. 'I saw one or two as we passed this morning. Fancy coming?'

Suzy was always eager for an excuse to abandon her book-keeping. 'Oh yes. Things are pretty much up to date. Fergus got everything in order for me before he left. It's been quite easy to keep it up since.'

'Oh God,' muttered Julia. 'Don't say he's an expert accountant as well as everything else.'

'I don't know about expert, but – Oh. You were being sarcastic. Do you really think having him stuffed down

187

your throat from birth gives you the right to hate him?'

'I don't *hate* him, I just get a bit fed up with hearing him described as the saviour of the human race, that's all.'

Suzy giggled. 'Not the whole human race, just us. Come on, Julia, lighten up.'

They didn't find many blackberries, but they enjoyed their ramble in the sunshine and were in sight of the boats shortly before the passengers were due back from the walk.

'I hope Mel hasn't been lonely,' said Suzy, who would have been. 'But she promised she'd be all right on her own.'

But Mel was not all right. And she was not on her own. In fact, the saloon seemed to be full when they arrived. There were two men sitting at the table, drinking lager from cans, and a girl on the steps, fiddling with her hands. One of the men was Jason. The other had a shaved head and a ring through his eyebrow.

'So Daddy's Little Princess has returned,' said Jason, draining his can. 'So now I can have the pleasure of throwing you off these boats.'

Mel was in the galley, looking white and shaken, but stubborn. The girl on the steps obviously felt awkward. 'Oh come on, Jace . . .' she said.

'They might as well know,' said the other man. 'And they might as well get off now as later.'

'What the hell are you doing here?' demanded Suzy. She frowned at the girl. 'Lisa?'

The girl nodded, but didn't reply.

'We've come because these boats are ours now,' said Jason. 'They've been sold.'

'Not to you?' said Julia.

Jason shrugged. 'Not yet. But we're running them for the rest of the season, and the next.' He sneered at Suzy. 'Your Uncle Ralph has sold out, sweetheart.'

188

'I don't believe you. He wouldn't do that and he's said nothing to me,' said Suzy, who had sat down. Julia's legs felt shaky too.

'But he has arranged to come and see you tomorrow?' Jason asked with all the venom he was capable of.

'Yes, but he likes to visit from time to time.'

'Well, tomorrow he's going to tell you he's sold the boats. We're just giving you a little advance warning.'

'Have you any proof?' asked Julia briskly. 'Bills of sale, transfer of ownership? Stuff like that?'

'No,' Jason said, with an upward inflection which implied such things were not necessary.

'Well, you surely don't expect us just to take your word for it,' Julia went on.

'I really don't give a shit what you think,' said Jason. 'We're here now, and we're taking over. You three girlies had better just pack your bags and split.'

'We're not going anywhere until we've proof that Ralph really has sold the boats. And then,' Julia continued, 'we'll want to see proof that whoever's bought them has been mad enough to appoint you as crew.'

Jason got up, insulted. 'Listen, you fat cow. There's no one on the cut handles boats better than I do. And no one cooks better than my Lisa.'

'Oh yeah?' said Suzy.

'Oh yeah,' repeated Jason, advancing on Suzy in a menacing way.

Seeing Suzy's fear, Julia found herself trying to deflect Jason's wrath. 'Well, I just hope your sidekicks are red hot on the customer-relations side, though that looks un-likely,' she said. 'Because you are such crap when it comes to dealing with people you'd drive every passenger you had away!'

Jason duly turned away from Suzy and directed his anger at Julia, pushing aside the chairs so he could get to her. She didn't move from her position on the banquette, but she did wonder if he would actually hit her. She was frightened, but prepared.

'Calm down, Jace,' said Lisa quickly, obviously not wanting the whole thing to escalate into violence. 'We can't just throw them out. We shouldn't have come, not until tomorrow. That's when the sale's due to go through,' she added, for the benefit of Julia and Suzy.

'Well,' said Julia. 'Until we've seen proof that there's going to be a sale, you have no right to be here, and can just leave. If Ralph really has sold the boats, you can come back when we've gone.'

'And who's going to make us?' The stocky sidekick – designed for strength, not for speed – cracked his knuckles, reminding Julia unsettlingly of a cartoon character.

'We are,' said Suzy.

'You and whose army?' Jason laughed. 'Give us another can out the fridge, girl,' he called to Mel.

'Wayne will give us a hand,' said Suzy. 'You haven't met Wayne, have you?'

'Is he the lad we saw going off with your passengers?' said Jason. 'Seemed like a nice boy, didn't he, Pig?'

'Yeah,' said Pig. 'A very nice boy. Pretty.'

Julia started to feel faint. It was so horrible to think they'd been watched. And there was no way they could get these three to leave by force, even with Wayne and the passengers as back-up. Wayne was perfectly fit and strong, but their bridge-playing lady passengers probably had brittle bones. Julia had a flash of longing for Fergus, Oscar and Sooty. Even Mrs Anstruther could have done something. Where were these people when you needed them?

'Listen,' said Julia. 'There's no need for violence. After all, if you are taking over the boats, you don't want to have to refit the saloon because it's been trashed, now do you?' Jason didn't react, but Julia carried on anyway. 'So why don't you ring up the people who employed you and tell them to bring us proof of purchase and we'll go quietly?'

Suzy squeaked indignantly. Julia ignored her. 'And when you've done that, Suzy will ring Ralph and get him to come down and tell us in person that the boats have been sold. When we've got both buyer and seller here, we'll all know where we are.'

'The passengers won't,' muttered Mel in the galley.

Julia got up and moved along to the galley door. 'Pass us the phone, Mel,' she said. Mel retrieved it and gave it to Julia, who then handed it to Jason. 'Go on. Ring up and get them down here.'

'They're a big operation. They don't just "come down here".'

'Don't they? Then they don't get their boats, do they?' went on Julia. 'And since when have hotel boats been such big business that "big operations" buy them?'

Jason looked disgustingly smug. 'That's how much you know, smartarse. They're multinational, they want the boats for corporate entertaining.'

He used the word as if it were unfamiliar to him, and for the first time Jason's story seemed to make sense. A big corporation might easily buy a pair of hotel boats for corporate entertaining, if they had more money than sense, or money they wanted to hide.

'Well, go on then,' said Julia, determined not to be disheartened. 'Ring up your "big corporation".'

Jason liked the sense of power the situation gave him. 'Got that number, Lise?'

Lisa dug about in the leather purse she wore round her neck and produced a bit of paper. She handed it to Jason.

'But I'm not phoning with you lot here,' he said. 'I'll go in the cabin.' He pushed past everyone and left the saloon.

Suzy moved away from the crowd by the steps and went to sit on the banquette. Mel left the galley and came into the saloon to join the rest of them. No one spoke. Lisa seemed extremely uncomfortable about the whole thing. The other man looked about him restlessly. He couldn't have been a potential member of the crew, Julia decided, not with a sobriquet like 'Pig'. He must have been brought along as extra muscle.

'The passengers'll be back soon,' murmured Mel to Julia. 'What should we do about dinner?'

Julia looked at Suzy, but she had hunched herself into a ball on the side bed. She looked totally miserable and turned in on herself. All her fight had gone.

'We'll have to feed them, whatever happens. You carry on cooking and I'll set the table.' Julia got up. 'If you wouldn't mind moving into the well-deck, we have to get on with dinner,' she said to Pig, who grunted a refusal until he realised that if he didn't move he was likely to be stepped on.

Lisa jumped to her feet immediately. 'Of course. Is there anything I can do to help?'

Suzy woke from her stupor and regarded Lisa in amazement. 'What on earth do you think you're doing, getting back with Jason? You must be mad!'

'He's not always like this,' Lisa said defensively. 'He can be really kind.'

Suzy raised her eyes to heaven in a gesture which told Lisa clearly that there was no hope for her.

Julia managed to move the intruders and Suzy out of the way and set the table. Then she put out the starters, while Mel got dinner to the point when it was only the vegetables which needed cooking.

Jason was a long time with the phone. When he emerged back into the saloon he looked thoroughly disgruntled. 'Took a fucking age to get through,' he said. 'Where are the others?'

'In the well-deck, do go and join them.' Leaving Mel in the galley, Julia took the phone out of Jason's hand and went with him outside.

'Did you get hold of the buyers?' Suzy demanded of Jason.

'Yeah. Took fuckin' for ever. They're coming over. So you'd better phone *Uncle Ralph*!'

Suzy snatched the phone from Julia. 'I will, but I'll do it in private.'

Julia could see Suzy was near to tears as she pushed through the boat towards the bedroom, and knew she didn't want to break down in public. When Suzy arrived back, she looked calm, but not exactly cheerful. 'Ralph's on his way,' she said.

'And so are the passengers,' said Julia, seeing them appear on the tow-path, with Wayne carrying all the bags.

'Right, you lot,' said Suzy. 'You bloody well stay out of the way. If you upset a single passenger, or do anything I don't like, I swear to you, I'll break every window, and fill the fuel tank with water. And then see if your fancy buyers want the boats, when they have to do a total overhaul on the engine!'

'Come on, Jace. There's no need for this,' said Lisa. 'Let's go and sit on the cabin top of the butty.'

'I'll go with you,' said Suzy. 'I'm not letting you lot out of my sight.'

Mel and Julia explained to the passengers that there was a bit of an upset, but it was not to trouble them. They served dinner, cleared up quickly, and then arranged a stool and a large piece of hardboard and a cloth, which created a makeshift card table.

'I'll leave the sherry decanter out,' said Julia, 'in case you fancy some later. It'll be on the house,' she added.

It was a great relief that these particular passengers were so self-sufficient. Provided they had comfortable chairs, good light, and their cards, they were perfectly happy.

At last a car appeared on the road bridge. Suzy and Jason both got up. They watched as it disappeared, and the whole group waited to see if it had gone for ever, or had parked. After what seemed an age, people appeared on the tow-path.

'Oh look!' said Suzy excitedly. 'It's Daddy! He's brought Ralph over. We'll see how well your bully-boy tactics go down, now you've got a real man to fight with!'

Jason turned to Suzy in bewilderment. 'That's not your "Daddy", princess. That's Max Boyd, the bloke who's buying the boats.'

Suzy gave Jason a look of absolute horror and Julia's heart lurched in sympathy. The thought that Suzy's father would buy the boats out from under her to make her toe the line made her feel faint.

'Daddy,' Suzy called, as Ralph, Joan and her father approached. 'Jason says you've bought the boats. Is it true?'

'Now, sweetheart, don't get all worked up. No one's doing anything except what's best for you.' He was a big man with a barrel chest and a lot of thick grey hair. He wore a suit and tie which, like the wearer, were more at home in a boardroom than on a narrow boat.

Suzy and the others jumped off the roof of the boat and Suzy's father embraced her. Suzy didn't exactly duck away, but she didn't hug him back.

'Christ, I didn't know he was Suzy's dad,' Jason murmured to no one in particular.

'Let's sit in the well-deck,' suggested Julia, when it looked like they were going to stand around on the tow-path all night, sharing confidences with evening joggers and cyclists.

'Or we could go into the butty cabin,' said Ralph.

'No we couldn't,' snapped Suzy. 'It's far too small and it's like an oven in there.' Even in a state of shock, she knew that the butty cabin would also reveal signs of her cohabitation with Wayne. Julia admired her quick thinking. Things were complicated enough without that.

Mel slipped away, muttering about writing letters; Wayne perched on the roof; and everyone else sat down in the well-deck. Jason, Lisa and their cohort sat on top of the mooring ropes coiled up on the fore deck with their legs hanging uncomfortably over the side. They probably felt the need to distance themselves a little from the family gathering.

Julia wondered if she should slip away like Mel but Suzy clutched her arm. 'No! Don't leave me!' she hissed.

'I'll just go and see if our passengers are all right.' Julia shot a sour look in the direction of Suzy's father and Jason for forgetting that the passengers should not be disturbed by takeover bids, management buy-outs and the like.

'You don't understand, chicken,' Suzy's father was saying as she rejoined the party, having replenished the ladies' decanter. 'I bought the boats because I knew you didn't want to let Ralph down.'

'So?'

'I knew you'd never be in a position to buy them, however hard you tried. You've made a brave stab, and I'm proud of you, but it's not fair on Ralph to keep him hanging on for the money when you've no real hope of buying him out.'

'Ralph didn't recover from his operation as quickly as we'd have liked,' said Joan. 'And Max has made a very generous offer.'

'And you don't really want to spend the summer sweating away taking old women for trips on the canal,' Max went on. He had glimpsed the bridge-players and assumed that all their passengers were over a certain age. 'It's probably been a lot of fun, but it's not something you want to do for the rest of your life.'

'Isn't it?' Suzy's eyes shimmered. Julia could see her holding her head back so the tears wouldn't fall.

'No, chicken. You're worth more than this. I didn't educate you at the best private schools in the country so

195

you could spend your life running around the country on a pair of canal barges.'

'They're boats, Daddy, not barges.'

'Well, whatever you like to call them. That's why we've arranged to buy them, so that Ralph and Joan can retire in comfort. We got Jason and Lisa to run the business, so you can come home and have a rest. I'm sure your friend could do with one.' His glance at Julia made her wish she had put on make-up.

Nobody spoke for a few moments. Then Suzy cleared her throat. 'Is it true that Daddy has offered you lots of money for the boats?' she asked her uncle.

'Yes,' Joan answered for him. 'And all in one lump. If Ralph sold the boats to you, he'd only get it in instalments. It might take years and years. You know that. We can't afford to turn down cash in hand.'

'So he's paying you in used notes, is he?' Suzy demanded. 'Well, I'm very sorry you can't wait for the money, Ralph. Because running these boats has been the most wonderful thing I've ever done.' She turned to her father. 'I've learned more about myself and the world than I ever thought I would. You gave me a wonderful education, tennis lessons, piano lessons, how-to-walk-down-a-catwalk-without-falling-over lessons. But none of them taught me anything except how to be a corporate wife, a trophy to hang on the arm of some fat executive.' Max Boyd sucked in his stomach. Suzy took a breath. 'I'm sure you all expect me to burst into tears and have a tantrum because my toy's been taken away. Well, sorry to disappoint you, folks, but I'm not going to. I can see I've been beaten by circumstances this time, but it won't be for long. I'll get a job, earn as much money as I can and save every penny. So I can buy another pair of hotel boats, and make a go of it.' She turned to her aunt, whose mouth was slightly ajar. 'I quite understand you worrying about Ralph's health, and I hope that having a lot of money will stop you worrying. I just hope Ralph doesn't mind seeing Jason and his crowd drive away every scrap of goodwill he and I have built up, him over years, and me over the past months. I hope he won't mind *Pyramus* and *Thisbe* being famous all over the cut as the worst hotel boats when they could have been the best!'

Chapter Sixteen

◈

There was a silence as everyone took in the fact that Daddy's Little Princess had metamorphosed into a very determined young woman. And then Ralph began to clap, slowly and deliberately, while Suzy's father, Joan, Jason and his cohorts looked on.

'Well done, girl,' he said. 'Very well done. I knew you had more pluck than Max gave you credit for.' He turned his attention to Suzy's father. 'Sorry, old man, but I can't accept your offer.'

There were small explosions of protest from several people. Ralph's voice was heard above the others. 'I always said I'd have to talk to Suzy about it, and that I wouldn't do anything until I had. I'd have told her about you wanting to buy the boats this weekend if you lot' – he cast a disparaging eye over Jason's party – 'hadn't jumped the gun.'

'But, Ralph – all those plans we made! You can't go back on your word!' Joan was distraught.

'No, I can't,' agreed Ralph. 'And I gave my word to Suzy.'

'I think you're forgetting that the boats don't make a bean,' said Max. 'You're not carrying enough passengers to break even, let alone make a profit. How is she ever going to earn enough to pay you?'

'Bookings may not be all they might have been this year, but they've made a video.'

Wayne, who hadn't said a word until now, wriggled forward. 'Yeah? Is it good? Have you seen it?'

'I've brought copies with me,' Ralph went on. 'But Sy Cline – that's my agent in the US – rang me immediately he got it.'

'And?' Wayne nearly fell off the roof in his eagerness to hear about his baby.

'He loved it, and everyone he's shown it to has booked. I've got more bookings from America for next year than I've ever had before. We're a third full already, and it's still only August. And they've only just started promoting it properly.'

'Yeah? Cool.' Wayne sighed happily.

'But, Ralph, you told me about all this,' said Max. 'Which is why I offered you such a good price and got another crew when we could have just used the boats for corporate entertaining and saved ourselves the trouble.'

'But you've just said, Daddy, that we're not even breaking even. Now it turns out you thought you could make money!' Suzy was spitting with rage. 'Make up your mind!'

'You have to make money, sweetheart. Business is business.'

Ralph broke in before Suzy could commit patricide. 'Anyway, I'm not selling to Max, not now. I want Suzy to go on running them on the terms we've already agreed.'

Joan was in despair. 'But Ralph! Your health! We were going to go on holiday to Australia so you could see the Great Barrier Reef before you die!'

'Calm down, Joan,' said Max. 'Ralph's not going to die, and I'm sure we can work something out. Suzy, darling.' He took hold of her hand. Julia could see her fighting not to snatch it back. 'I didn't realise how much this boat thing meant to you. I would never do anything to hurt you, you know that. And if you want these boats so much, I'll buy them for you. That way Ralph gets his money straight away, and doesn't have to wait for it.'

'No, thank you.' Suzy withdrew her hand. 'If Ralph

really needs the money up front, he'd better sell to you, but if he's selling them to me, I pay for them, not you.'

'But it's the same thing, sweetheart!'

'No it's not. I want to buy the boats, myself, with money I have earned with the sweat of my brow. I don't want you to give them to me, as if they were another little hobby I was bound to give up after five minutes.'

'Good for you, girl,' said Ralph. 'I don't mind waiting for my money.'

'Oh Ralph! When will you learn to take care of yourself?' said Joan.

'But, Suzy, why won't you let me pay for them?' Max was bewildered and hurt. To him, Suzy refusing his money was the same as refusing his love.

Recognising this, Suzy took hold of his hands this time. 'Don't you see, I've been indulged all my life? I couldn't have had better parents, you've provided me with everything I wanted and a whole lot of things I'd no idea I needed. But I'm your daughter, Daddy. Like you, I want to build my own little empire. You never had a father who bought your first business.' Suzy had many times heard the story about how her father started off selling petrol at weekends and ended up with a chain of petrol stations which were just the start of it all. 'I want to work for myself, just like you did. I really look up to you, Daddy. And I want to be like you.'

Julia wanted to give her a medal for manipulation. Max looked as if he was going to burst into tears of pride that his little girl had turned out to be such a chip off the old block. He took her in his arms. 'Sweetheart, I'm so proud, so proud. But you must let me help you a little bit. Let me get you another car.'

Julia could see Suzy pretend to consider. 'I think you'd better buy Ralph and Joan tickets to Australia.'

'Yes, of course, but a nice little car for you too? Please let me.'

'Very well,' said Suzy, releasing herself. 'If it would make you happy.'

'So where does that leave us?' asked Jason.

'On the tow-path, out of a job,' said Suzy. 'So piss off!'

Jason instantly broke into loud, abusive protest.

'If you're going to blaspheme, do it out of earshot of my passengers,' Suzy went on. 'Daddy, could you please sort Jason out? On the tow-path? Joan, Ralph, come in and say hello to our ladies and I'll make some tea or something.'

'I'll do that, Suzy,' said Julia, taking her cue.

She introduced the passengers to Joan and Ralph. Ralph was his usual charming self and Joan turned out to know someone who lived in the same village as the ladies. Julia made tea and produced cake. Everyone had some except Max, who returned from disposing of Jason looking disgruntled. There had obviously had to be a pay-off and he hated not getting value for money.

'Brandy?' suggested Julia.

Max looked longingly at the bottle she was holding. 'Better not, I'm driving.'

'We've got two spare cabins, you could stay the night,' said Suzy. 'Why don't you? See what we get up to.'

Max exchanged looks with Ralph and Joan.

Ralph said, 'We could ring Emily – our neighbour,' he added for the sake of the ladies, 'and get her to collect the dogs for the night. What about it, Joany?'

Joan was looking happier and Julia wondered if Max had confirmed his promise of a ticket to Australia. 'I suppose so. If that's what you want.'

'Oh yes. We could go with them for a little way up the canal in the morning, if that's all right with Suzy. And Julia.'

'Yes,' said Suzy, 'we're a team.'

'So, would you like brandy?' asked the other member of it.

'Yes, please,' said Max. 'Large ones. But I'd better ring your mother.'

Julia poured brandy for everyone, including the bridge-playing ladies, who had abandoned their game in favour of flirting with Ralph and Max who were real experts at it.

Julia, although very tired, felt as proud of Suzy as she would have done had she given birth to her. Of course, she was still Daddy's Little Princess, twisting Daddy round her little finger. But it was on her terms. And if she got her own way by manipulation, well, so had women for thousands of years. And Suzy had made a brave decision. It would have been very easy to let her father buy the boats for her.

Eventually, the ladies went to bed, Joan following them, having been settled into the front double cabin, leaving Max free to indulge in a little interrogation. Julia rose to go as well, but Suzy pulled her back down on to the banquette. 'Don't leave me now!' she whispered.

Julia resigned herself to a late night, and remembered with a yawn that it was her turn to cook breakfast in the morning. She sent mental messages to Mel, pleading with her to do it, seeing as she had been able to go to bed hours ago.

'Now, young man,' Max turned to Wayne. 'We haven't heard a lot from you. Tell me a bit about yourself.'

'Well –'

Suzy rushed in like a hen to defend her chick. 'He's been wonderful, Daddy. When Jason pushed off, Wayne just stepped in. He picked up boating just like that. He's been brilliant.'

'And how did you meet my daughter?'

'In Tewkesbury,' his daughter answered. 'It was so handy that he should have been there just when we needed him.'

'He made an excellent video,' said Ralph. 'A bit off the

wall, but the Americans loved it. What was that dog doing on board?'

'Oh, Sooty. He came with Oscar, a friend of Julia's . . .'

'An ex-friend of Julia's,' said Julia.

Suzy giggled. 'Yes, well, she did push him in.'

'Only after extreme provocation,' Julia said, trying not to sound defensive. 'He was very rude to the Health and Safety Inspector.'

'My God! Did they catch up with you?' Ralph was horrified. 'What happened?'

'He was a sweetie,' said Suzy. 'The first time he left a list of things to do. Fergus – he's another friend of Julia's – did all the bits of DIY necessary: fitted the thermometer to the fridge, stuff like that, then the Inspector came back and said we were fine. Julia and me've got to go on hygiene courses in the winter. But then we're OK. I don't know why you worried about it so much, Ralph.'

Ralph hunched his shoulders. 'Just assumed they'd be a load of jobsworth civil servants, I suppose.'

'That's what Oscar thought, which was why Julia had to push him in.'

Max regarded Julia. She didn't look the sort of woman to set the world on fire, but she seemed to have a lot of friends. 'And how have you enjoyed hotel-boating?' he asked her. 'And will you come back next year to support my Suzy?'

'Um – well, I'd like to. But it may not be possible.'

'Why not? Not getting married, are you?' He seemed to find this idea rather extraordinary. After all, she was over twenty-five, and therefore past it, in his book.

'Good gracious no,' said Julia, aware of all his disparaging thoughts. 'But Suzy and I haven't discussed it.'

'You do want to come, don't you, Julia?' Suzy asked. 'Next year we'll have four crew right from the beginning.'

'Yes, how is that other girl working out?' asked Ralph.

'She's an angel with the strength of an ox,' said Julia. 'And of course I want to come. I'm just not sure how things will turn out, that's all. You know how it is.'

Losing interest in Julia, Max turned his attention back to Wayne. 'And so, young man, where do you see yourself in ten years' time?' he asked, reverting to interview mode.

Wayne cleared his throat and glared at Suzy, success-fully preventing her from answering the question for him. 'I've always been interested in film. I want to write, direct and produce my own work. I've already made some films and a video for a band. They went into my portfolio for college. I'm only really going to college to make the right contacts, to meet people I can work with in future. But I'm going to get there. It might take some time, but I'll make it.'

Julia wanted to clap. He was a very beautiful young man, and his long vowels and slightly husky voice added to his already ample sex-appeal. Wayne could have sailed through life trading on his good looks and easy-going personality. To have such clear-cut ambitions before he had even gone to college was admirable.

'Well, that's all very fine and large, but what are you going to live on while you're at college?' said Max.

'That's none of your business!' Suzy was furious. 'Anyway, he's going to live on the boat. There's a canal quite near where he's going to be and we're going to move it there.'

'That's not what he meant,' said Wayne. 'And Suzy's right, it is none of your business. But I'll tell you anyway. I'll get a job, like I always do, like I've done since I was thirteen. My parents aren't wealthy, they provided me with a good home but they could never afford the extras. Those I've always paid for myself. College is an extra, so I'll take care of it.'

Max was obviously a bit taken aback. Young people who didn't depend on their parents for everything hadn't crossed his path before and he didn't know how to deal with them. 'Hmm.' Max changed the subject. 'Any more of that brandy?'

Julia found another bottle hidden behind a bag of soap-filled pads and poured out seconds.

'Don't you want any, Julia?' asked Suzy.

'No thanks. I'm too tired to drink.'

'Don't let us keep you up then,' said Max. 'You two girls go off to bed.'

'Well, I don't know,' said Julia, after an exchange of frantic looks with Suzy. 'It seems a shame to miss a party. Pass the bottle.'

Eventually the moment had to come. Suzy and Julia both failed to get the men to go to bed first, and unless they were prepared to stay up until one in the morning, the risk of Max finding out about Wayne and Suzy had to be taken.

'I think I must go to bed now,' said Julia, who felt sick with exhaustion. 'Coming, Suzy?' She could hide Suzy in her bedroom until she could slip over to the butty.

'So if you've got three crew,' asked Max, just when they'd hoped he would have forgotten about Mel. 'Where does Wayne sleep?'

Suzy raised her eyes to heaven. 'Oh, Daddy.' She put her arm round his waist. 'You always think the worst, don't you? Wayne's got a tent!'

Max visibly relaxed. 'Well, I'm glad you're not sleeping with the help. It doesn't do to get too familiar with your employees, you know. Makes it difficult if you have to pull them up about anything.'

'Quite right, Daddy.' Out of sight of her father, Suzy winked at Julia and Wayne. 'Now, shall I see you to your cabin? I don't want you bursting in on any of my ladies by mistake.'

Julia was washing glasses when Suzy reappeared. 'Tent, indeed,' she said.

'Wayne has got a tent.' Suzy was indignant. 'He just doesn't sleep in it.'

Julia laughed. 'You were brilliant today, Suze. I felt really proud of you.'

'Did you? That's lovely. But it was funny. Daddy has always frightened me, just a little bit, he does tend to shout so. But I just knew what I wanted, and I knew I couldn't take his money for it, it had to be something I earned myself.'

'So you won't take the car, then?'

'Julia! He's an old man! I can't refuse him every little thing!'

'Of course not.'

'But I wasn't so sure about you, Julia. I thought you loved the canals as much as I do, and yet you didn't sound too keen on coming back next year. I could pay proper wages. I had a word with Ralph and he says we'll have no problem filling up next year.'

'It's not that I don't want to come back, I'm just not sure if I can.'

'Why? What could stop you, if you want to?'

'The thing is, Suzy, I think I might be pregnant.'

Chapter Seventeen

❧

'Oh my God!' said Suzy and then clapped her hand to her mouth. 'Oh, I am sorry! I shouldn't have said that. I just don't know if it's good news or bad!'

'Nor do I!'

'It's Fergus, isn't it? It couldn't be anyone else. Oh God! It was that time after you pushed Oscar in. I knew it!'

'Did you? I thought no one knew.'

'I didn't know for certain, there was just something about you. And I'm sure no one else had the slightest idea. Oh God, sorry to be so hysterical but it's been a long day and I never thought I'd be in this position.'

'What position?'

'Counselling someone who's pregnant. I always thought it would be the other way round . . . But are you sure?' Suzy went on, when Julia didn't reply. 'Have you taken a test? How late for your period are you?'

'Three months. I mean, I've missed three and I keep needing to wee, and I can't face coffee. I remember my sister telling me that was what first got her.'

'Are you feeling sick at all?'

Julia made a face. 'Only in the mornings.' She sighed, long and hard. 'This is the first time I've really acknowledged I could be pregnant. I kept trying to put the missed periods down to stress and things.'

'So how do you feel about it?'

'I don't know! I haven't had time to think. But I didn't really want children.'

'Not ever?'

'No. Just not yet.'

Suzy coughed and looked down at her hands. 'I don't want to be unkind, but you're not exactly a spring chicken. For having babies, I mean.'

'Thanks a lot.'

There was silence while Suzy considered what to say next. 'You could always –'

Julia stopped her finishing the sentence. 'No, I couldn't. Out of the question. I'm not saying abortion is always wrong, it just is for me. In these circumstances.'

'Have you always felt like that about it?'

'No,' said Julia slowly. 'I haven't.'

'Well then, that makes it all a lot simpler. You keep the baby. At least you know your mother will be ace about it.'

'Do I? I know she's always wanted me and Fergus to get married and have babies, but I don't think this is quite the way she had in mind. Which is why,' she went on, suddenly threatening, 'she must never find out who the father is.'

'But she's so cool! She wouldn't make you get married against your will or anything!'

'Oh wouldn't she!'

'I'm sure she wouldn't. She knew about me and Wayne and never turned a hair.'

'You're not her daughter. She's very tolerant about other people's unconventional life-styles, but her daughters are different.'

'No, no, she'll be cool, I'm sure. My mother would just *die*, but then she's terribly conventional.'

Julia didn't bother to explain that her own mother's unconventional veneer was very new, not really a hardened surface: it could easily be scratched. 'Well, I won't say anything until I'm sure I'm pregnant,' she said, although she was sure.

'No, of course not,' Suzy agreed, equally certain. 'You may be worrying quite unnecessarily.'

Julia ran her fingers through her hair. 'Who am I kidding? What other possible reason could there be for me missing three periods? And I did have unprotected sex.'

'Only once?'

'Of course only once!'

'All right, all right. It's just terribly unlucky getting pregnant after only once, that's all.'

Julia instantly felt defensive about her situation. 'Or lucky?'

Suzy stifled a yawn, aware that Julia's feelings about this were far from straightforward. 'Do you want to talk about it?'

'No, we're all completely knackered. Let's go to bed and think about it in the morning.'

'Are you sure? If you want to discuss things, I don't want to just abandon you.'

Julia couldn't wait to be abandoned. She had, after all, had longer to get used to the idea than Suzy, and now all she wanted was to get some sleep. 'No, really, it's all right. Let's just go to bed. I'm so tired I'm falling over.'

At last Julia managed to convince Suzy that she wouldn't be deserting her if she went to bed, and so Julia could go too. Tomorrow she would consider how best to plan her future, but she needed a good night's sleep first.

Mel, aware of how late it was when Julia got into bed, did get up early to make breakfast, but Julia got up shortly afterwards and helped her.

'I might as well tell you,' Julia said as they cut grapefruit together, 'as I've mentioned it to Suzy, that I think I might be pregnant. But it's all right' – Julia put out a soothing hand – 'I don't need counselling.' She couldn't bear another question-and-answer session which might involve telling Mel that her erstwhile tutor was responsible. She smiled brightly. 'In fact, I'm fine about it.'

Mel gulped and, like Suzy, tried to calculate whether

congratulations or commiserations were in order. 'I don't know what to say.'

'It's all right. Just carry on as normal. Really, I'm perfectly OK.' Just then a horrible churning inside her caused her to belch, put her hand over her mouth and rush out of the boat into the fresh air. 'Or, perhaps I'm not perfectly OK,' she said to the beautiful summer day which greeted her.

Fortunately for Julia, Suzy was so much taken up with proving to her father and Ralph how good she was at hotel-boating, she didn't have time to talk to Julia about her pregnancy. Which gave Julia time to consider her own feelings, which swooped alarmingly from a sort of startled excitement to despair and back again.

If it weren't for the guilt which seemed almost over-powering at times, the excitement would have had a chance. The thought of a tiny, growing life inside her was thrilling, but horror at her own irresponsibility and at the thought of the reactions of her friends and family kept swamping it. How could she dream of bringing a child into the world, knowing it would only ever have one parent, and thus no chance of a normal family life?

But sometimes her guilt was replaced by delighted hysteria as she considered her options. Should she ask Oscar to take on another man's child? The thought of his face made her giggle like a schoolgirl. It would certainly rid the world of his mother, who would die of apoplexy if she even had a sniff of the notion. The thought of her brother's reaction also had its funny side. He would be so desperately disapproving he would want to forbid his children to have any contact with her, in case she contaminated them with her wild immorality. How his wife would react, she couldn't tell, she'd never got to know her well enough.

Her sister, she knew, would be very supportive, once she had got used to the idea of her sensible older sister having been silly enough to get pregnant. She would pass on baby paraphernalia and advice, and would support her however her mother reacted.

The only person whose feelings she didn't try and anticipate were Fergus's, for the simple reason that she had no intention of telling him. She couldn't quite argue that it was none of his business, but it really had very little to do with him. It was pure chance that a baby had been conceived after their one encounter. They had no relationship. But what really made her determined he should never know was the fear that he might suggest an abortion. Even the idea that this might be the best solution would be devastating.

On the other hand, if her mother was to be believed, he might be delighted. If his ex-wife was organised enough not to become pregnant so she could carry on with her career, he might be thrilled that he'd caught Julia off guard. Her mind drifted back to that golden afternoon. No, she couldn't blame Fergus for this. He had tried to be sensible. This was entirely her own responsibility.

When at last Ralph, Joan and her father had gone, Suzy turned her attention to Julia. 'Have you told Mel?' Julia nodded. 'Do you mind if I tell Wayne? It's just that I know you mustn't do anything heavy, and it be would easier if he knew.'

'I think I've already done something heavy, Suzy.'

Suzy put her arm round her and hugged her, and Julia surprised herself by crying.

Wayne smiled his lazy smile which seemed to congratulate her fertility. In spite of his plans for a film career, Julia couldn't shake off the feeling that Wayne was born to make love to country girls in hayfields and, if he made them pregnant, feel pleased at the thought of being father to strings of plump, contented babies.

'We must get you a test as soon as possible,' said Suzy. 'But I have to admit, if it was negative, I think I'd be quite disappointed now. Even though it would mean I wouldn't have to worry about crew for next year.'

The test, when Julia found time to do it, proved positive, and in spite of the guilt and ambivalence which still washed over her, knowing she really was pregnant was awe-inspiring. She, Suzy and Mel thought up wild schemes by which Julia and the baby could be supported in the lap of luxury.

'You could find an heirless millionaire, and marry him,' suggested Suzy. 'Then he'd die and leave you all his money, while the disinherited children of his first five marriages hated you from a distance and tried to sue.'

'Nah, don't like bald men,' said Julia.

'You could sell your story to the tabloids and live on the profits,' suggested Mel. *'I was impregnated by a Martian.'*

'They'd take their money back if the baby didn't have two heads. No, I think I'll just do something from home. A catering business or something.'

Suzy suddenly got excited. 'You could cook dishes for us. I'm going to get a freezer for next year, and if it was filled with your wonderful cooking it would make life so much easier.'

'But how on earth are you going to afford it?' asked Julia, jealous of next year's crew's improved facilities.

'Oh, Daddy said he'd pay for it.'

'Honestly, Suzy,' said Julia, glad not to be the topic of conversation for a moment. 'You make a wonderful declaration of independence and then you go and let your father pay for things! I'm shocked.'

'The trick is not to let him pay for everything. I don't mind him buying the odd thing.'

'The odd car, the odd freezer . . .'

'But I don't want him taking over. He's very apt to do that, you know.'

'So's my mother,' Julia said glumly. 'Think how she was in the galley. She's worse with her grandchildren. My sister's husband had to be terribly firm, and I haven't got a husband to protect me.'

'No? You don't want Fergus to marry you, then?' asked Suzy.

'Fergus!' Mel shrieked. 'You mean the baby is Fergus's?'

Julia looked at Suzy in horror. She had forgotten to warn her not to tell Mel who the father was. 'You won't tell him?' she said to Mel. 'And not anyone else, either. He might get struck off or something.'

'No he won't – you're not his student,' said Mel. 'But why don't you want him to know?'

'It's complicated. But if he knows it'll get more complicated. Really, it's nothing to do with him. It was my fault.'

'He was there too, presumably,' Mel went on. 'It's as much his fault as yours.'

'No, not really,' said Julia, who blushed at the memory of her wantonness. 'And I really don't want him to know.'

'But why are you so unwilling to let him take his share of responsibility?' Mel persisted.

'It's difficult to explain. His mother and mine are very old friends. He'd probably feel obliged to offer to marry me, which I really don't want.'

Mel shrugged. 'Well, it's up to you. I can think of worse fates that being married to Fergus though. A lot of the undergraduates have crushes on him.'

'But that's disgusting, he's quite old!' objected Suzy.

'Not everyone wants their man fresh out of school,' said Mel. 'I like a more mature man myself. I've nothing against an older woman showing a boy the way, but I don't want anyone practising on me.'

Julia was with Mel on this one, but didn't comment, hoping for a change of subject.

She didn't get one. 'But going back to Fergus,' went on Mel, 'even if you don't want to marry him, I'm sure he'd do the decent thing about child support and stuff. I think you should tell him.'

'I absolutely don't want to. I want to bring this baby up on my own, with no interference. Which, given my mother's particular personality, may be quite difficult to achieve.'

'But Fergus loves kids!' Mel persisted. 'According to college gossip, his wife didn't want children because of the effect it would have on her career, which was why they broke up.'

'Which proves he's got antiquated notions of women's role in society! So I don't want him near me.'

'You must have wanted him near you that once,' said Suzy.

'That's different. You of all people should understand.' Julia picked up a kitchen knife in a business-like way, although she had no real idea of what she wanted to chop with it.

'I still think you should get him to marry you,' persisted Mel. 'He'd make a lovely husband. I gather he can cook and everything.'

'He may make a lovely husband, but not for me. We don't get on, so even if we married for the sake of the baby, we'd only end up getting divorced. Far better for the baby to get used to the idea of not having a father from birth.'

'Come on, Suze!' said Wayne impatiently. 'The taxi's waiting!'

At last Suzy squashed herself into the back with Mel and Wayne. Julia, in honour of her condition, had the front seat. They were off to the house of one of the bridge-playing ladies, who lived quite near. Wayne, using his considerable charm, had persuaded her to let them come and see the video. They had thrown themselves into the Saturday chores like mad things so they'd have time.

They all trooped into the lady's tiny, perfect cottage and

sat awkwardly on her antique furniture. But as she had only just arrived home after a week away herself, she was in no mood for ceremony.

'I'm going to collect my dog from the kennels,' she said. 'You just make yourselves at home.'

'We mustn't really,' said Julia, observing the delicate legs of the table on which rested the television and video. 'If you lean back in your chair, Wayne, it may break.'

'Don't worry, I just want to see the vid,' he said, using the remote control to fast forward to the beginning.

Suzy, Julia and Mel were in the mood to giggle at it. Wayne took it very seriously, commenting on bits where he felt his camera angles hadn't quite worked and where he felt his friend should have edited it differently.

Fergus, Julia silently acknowledged, came out very well. Tall and tanned and strong, he was an older woman's heart-throb. But she was appalled at how harassed and red in the face she was in it. 'I look awful!'

'Well, if there were only the three of you, and you had those awful passengers, I'm not surprised you seem a bit fraught,' said Mel kindly. 'Sweet dog though. Who did he belong to?'

'The large man with the loud voice. He's the son of the thin woman who looks like she's got a lemon stuck up her arse,' said Wayne. 'I tried to keep her out of shot most of the time, but although she moaned on and on about having her privacy invaded, she got her nose in everywhere.'

'The canals look heavenly,' said Suzy, who could look at her own form in shorts and vests with perfect equanimity. 'So does the food. No wonder the Americans liked it.'

'It must have been such hard work with just the three of you,' Mel repeated, still incredulous. 'Who did all the cooking?'

'Julia,' said Suzy.

Mel whistled. 'And you pregnant, and all.'

215

'I suppose I was pregnant then, but I didn't know about it.'

'Still, think of how your hormones must have been rushing about, sending you crazy,' went on Mel.

'I don't actually mind being pregnant,' said Julia firmly, and not quite truthfully, 'but I don't much like talking about it.'

'And I want to watch this video,' said Wayne. 'This could be the start of my career!'

Whether or not the video was the start of Wayne's career, it was certainly the start of a spate of bookings from America for next year which had them nearly half full before the end of the season. Ralph had also sent a copy to one of the holiday programmes on television, which, he told them gleefully, meant they would come and do a feature on them. This, he said, was almost a guarantee of success.

They learned this at the beginning of the last week of the season, and Suzy was thrilled.

'Wayne, you're a star! I'll be able to prove to Daddy that I can do things, and I'm not just his Barbie doll!'

'I think he knows that already,' said Ralph, who had brought the news about the bookings along with the laundry. 'He's really proud of you.'

'Good. But more importantly, I'm proud of myself. Because I'd never tried to do anything on my own, I wasn't sure if I could. Not that I have been on my own, exactly,' she went on, putting a hand on Julia's sleeve. 'I couldn't have done it without you.'

'Nor could Superwoman,' said Julia. 'You hired me, you have to take credit for that.'

'I do. And I'm so glad that I'll be able to give you some wages. The business account's quite healthy, now we've got all these deposits.'

'You mean you've had the poor thing slaving away all

summer with no wages?' Ralph was horrified. 'Why didn't you walk out on her then, girl?'

'Nowhere to walk to. I'd let my house . . .'

Suzy's mouth formed an 'O' of horror before she realised that Julia was joking. Ralph laughed.

'Well, Suzy, you're an even better businesswoman than I thought you were, if you can get and keep staff without even paying them. Did you others get paid?'

'Oh yes,' said Wayne. 'Every week.'

'I got paid in a lump sum before I came,' explained Mel. 'Suzy sold her pearls to pay for me.' She regarded Suzy anxiously. 'That wasn't a secret, was it?'

'Only from Daddy,' said Suzy blithely. 'If he found out about it, he'd buy me some more, and I'm getting really fed up with all these possessions. They just tie you down.'

Ralph raised a somewhat sceptical eyebrow. 'Well, you have grown up,' he said in a manner which wondered if the change was permanent. 'So, what are you going to do now, Julia? Have you developed a taste for life on the move, or will you go back to what you did before?'

Julia didn't know the answer. 'I have really loved my time on the canals. It was terribly hard work, but worth it. Anything I do now will seem rather tame.'

Julia noted that she had developed Suzy's trick of telling the truth while lying through her teeth. She still hadn't decided how to support herself and her growing baby, which had reached the stage when she had to leave the button of her jeans undone and pull her T-shirt down over it. But what was preoccupying her now was the fact that she hadn't yet told her mother. A baby due in February would have to be admitted to before Christmas, even if she didn't see her mother before then.

Her sister already knew and, having OhmyGoded and Howdidthathappened? a bit, was being as supportive as Julia had thought.

'It may seem an awful shock now, Ju. But having a baby is lovely really.'

'What? Even the "having it" part? All that agony you went through was lovely, was it?'

'Well no, not lovely, exactly. But terribly exciting. It's not like being at the dentist, when you just lie there passively. You're actually doing something.'

'I never minded the dentist.'

'Because you had good teeth. Now, do you want me to tell Mum for you?'

'Oh Angela.' This was true self-sacrifice on her sister's part. 'I wish I could take you up on that amazing offer, but I'd better not. She'd never forgive me if she got the news second-hand. I'll let her tell Rupert, though.'

'Good thinking. She won't let Rupert think she's anything but thrilled about it. Talking of our dear brother, have you heard any more about Strange's suing you lately?'

'Now you mention it, no. And what with one thing and another, I'd forgotten all about that. Perhaps Darren found what they'd lost. I couldn't really believe they'd actually think I'd stolen anything.'

'Then you could counter-sue for defamation of character.'

'Somehow, Angela, I've got more important things on my mind right now.'

Chapter Eighteen

The last week of the season had come horribly suddenly. 'Probably,' said Suzy, 'because we're having such a good time. We know what we're doing, we've got help and we know the boats are truly ours.'

Julia, knowing that soon she would have to make a lot of important decisions, was as sad to see the season end as Suzy. 'We'll have to make the last week really good,' she said. 'Go out on a high note.'

'Well that shouldn't be difficult. John and Betty are coming back. Do you remember, our steam-freak and his wife, who came up Tardebigge with us the first time?'

'It's so lovely of you to come back!' said Suzy, after she had hugged both Betty and John with enthusiasm. 'It shows such faith in us.'

'Well, we said we would, didn't we?' said Betty. 'And I love the countryside at this time of year. It's not too hot, and with the trees just beginning to turn, the scenery's at its best.'

'Ooh,' said Suzy. 'It's a pity you weren't here when Wayne was making his video. You could have said that to camera.'

'I'm glad to see that Julia's got someone to help her with the cooking,' went on Betty.

'Yes, Mel's brilliant,' Julia agreed. 'She made those brownies you're eating.'

'I don't know how you managed,' said Mel, looking at the photos John had produced, 'with just the three of you.'

'We relied heavily on our passengers,' said Julia. 'And they never let us down.'

'Mmm,' said Suzy. 'But we never had another passenger who got the hang of the block and tackle to give the butty a kick-start out of the lock.'

The other passengers were a retired vicar and his wife and a pair of backpacking American girls who had booked in for a week of luxury in between hitching round Europe. With John and Betty as examples, they settled in quickly, and were soon back in the saloon drinking tea and eating brownies. The vicar's wife looked at John's photos uneasily. 'Do the passengers have to work? I've got a dicky back.'

'Only if you want to. Passengers helping is entirely voluntary. Except for John, of course. We need him,' said Suzy. 'Now, more tea, anyone? Or shall I open the bar?'

The American backpackers, as relieved as the vicar's wife, opted for cold beer.

On Wednesday morning, when Julia had washed up breakfast, Mel appeared to hustle her out of the galley.

'Get some fresh air. Go and set locks or something.'

Julia allowed herself to be bullied and went to fetch a sweater. A hot August had drifted into a September rather full of seasonal mists and not so mellow fruitfulness. But although some of the heat had gone out of the sun and the days were shorter, the passengers spent most of their time off the boats, either helping to work them or wandering along the hedgerows picking huge quantities of black-berries. The vicar and his wife brought back mushrooms from their early morning walks.

They were on their way from Oxford to Stratford and had reached the Grand Union where the locks were broad and the boats could travel together, so John, deprived of his beloved bow-hauling of the butty, was probably setting locks instead. But Julia tucked a windlass into her belt anyway. Some time on her own would be welcome, for although their last week was going extremely well, the passengers a happy, harmonious, heavy-drinking group, Julia's spirits were not as high as everyone else's. She still had to tell her mother about her pregnancy.

John was not at the next lock as she expected, but as she approached it she was met by a very distraught pair of women, one of whom had a handful of large dogs straining at their leashes, threatening to pull her into the canal.

'The boats are stuck in the lock!' they screamed as they saw Julia. 'They're going to sink!'

Julia ran to the lock and looked down. There were two small cruisers jammed together, tipping inwards perilously as the water drained from under them. The lock was a tight fit for two cruisers side by side, and something in the brickwork had caught on their fenders, wedging them in the lock walls.

'Right. Drop those paddles,' she ordered, but saw the dogs were winning their battle to tow one woman to wherever their master was, and the other was now having hysterics.

So Julia ran to the end of the lock herself, pulling her windlass out of her belt and got the paddles down. Then she bolted back to the other end and opened one paddle, and then the other. The boats hung perilously, grinding against each other and the wall, but gradually, the lock filled and took the weight of the boats, so they were no longer in danger of crashing down several feet and possibly turning over as they did so.

'Right,' said Julia, when the women returned, 'now get a line off each boat and ease one back so one of you goes behind the other, and hold the boats in position while the lock empties.'

'Bastards, going to the pub and leaving us to do this by ourselves,' said the woman who had had hysterics, reluctantly doing as she was told.

Julia looked at her carefully. Something about her voice was familiar. Then she remembered, she was the woman who had screamed at her to get out of the way her first day on the cut. She felt slightly relieved that although the woman would recognise the boats when they passed, it was unlikely she would recognise Julia, who had changed a lot since their first encounter. Julia was now sun-tanned, confident, and, in spite of permanent nausea, fit. None of which she'd been way back in early spring.

John, who'd gone off exploring, appeared and together they helped the women tie up their boats, once the lock-gates had opened to allow them out. The women then went in search of their menfolk.

'What was all that about?' he asked as they walked back up to make the lock ready for *Pyramus* and *Thisbe*.

'Oh, they tried to go in the lock side by side instead of one behind the other,' said Julia. 'They got hung up on a protruding brick or something.'

'Well, you obviously saved the situation. Well done. When we first came on holiday you weren't so handy with the boats, though you were a whizz in the kitchen.'

Feeling guilty for the reason she wasn't in the kitchen, Julia blushed.

'And they didn't even say thank you,' John went on indignantly.

'They felt stupid, I expect. Saying thank you would make them feel worse.'

'That's no excuse. People should face up to their responsibilities.'

'Yes,' agreed Julia, realising she mustn't put off telling her mother any longer.

'So why do you want to ring your mother just as we're going into a tunnel?' said Suzy, clutching the mobile phone, which Julia had asked for. 'You've waited this long to tell her you're pregnant, another half an hour won't

222

make any difference. You'll only lose the signal and be cut off the moment you've broken the news.'

'That's the idea.' said Julia, who had planned it carefully. 'And if I time it right, she won't be able to get through if she rings back. So she'll ring my sister, to tell her. Angela will say she knows already, but the whole conversation will take some time. By the time she finally manages to get back in touch with me, she will have got used to the idea. But unless you give me the phone soon, I'll have to blurt it out straight away, or we'll be cut off during the "How are yous?"'

'But won't you dread her ringing back? Wouldn't it be better to get it all over with at once?'

'Don't think so. I think she might calm down once the first shock is over. Angela told me she's planning to say something like, "You wouldn't want Julia to die childless, would you?" Mum'll say, "Well, couldn't she get married and have them like a normal person?" but Angela will tell her that all the good husbands have been spoken for, and only the wimps and the wife-beaters are left. Which should help.'

'I really can't imagine your mother being anything other than totally supportive.' Suzy clung on to the phone with the same tenacity as she clung on to her impressions of Margot.

'I have tried to tell you about her. And she will be supportive when she's got over having to tell her friends her unmarried daughter is pregnant, and having them mutter about young people these days, although that hardly applies in my case, God knows.' Anxiety was making Julia ramble rather. 'But at first, she'll go mad. Believe me.' Julia put out her hand for the phone again.

Suzy shifted so it was still out of Julia's reach. 'I'm not happy with this hit-and-run idea. I don't think it's fair on Margot. You have to consider her feelings.'

A little tornado of indignation whirled inside Julia and

then subsided again. Suzy had grown up a lot since the beginning of the season, but she still wouldn't be able to see the irony of this remark. 'I didn't notice you being particularly sensitive towards your father the other day,' she said mildly.

'Yes I was!' Suzy didn't bother to hide her indignation. 'I took the car, didn't I?' But taking the point, Suzy handed over the phone. 'I'm still not convinced you wouldn't be better to do it when you're settled back home. Then you could reassure your mother that you've got all sorts of plans of how you're going to manage. She only wants the best for you, after all.'

'I know!' Julia was getting frantic. 'But if I waited until I had my life plan worked out, the baby would be about ten, and I don't suppose I'll be able to avoid seeing her this Christmas, let alone Christmas for the next decade! Now, please! I must do it now or my timetable will go to pieces!'

Julia's gauge of her mother's reaction turned out to be pretty accurate. 'My God!' was all she managed to say before she was cut off, but it seemed to echo round and round the Stygian blackness of the tunnel for its entire length. And when, a little later, her mother rang back, along with a lot of 'How can you have been so stupid?' and 'I always told you about contraception, there's no excuse for a woman of your age to get caught out' Julia had taken deep breaths to prevent herself from telling her that she was delighted about the whole thing, not because it was entirely true, but as a reaction against her mother's horror. Her mother had even subjected her to what Julia had dreaded most, mutterings along the lines of: 'These days, surely no one needs to have an unwanted baby', which was code for: 'Why don't you have an abortion?'

Margot, who had been born before the days of legal abortion, had, like many of her generation, a more pragmatic attitude to it than younger women. Unlike

224

them, she had not, in her impressionable youth, been exposed to pictures of unborn children and didn't see it as murder. Julia's fear that her mother would suggest an abortion was one of the things which had made her put off telling her.

However, as predicted, Margot's phone call to Angela had softened her outrage a little. Angela, whose respectability was established by her husband and three children, had managed to convince her mother that everyone had babies out of wedlock these days, and that her friends wouldn't ostracise her because Julia had become pregnant. Margot claimed to tell the truth and shame the devil, but actually she was as eager for approval as her daughter. Angela, working hard on her sister's behalf, managed to imply that only a mother as cool and sophisticated as Margot would be able to handle it so well.

So when Margot was telephonically reunited with Julia, while still not *aux anges* about the idea, she was a little less traumatised by it.

'So who's the father? Will he make an honest woman of you?'

'It was a very casual encounter. I'm not even going to tell him. There's no reason why a young life should be messed up because I was careless.' Another case of the truth masking an untruth. The word 'young' might deflect her mother from thoughts of Fergus.

'So it wasn't –'

'No. I know I've been really silly and totally irresponsible – not to mention sluttish – but I don't want anyone else's life to be affected.'

Margot was silent. 'Well, I suppose it's better to be an unmarried mother than be married to someone totally unsuitable . . .' She didn't sound entirely sure.

'Mummy, you wouldn't want to see me stuck in a high-rise flat somewhere, with a baby and the lift not working, now would you? Much better that I stay in my own little home.'

'But you've let it!'

'But it'll be empty again next week. I always meant to go back to it after the end of the season.'

'What if you can't get the tenant out?'

'Mummy darling, can you remember what I did for a living before I came on the canals? The contract was watertight, and anyway, the girl I let it to has plans of her own. I rang her to make sure last week and she said the garden was full of runner beans.'

Having soothed her mother somewhat, Julia, shaking slightly, went to join Suzy at the stern of the boat.

'I told you she'd be fine about it,' said Suzy, before Julia had time to speak.

'Yes.' Julia didn't disillusion her. 'In a manner of speaking. Now what are we going to give our passengers for our very last dinner of the season?'

'Champagne and smoked salmon,' replied Suzy.

Julia shook her head. 'We can't afford that. We might get some smoked salmon scraps and make a mousse though.'

Affordable or not, the last dinner on board did include champagne, and as everyone got slightly tipsy and very sentimental, praise for their prowess as hotel-boat operators became more and more extravagant.

'You're a good girl,' said the retired vicar to Julia. 'Even if you are pregnant. Mistakes can happen to anyone, can't they, dear?'

The 'dear' in question flushed. 'She was a honeymoon baby, a little premature.' His wife said her lines as if she'd said them many times. 'She went to Oxford, you know.'

Julia, who had been told before, nodded. 'You must be very proud.'

Once the boats had been safely delivered to a local boatyard, who were going to give them a check-over, Suzy was going to drive Julia home in her new car. Wayne was going back to Tewkesbury to see his parents and insisted he could manage by bus.

'You must let me take you to the bus station, then,' Suzy said tearfully, and rushed out muttering about warming up the engine of her car.

Julia had also been sad to say goodbye to Wayne. He had proved himself to be so much more than just the beautiful boy Suzy had picked up from the riverbank. He had learned a whole new craft, and had made a business-saving video. He had blushed when Julia had told him this, and kissed her cheek.

'Good luck with the baby, Julia. Let me know what it is,' he had said.

Suzy, having seen him safely on to the bus, returned to the boats quite cheerful. 'I'm going to be seeing him quite soon, anyway. As soon as the boats have had a once-over, we'll bring them down so he can live on them. Save him accommodation fees.'

Together they packed Julia's strangely increased possessions into Suzy's car and set off towards Lechlade. They chatted about Julia's plans, the prospects for next season and how Suzy would manage for crew before Wayne and Mel could join her. 'I'll put another ad in *The Lady*,' said Suzy. 'It worked so well last time.'

Julia chuckled. 'It's very kind of you to give me a lift, Suzy. Getting all this lot home by public transport would have been no picnic.' They drew up in front of her cottage. 'Oh.' There in their garden, tying up their chrysan-themums, were Daisy and Dan, her elderly neighbours. 'Telling them I'm pregnant isn't going be a breeze, either. Will you come in?'

Rather to Julia's relief, Suzy refused, only staying long enough to help Julia in with her bags. Then she hugged Julia very hard. 'You've got your cheque?' Julia had, a far larger one than she had expected, everything considered.

'Well, you've been an absolute star. I couldn't have managed without you. I can never, ever, thank you enough.'

'You don't need to thank me.'

'Yes I do, and I'm going to come back and see you very soon, and make sure you're all right.' Another hug, and she was gone.

Julia waved to her as she sped away and then turned to her neighbours. 'Did you get on all right with Alice, my tenant?' she asked them after the initial greetings.

'Oh yes. She was a nice girl. Said she's left a note for you with her forwarding address and that. But we got on fine. She dug you a very nice veg garden up at the top end where all those nettles were. I gave her quite a lot of spare plants to put in it. Pity you'll never be around long enough to keep it up.'

'Actually' – Julia seized this opening – 'that may change. But I'll come over and see you properly when I've got a moment,' she said. 'I've got rather a lot of sorting out to do.'

'The kettle's always on, you know that, dear,' said Dan, prevented by bad eyesight and a dry-stone wall from seeing her condition.

As she opened the windows to let out the smell of joss-sticks which she found made her sick, made a fuss of her cat and searched for the few things she actually needed among the many she did not in the plastic-bag-filled loft and spare room, she realised she dreaded Dan and Daisy's disapproval more than her mother's. After all, she knew that her mother would never actually cut her off, however many illegitimate babies she had. But Daisy and Dan could easily decide to withdraw their friendship.

They were in their eighties, and had lived in the cottage all their married life. They gave Julia surplus vegetables from their garden, and in return she made jam from their plums and mincemeat at Christmas. They fed her cat when she went away on business, and when they went to visit their son, Julia watered their garden, opened and closed the curtains, and generally made sure their house was looked after. They had been neighbours for five years and there'd never been a cross word. How they'd feel about an illegitimate child adding several decibels to the local noise level, Julia couldn't predict, but felt it couldn't be positively.

While she'd been right about her mother's reaction, she was completely wrong about her neighbours'. 'I've got a bit of news for you,' said Julia, having drunk one cup of tea and eaten a rock cake. 'I'm very – quite – pleased about it, but you may not like it.'

'What's that, dear?' said Daisy, concern wrinkling her already well-lined brow. 'You're not moving away, are you?'

'Oh no.' Julia smiled reassuringly. 'It's nothing like that. I'm going to have a baby.' There was no dropping of crockery or horrified gasps, so she went on. 'And I'm not married, and not going to be, either.'

Still the silence was punctuated only by the grand-mother clock, ticking steadily away, a lot slower than Julia's heart happened to be doing. The old couple exchanged anxious glances, but then Daisy said, 'Well, my dear, it doesn't do to leave things too late.'

Her husband said, 'And I expect the man'll come round to the idea of being a father and do the decent thing. Don't you worry, my dear. We'll be glad to have a baby living next door, won't we?'

His wife nodded. 'There hasn't been a baby born from that house since little Christopher Jones.' She suddenly smiled. 'He'll be nearly sixty by now, I reckon.' Then she leaned forward to touch Julia's knee. 'Don't you worry, my dear. Things aren't like they were in my young day. A woman's not spurned by her neighbours for having a slip-up nowadays.'

Julia found tears springing to her eyes, something which happened increasingly frequently. 'You're very kind.'

More tea was poured in honour of the occasion and when eventually Julia took her leave, having presented them with a painted jug to add to their collection, she rang her sister.

'It's so ironic,' she said. 'There's Mum, thinking she's so New Age and liberal and yet she reacts like a Victorian vicar's wife when she hears. And there's Daisy and Dan, who've hardly noticed that Victoria isn't still on the throne, being perfectly fine about it. Honestly!'

'I expect in their day it was quite common to get pregnant outside marriage. You just got the boy to make an honest woman of you. Nowadays whizzy career women go it alone.'

'Mmm,' Julia mused, ignoring this dig at her previous life which now seemed as if it had been lived by some quite different person. 'I never liked the thought of being "made honest" by someone else. Either it's wrong to make love, or it isn't. Getting married doesn't really change anything.'

'Talking of changing things,' said Angela, who, a mother already, didn't have time for all this philosophy. 'Your niece would appreciate it if I changed her. A situation you'll soon find yourself familiar with. I'll speak to you soon. Bye.'

It was a few days later, having unpacked and washed her clothes, and told her brother, who managed hardly to refer to Julia's condition, that no, she really was sure she hadn't got Strange's papers (Darren apparently not having found them), that she decided to tackle the spare room. Not nesting, she told the cat, who wasn't listening, just making a little space, in case she needed to take in a lodger.

And there, stuck at the back of the wardrobe, where she had thrust it in fury, she found her briefcase. It was not, as she had previously supposed, empty, but contained some papers she had a feeling certain people had been looking for.

A cold sweat broke over her. She suddenly felt sick. She'd been so sure of her innocence, she'd hardly given the matter a thought. But now she was confronted with papers that could, presumably, put her in jail. She sank on to a bag of jumble, her knees trembling. 'Oh my God!' she said to the cat, who was now washing itself. 'What the hell do I do now?'

The cat hardly had time to think of an answer before there came a knocking on the door which made her scream. For a split second she felt like a burglar caught in the act. Then she remembered that she hadn't actually *stolen* the papers. Strange's were sure to see reason when she explained how they came to be in her possession when she had denied all knowledge of them. And whoever it was at the door, even if it was a policeman, was unlikely to kick it down in order to arrest her. This was not, she reminded herself firmly, still shaking, an episode of *NYPD Blue*. But she went downstairs feeling decidedly guilty.

Chapter Nineteen

It was Fergus. He stood there with rain glistening on his shoulders and hair and, back-lit by a streetlight, he seemed particularly tall and menacing.

Julia's wits were already jangled by her awful discovery, and her guilt button had not so much been pressed as stamped on. It took her precious moments to remember that she hadn't yet done anything dreadful to Fergus. She mentally shook herself. It was everyone going on about how she should tell him she was pregnant that was doing it. Well, she wouldn't have to bother with that any more; he'd have worked it out for himself.

'Oh. It's you,' she said. 'What are you doing here?'

'I came to see you.'

'Oh. Do you want to come in?'

'That is why I knocked on the door, instead of just standing outside it.' He pushed past her into the sitting room and shook himself. The way the rain showered off him reminded Julia irresistibly of Sooty. Except that Sooty never looked anything but benign.

Fergus seemed large and out of place in her small sitting room which was still dotted with cardboard boxes, waiting to be unpacked. Julia removed a couple from a chair and pulled herself together. He didn't know anything about Strange's suing her, and what she had just discovered in her briefcase. And he might not even realise he was the father of her child. She put on a social smile.

'Well, this is a surprise. Can I take your coat?'

He unbuttoned it, took it off and handed it to her.

'There's no need to play the hostess for me. We're not on the boats now, you know.'

Julia, sinking slightly under the weight of the coat, smiled more brightly. 'It's soaking. I'll go and hang it up in the kitchen. Can I get you anything to eat or drink?' she added, hoping to buy herself precious time alone, so she could work out why he'd come.

He wasn't having any. He followed her into the kitchen. 'You're pregnant,' he thundered at her, giving a perfect, if unnerving, impression of Mr Barrett of Wimpole Street.

There didn't seem any point in denying it. It was rather like when people told you that you'd had your hair done, as if it might have happened without you noticing. 'I know. Who told you?'

'My mother! Your mother told her!'

Julia felt suddenly weak and hooked a chair out with her foot and sat on it. She had thought her own mother might have kept such devastating news to herself, at least for a bit longer. It couldn't have been easy for her, telling the mother of the perfect child that her own child was virtually a fallen woman.

'Was Lally furious?'

'Why should she be? She doesn't know I'm the father.'

Julia toyed for a nanosecond with the idea of denying that he was, but decided against it. She was in enough trouble already. 'So you didn't tell her?'

Fergus winced at the stupidity of this question. 'No, actually I didn't. When she said, "You'll never believe this but poor Margot's daughter Julia – that's the unmarried one – is expecting a baby?" I didn't say, "Then I must be the happy father!"'

'No need to be sarcastic, a simple "no" would have done.'

Fergus pulled out a chair on the opposite side of the table and sat on it. 'I wouldn't tell anyone anything without discussing it with you first. But why the hell didn't *you* tell me? It's not easy hearing you're about to be a father from your mother.'

'I thought you might shout,' said Julia, not because she had thought it, but because it might stop him shouting now. It didn't.

'I wouldn't have shouted,' he thundered on, 'if I hadn't heard the news third-hand!'

'Did – does – did your mother say anything to mine about who the father is?'

'For Christ's sake, why should she? I didn't write her a postcard saying: *Having a lovely time, slept with your best friend's daughter*. But haven't you told Margot yourself?'

'Good God no!'

'Why not? Are you ashamed of me?'

'No, but I didn't want us rushed to the altar with a shotgun at our necks.'

'Would your mother have done that?'

'She'd have had a damn good try.'

Fergus subsided. 'I thought she was a pacifist.'

'Only in theory. Where her children are concerned, she's an old-fashioned tigress.'

Fergus pushed his hair back from his eyes. 'You couldn't lend me a towel for my hair, could you? It's dripping down my neck. I had to park the car miles away.'

Julia got up, relieved to be back where she knew what she was doing, looking after people. 'Yes, of course.' She opened a cupboard and produced a towel, which, rather to her surprise, had been ironed, presumably by her tenant. 'Can I get you a drink or something?'

'What are you offering?'

'Well, coffee, tea, cocoa, any amount of weird herb and fruit teas that the girl who rented my cottage left, or alcohol.'

'What sort of alcohol?'

'Um . . .' She inspected a dusty bottle. 'Elderberry. My

234

mother gave it to me last Christmas. I'm afraid I haven't got anything else. I'm off it myself and haven't got round to buying anything for guests.'

'Especially not uninvited ones?'

'Guests are guests,' said Julia, blushing. 'Now, what do you want to drink?'

'It had better be coffee. I am driving, after all.'

'Coffee,' Julia repeated. 'I'm off that even more than alcohol. If I found you the things, would you mind making it yourself?'

'Not at all. Or I could have tea. I don't want to make you feel sick.'

Julia turned away, in case the words: 'You've already done that by making me pregnant,' slipped out. 'What about a biscuit?'

'I'm not sure I can cope with you when you're so polite,' said Fergus. 'It seems out of character, somehow.'

'Not at all. I spent most of the summer being polite.'

'When you weren't trying to drown people.'

'That was a one-off. Most of the time I had the patience of Job.'

Fergus grinned. It caused a pang of something quite unacceptable to thump in her solar plexus. 'You didn't show me your patient side much, though.'

'I'm showing it now. I still don't know what you want to drink.'

'Oh. What are you having?'

'Ginger tea. It's very good for indigestion.'

'Is it? I'll give it a go, then.'

Julia took her time with her preparations, finding the ginger, peeling it, and slicing it finely before putting it into china mugs. Such care was not entirely necessary, but she knew that when she and Fergus were finally provided with drinks and biscuits and anything else she could persuade him to have, there would be a confrontation, and she was not looking forward to it. She handed him his mug. 'Shall we stay in here, where it's warmer? Or go through to the sitting room?'

'Let's stay here. I'm still fairly damp.'

'Are you sure you wouldn't like me to make you a scrambled egg or something?'

'No, really. I ate before I came.'

'You should have rung, really.'

'I would have done, but I thought you might arrange to be out.'

Julia opened and shut her mouth as she considered this and decided that she might well have done. 'Where did you get my address?' A horrible thought struck her. 'You didn't ask my mother for it, did you?'

'No, I just looked it up. Do you think it's wise for a single woman to be in the phone book?'

'I've never had any trouble before.' She made a face so he would take her meaning. 'But if you'd asked my mother for it all hell would have broken loose.'

He nodded, sipped his tea, grimaced and put down his mug. 'You don't deny it's my child?'

'Would there be any point?' This was not a rhetorical question, she wanted to know if she would have got away with it.

'No. I don't think you're promiscuous.'

'Good.'

'So, shall we get married?' He said this in the casual way he might have suggested going out for a curry.

'No.'

'You've thought about it?'

'Not really, only long enough to know I don't want to do it.'

'But why not? Surely you don't want to bring up a child on your own? You'd have to give up your career. '

'I gave up my career, as you call it, last spring. I wanted a complete change and I've got it. And I'd never get married just because I was pregnant, even if I did want to.

236

Be married, I mean.'

'And I don't have a say in all this?'

'I don't think you do, really.'

'But you have acknowledged me as the father of the child. I do have some rights!'

'I know. I won't be at all difficult about access or anything. You can take it to the zoo or McDonald's as often as you like, as long as you don't turn out to be violent, of course.'

Fergus seemed to have to struggle not to be for a few moments. 'Being a father involves a lot more than few outings to fast-food outlets!' He spat out the words as if he were talking about crack-houses.

'Well, I agree that too much junk food is a bad thing. You could take it to museums instead. The Corinium Museum in Cirencester has got a lot of Roman artefacts.'

'I know that! The point I'm making is that going on trips is all very fine and large, but it isn't being a father!'

'No, I know it isn't. But I'm afraid it's what happens once the parents have split up.'

'But we haven't split up. We haven't even got together! And I don't want my child brought up in a single-parent family.'

Julia couldn't help sympathising. According to everyone, he'd wanted children when he was married. It must be galling to have one now, when he wasn't. But she didn't see how she could help. 'Staying together for the sake of the children is one thing. Getting together is quite another.' She held up her hand as he started to protest. 'It's not as if we were actually going out together first. And shotgun weddings rarely work.'

'I don't see why they shouldn't.'

'I don't see why they should! God knows, marriage is hard enough for people who are in love with each other!'

'But they *do* work. It's a good institution.'

'So are mental hospitals, but I still don't want to be in

one.' Julia touched his wrist. It was warm and satisfying under her hand, momentarily distracting her from her intention to reassure him. 'I know single-parent families aren't ideal, but I plan to be a very good one, the very best possible.'

'Oh do you? You'll give up work and look after the baby full time, will you?'

He obviously expected her to say no, and mutter about crèches, day nurseries, and childminders. His expression of surprise when she nodded almost matched the surprise she felt herself. She hadn't wanted a baby, but now she was having one, she didn't want anyone else bringing it up. She also remembered her colleagues at Strange's discussing the difficulty of finding work with appropriate hours, and how to cope when the children were ill. 'Yes I will,' she said. 'Until it goes to school, at least.'

'But how will you support yourself? I'm perfectly willing to support the baby, but you wouldn't want to take money from me, would you?'

She shook her head. 'Certainly not. And I don't want you to support the baby, either. It's my responsibility. I shall keep us both.'

'How?'

'Outside catering, dinner parties, filling people's freezers, stuff like that. I've started already.' This wasn't quite true, but she had put up some postcards in local shops. She reckoned she had about four months' money saved before she ran out.

'You'd never earn enough to keep the two of you.'

'How do you know?' Julia wasn't entirely confident herself, but she didn't need him to make pessimistic assumptions.

'I don't know for a fact, I just think it's unlikely. And you can't forbid me to give you child support. It's against the law, for one thing.'

'Not if I'm not claiming benefit. If I earn enough for the

baby and me, you don't have to do a thing.' And please God, she would.

Fergus got up, sat down and then got up again, standing with his back to the stove. He didn't know how financially insecure she felt, or that upstairs she had evidence of a crime which might put her in jail, but she still felt threatened. 'Don't you understand, I want to help you look after the baby? It's my baby as much as yours.'

'No it's not! You're not giving birth to it!'

'That's a mere biological detail! A baby needs two parents, both to be conceived at all, and to live. I'm the father! Which makes it half mine.'

'Babies don't come in two halves! We can't divide it up and share it!'

'We could share responsibility for it!' Aware that he was shouting again, Fergus took a breath. 'I might not ever have another child.'

'Why on earth wouldn't you?'

'For all the reasons you might not either.'

'Are you saying I'm old!'

Unexpectedly, Fergus chuckled. 'No, I'm saying I am. We're both rather old to be first-time parents. That's why I don't want to waste the opportunity to be a proper father.'

Julia rested her head in her hands and it stayed there for a long time. 'I suppose you're right. I suppose it's only fair. So I will let you help me support it, if you really want to.'

'Generous!'

Not so much generous, as not entirely stupid. 'But nothing else. Access visits will be at my discretion. If we're not married, I don't think you can claim what I don't choose to allow you.'

Anger flickered in his eyes, but he suppressed it. 'But why can't we be married? Then you wouldn't have to work. I could support you both and you could just look after our child. It will be so much better for the baby.'

'Do you really think the baby will notice having had two

parents for the six months or however long it is we can stand being married? No. By the time it's conscious, our marriage will be over and it'll be back to being the child of a single parent again. Only then, the access visits are likely to be full of acrimony and bitterness. No, it would be far better for the child to be just mine from the beginning.'

'I think we should give marriage a chance. Why are you just assuming we'd break up?'

'Two out of three marriages do,' she said, glad to have stored this titbit from the newspaper. 'Ours would have had a worse start than most, being entirely for the sake of the child.'

'I don't think you can possibly say that. We haven't so much as been out for a drink together in the normal way. We might get on like a house on fire.'

'Fergus! This is my point! We don't really know each other, and it's too late to do anything "in the normal way".'

Fergus scowled. 'Well, we could live together to see how we do get on.'

Julia shook her head. 'There's no point. I know I don't want to marry you or anyone. It would be a whole lot of upheaval for nothing.'

'Not for nothing! Isn't it worth even giving it a try, for the sake of the baby?'

'I really don't think it could possibly work under those circumstances.'

'But I want to be a father! When my mother told me about it, my first reaction was huge excitement! It was only when she was going on and on about how surprised she was that a daughter of Margot's could possibly have got herself into this position, that I started to feel angry.'

Julia faltered, finding herself unexpectedly in sympathy with him. Her reactions had been equally confused: horror crossed with elation. 'I'm sorry, Fergus,' she said more gently. 'I could never marry anyone who didn't want to marry me for me, and not just for the baby.'

Fergus was silent for a long time. 'I could marry you for you.'

For a moment she allowed herself to wonder if, in entirely different circumstances, this could ever have been true. She would never know. She shook her head. 'Even if you could, which I don't believe for a second, I would never know that you had. I would always think it was for the baby.'

'Very well,' he said, after what seemed like hours. 'I realise I have to accept whatever you choose to allow me, but I can ask for you to be fair.'

'Oh, I want to be as fair as possible,' said Julia, rushing in with relief. 'And while you may not have many rights, you do have feelings.'

Fergus relaxed. It was only when some of the tension went out of his body that Julia realised how much had been in it. 'Well, thank you for appreciating that.'

She smiled warmly at him. It must have been a dreadful shock to find out about the baby from his mother. Particularly as she had obviously delivered the news with the delight disguised as shock with which some people regard other people's misfortunes. 'You're welcome. And anything you feel I could do to make this situation easier for you, just say.'

A moment after the words left her mouth she realised she'd made a mistake. 'Good,' he said. 'Then you won't object if I make a few stipulations about your preparations for the baby's arrival?'

Julia stiffened visibly. 'What are you talking about? Are you asking me not to decorate the nursery with pink lambkins?'

Her question confused him. 'No! Honestly, where did you get that idea from? If you want the baby to wake up surrounded by pictures of anthropomorphised animals' – he shuddered at the idea – 'that's up to you.'

'I never thought I'd hear that word in conversation.'

He ignored this. 'No, what I'm talking about is your preparations for becoming a mother.'

Julia felt very tired. 'Look, I've already been to the doctor. She says I'm fine. I've had a scan.' Briefly, she let her mind flit back to the excitement she had felt, seeing her baby moving about on a television screen. 'I'm taking my vitamins; I'll start to go to classes on how to look after it soon.' She glared at him. 'I'm doing my pelvic-floor exercises.' He didn't flinch. 'But actually, I've looked after all my sister's children since they were tiny, on and off.' She didn't tell him how much they terrified her when they cried and cried for no apparent reason.

'You're still not with me. I mean, how fit are you to be a mother? I'm talking life skills here.'

'How fit am I? Life skills? What are you . . .?' Then the first week of the season floated back into Julia's memory. 'Oh, you mean Suzy's thing about opening champagne bottles?'

'Yes, but even more important, I remember you said that you didn't drive.'

No wonder he'd done so well in his exams, he had a twenty gigabyte memory. She dragged her lesser mind back to the conversation. She'd been learning to steer the boat, if she remembered rightly. Now her problems were somewhat different. How could she explain to Fergus that she couldn't afford driving lessons or to run a car without implying she was short of money? Tricky, even for a brain not addled by anxiety, hormones and fatigue. 'I don't think . . .'

'It's all right, I know you can't afford it.'

Julia tensed, waiting for him to offer to pay for lessons and thinking how best to refuse.

'I'm offering to teach you, in my car.'

Julia's bubble of tension burst. She giggled. 'Fergus! That's the most ridiculous idea I've ever heard in my life!'

'Why?'

'Why? Because we don't get on that well now. How on earth would we manage to remain speaking to each other if you tried to teach me to drive? Well-established relationships have foundered because one tried to teach the other to drive!'

'And well-established couples have continued to be well established because one taught the other to drive. The idea that men – people can't teach their partners to drive is just a stereotypical myth.'

'You may be right about it being stereotypical, but you're talking about couples who get on, not couples who don't.'

'We're getting on all right now.'

'Are we?' The notion that she and Fergus could have a conversation without quarrelling was novel, but perhaps he was right. They were discussing some pretty controversial things here, but no blows had been struck.

'We are,' he went on. 'And I don't see why two adult people with a common problem –'

She ignited instantly. 'I refuse to see my baby as a problem!'

'I didn't mean the baby, idiot!'

Secretly she was pleased by this reaction but she wasn't going to tell him. 'Ah! You see? You called me an idiot: we're quarrelling! I told you we didn't get on.'

Fergus took a patient breath. 'There's no need to sound so happy about it, it's nothing to be proud of. The problem we have in common is that you need to learn to drive, and I don't suppose if I offered you the money to have lessons you'd accept.'

'No, of course not.'

'So I'll have to teach you.'

'No you won't. I can manage without driving. When I can afford it, I can pay for my own driving lessons.'

'You'll find it terribly difficult bringing up a child

without a car.'

'So you're the expert all of a sudden?'

'I do have friends with children. I happen to know that they find it very difficult to manage without transport. They ask me for lifts, sometimes.'

'I've got transport. My sister's giving me her pram. I can transport it into town, which has everything I need.'

'What about when you want to take it swimming?'

'There are buses. Oxford isn't that far away. And if more people used public transport instead of depending on the car, pollution problems would be a whole lot less. This is all terribly one-sided,' she went on. 'I'm sure you don't have all the necessary "life skills" for fatherhood. What are you going to learn?'

'I'm totally depending on you to teach me how to change a nappy, bring up wind, get the baby off to sleep, and all those other things.'

A vision of Fergus with a tiny baby on his shoulder, patting its back, brought tears to her eyes. For a moment she wondered if she was depriving her child by refusing to marry Fergus. But how healthy was it for a baby to grow up with parents who fought all the time? Surely it was better to see Daddy as a friendly visitor, not an in-house enemy?

'Well of course I'd do that if you wanted me to, but when the baby was tiny, I'd always be there to do it.'

'What do you mean? I thought my role as absent father involved trips to the zoo and hamburger-joints?' He managed to convey his distaste without changing his expression.

'Yes, but when it was tiny, I'd have to be with it.'

'Why? I am perfectly capable of looking after a baby, you know. Or at least, I would be if I were shown what to do.'

'But even if we were married you wouldn't be able to breastfeed it,' pointed out Julia.

A lot of Fergus's antagonism melted away. 'You intend to breastfeed, do you? I'm so glad. Apparently it's much better for the baby.'

'So they say.' Actually, Julia hadn't thought about feeding methods in great detail yet as there seemed to be a lot of other things she had to sort out first, but she realised that if she breastfed the baby, it would give her a hold which Fergus couldn't take away from her. She studied him thoughtfully. There was no doubt about it, having Fergus willing to help with the baby was a comforting thought. With her mother in the Lake District and her sister tied up with her own little ones, there would be times when she might feel very lonely.

As if sensing her softening attitude, Fergus went on. 'And you must let me know if you have any alterations to the house that might need doing.' His eyes went to a pile of plastic boxes stacked in a corner of the kitchen.

'There's not a lot to do,' Julia assured him. 'Those boxes are just things I packed away to give my tenant a bit more room.'

'Where are you going to keep the baby?'

'It's not a horse or a hamster, it can share the house with me!'

'Your bedroom?'

'In the beginning, certainly.'

'And have you got room for a nursery?'

'There is a small room suitable, yes.' Julia was wary, lest Fergus ask to see it. Not only was it was piled high with surplus furniture and plastic bags full of old clothes that she'd never got round to giving away, but it had her briefcase, full of important papers that she shouldn't have. 'It only needs a lick of paint. And I don't need help decorating,' she went on hurriedly. 'I'm very good at it.'

'What about all the filling and sanding? How good are you at that?'

Sexist pig, she thought, but kept it to herself. 'Excellent.

245

My polyfilling would win prizes.'

'Oh? Perhaps you could come and do some at my house. DIY isn't really my thing.'

'How would you have managed if I'd asked you to decorate the nursery, then?'

'I'd get someone in to do it, or look it up in a book.'

'You are so cerebral!'

His eyes narrowed, in a way which Julia was forced to acknowledge was rather sexy. 'Thank you.'

'I didn't mean it as a compliment.'

'I know.'

Julia found herself rather short of breath. Having Fergus looking into her eyes in that way was unnerving. She got up. 'Are you really comfortable in here? Or shall we light the fire next door? I know it's only October, but it's a filthy night.'

Surprise flickered across Fergus's expression. 'Will you let me light it for you?'

Julia, who realised that she'd now invited Fergus to spend the entire evening with her, when he had probably intended to go home and watch a documentary on nuclear physics or the effect of microorganisms on the cosmos, narrowed her own gaze, keen to claw back lost ground. 'I'll have you know, Fergus Grindley, that making fires is one of the things I do best.'

'I'm sure,' he said. 'But I'm hopeless at making cocoa.'

'Cocoa? That's a bit domestic, isn't it?'

'I don't suppose you want to drink anything stronger? I thought not. So you'll have to make it, while I get the fire lit. Unless, of course,' he added dryly, 'you have a book with a recipe for cocoa in it. Then I'd be fine.'

Julia conceded defeat with a roll of her eyes. 'Oh God! Didn't they teach you anything useful at that posh school of yours?'

'No,' said Fergus meekly.

Chapter Twenty

Julia made cocoa, aware that somehow she'd been manipulated into greater intimacy than she had intended. The feeling that she was going to quite enjoy sitting in front of the fire with Fergus nagged at her more than the thought that he was showing signs of wanting to take over her life. This shift was quite worrying. After all, she had intended not even to tell Fergus she was pregnant. She'd have to watch herself, or she'd find herself thinking that marriage would be a good thing.

Fergus had got the fire going fairly well, but Julia added a candle end to it, just to stake her claim as the fire queen. Fergus didn't comment, but there was laughter in the back of his eyes. Julia handed him a mug of cocoa, annoyed with herself. Everything she did seemed to work better for Fergus than for her.

There was a rocking chair near the fire and a sofa opposite it. Fergus was sitting on the sofa, which gave Julia the choice of sitting next to him, or taking the rocker. It had been a present from her mother, and Julia had been pleased with herself for being able to assemble it from its flat-pack. It wasn't very comfortable, but she kept it by the fire because it looked pretty. Should she now sit on it and suffer? Ask Fergus to move? Or just sit next to him on the sofa, which had the right amount of cushions for her to pull into the small of her back? She sat next to Fergus, sipping her cocoa, eyes lowered.

'So, have you told many people about the baby?' he asked.

'Well, Suzy knows, of course. I had to tell her because she wanted me to go back to the boats next season. My mother, who told my brother, who was horrified, but hardly mentioned it to me it all. My sister, obviously. And my neighbours. What about you?'

'I had hoped, faintly, I was going to be able to announce our engagement first.'

'Oh Fergus . . .'

'Don't worry, I accept your decision. But I don't understand why you're so against marriage. You got engaged to Oscar, after all.'

Julia shuddered. 'I must have been out of my mind. I was working away a lot and he didn't want much in the way of conversation. He's terribly into wine and because he couldn't ever drink more than a glass because he was driving, I used to finish the bottle. I think I must have been drunk, or half asleep, and not heard what he said when I said yes. There doesn't seem to be any other excuse.'

'You don't think, subconsciously, you felt it was time to settle down and have a family?'

Julia gave a little shriek of horror. 'It must have been pretty deeply unconscious! More likely it was a subconscious attempt to shut my mother up about marrying –'

'Who?' He spoke very, very, quietly, as if he knew the answer.

'You, actually. Let me explain!' she went on hurriedly. 'My mother, for all her New Age hippy exterior, really thinks that women can only be fulfilled by getting married and having children. And apparently, your mother and mine have always thought what fun it would be if we got together.' She shifted a cushion into the small of her back. 'Anyone would think our "estates marched together" or something. But Mum has been going on about me marrying you since I hit twenty-five and was still unhitched. You getting divorced and me breaking up with

Oscar brought it all up again.'

'I can begin to see now why you don't want your mother to know that I'm the father of your child. But she's bound to find out sometime. What did you tell her when she asked?'

'I said there was no reason why a young life should be ruined because I was careless, among other things.'

'She probably thinks it was Wayne.'

'Oh God! I never thought of that! Poor Wayne! I was so intent on distracting her from any thoughts of you, I forgot all about him. I hope she doesn't find out his address and harass him!' Julia frowned at his disbelief. 'You don't know how bossy my mother can be.'

Fergus sighed. 'I can see that she's completely put you off the idea of marrying me. Perhaps if I'd known all that, I would have resisted you when you lay there asleep, looking so sensual and abandoned, all your spikiness gone.' He pulled himself upright. 'Still, I didn't know, and I didn't resist and now I'm going to be a father, and I can't tell anyone.'

The dreadful sentimentality, to which she was so prone lately, pierced her. He'd always wanted children and now he couldn't tell anyone he was going to have one. Perhaps she *should* accept his offer of marriage? Her feelings for him were not really in doubt: either love or lust or a mammoth crush, otherwise she would never have made love to him. But what about his feelings for her?

He had obviously desired her, that one time, but that wasn't enough to sustain a marriage. What would happen when the baby was less of a novelty? When she was too tired to make love, too fat to get into any of her clothes, and too busy to wash her hair? Would he go off with one of the lissom young students who surrounded him? And even if he was faithful for the sake of the baby, would she eventually feel jealous of her own child, when he loved it but did not love her?

'I expect you could tell a few close friends. After all, you might be spotted at the swings and unless you could pass the baby off as a nephew or niece, it might be awkward.'

Fergus stood up, putting his cocoa mug down hard. 'I think I'd better be going. The thought of being obliged to "pass" my baby "off" as a nephew or niece is making me angry.' He took a breath. 'Particularly as the main reason seems to be because of a lot of nonsense talked by our mothers where we were children!'

Julia didn't speak while she retrieved his coat. Without admitting her feelings to him (when she'd hardly admitted them to herself), she couldn't explain that her mother's matchmaking was only a tiny part of her reasons for refusing his offer of marriage.

'I'll be in touch pretty soon about the driving lessons,' he said.

'I'm not going to let you teach me to drive,' she said, when half the door was between her and him.

'We won't argue about that now,' he said, and strode off into the night.

Slowly, Julia went to bed, not even letting herself look at the door of the spare room, or think about the wretched papers. She'd sort it out tomorrow.

She still hadn't decided what to do about them the following afternoon, when the phone rang. Her heart leaped, half hoping, half dreading that it was Fergus. It was Suzy.

'Can I come over? I've got a proposition for you.'

'That sounds frightening,' said Julia calmly. 'Will I like it?'

'You may do, a lot. It means money.'

'In that case, do come over.'

Suzy, curled up on the sofa, cradling a glass of the wine she had brought with her, was bubbling with excitement.

'I just happened to be in Oxford, doing a little

shopping,' she began.

'I thought you were supposed to be taking the boats to Wayne's college?'

'Well, I had to pop home for a bit, pick up some things. I've found an ace freezer for next year, by the way, runs on gas. Anyway, after I'd done my shopping, I just went down to the canal, to see if anything was going on.' Julia had a feeling that something was. 'And I saw that restaurant boat, you remember? The one we saw?'

Julia didn't remember, but she had probably been cooking when they passed it. 'Carry on.'

'Well, they were taking it to be dry docked. They do that every year, but they've got to put a new counter on it and it's going to take ages.'

Julia remembered that the counter was what you stood on to steer and felt proud of herself.

'They're worried that they're going to have to be away too long, and people will forget about them.'

'That would be sad.' Julia stifled a yawn.

'So I asked them if they'd like it if we brought *Pyramus* up and stood in for them while they were having the work done.'

'But surely *Pyramus* will be – sorry, my memory's gone – wherever Wayne is.'

'She doesn't need to be. Wayne could perfectly well live on the butty. *Pyramus* could be an understudy restaurant boat.'

'It's not really designed right, is it? With people all sitting together?'

'Derek, who runs *La Barge Baguette*, says that people mostly book as parties, and that *Pyramus* sounded fine. He hasn't seen her of course, but he's coming up this weekend. Apparently they shut down in November because it's so slack, but we must be ready for the first of December. Lots of colleges have small get-togethers on it, and there are some bookings already, made before they realised how much the boat needed doing to it. They don't want to cancel as it looks unprofessional and people would find it difficult to book somewhere else this near Christmas.'

Julia hadn't previously considered October as near Christmas. 'So where do I fit into your plans?'

'As the cook.'

Julia swallowed and took a deep breath. 'Suzy, dear, look at me. *Pyramus* is a narrow boat, and no longer could I be described as narrow. And I've still got time to go.'

'You're not that big. From some angles it hardly shows. Anyway, the thing is, Derek will pay us a small retainer for being there, and anything we make, we keep. Or rather you do, as Daddy' – she looked down at her fingers, as if concerned to see a catch in one of her nails – 'really wanted to give me a little allowance. Compensation for all the hassle he caused us.'

'Suzy!'

'But think what perfect advertising for us it will be! We can give every diner a brochure. It won't be nearly such hard work as running the hotel boats, because it's only one meal. And you could cook lots of it here, at your leisure, and just bring it along and do the fresh stuff.' Suzy drew breath. 'Why aren't you looking more enthusiastic?'

'Because I haven't got transport. It would mean you picking me up and taking me back each night, and that will be a dreadful nuisance for you.'

Suzy frowned. 'Yes it will, because I'm going to be in Farnham some of the time, with Wayne.'

Julia sat bolt upright and the baby kicked hard. 'What? And you wanted me to drive the boat and cook at the same time?'

'No, no! *La Barge Baguette*'s crew will do that. And they've got a waitress for when I'm not there. You only have to cook. Which is why you keep the money. There seems to be quite a lot of money in it. You can charge people for the romantic setting.'

'How do you know, and what's quite a lot?'

'I asked, because you're not the only shit-hot businesswoman around here.' Suzy mentioned the figure Julia was likely to earn. It was enough for about six months' mortgage payments.

'The transport problem still remains, only worse,' said Julia. 'I could take taxis back, I suppose, but it would cut into the profits.'

'It is a pity you don't drive. Derek has got a van he could lend you. It's got the name painted on the side and everything. Not our name, of course. I wonder if I could get it redone?'

Julia stepped in before Suzy's ideas got ridiculously grand. 'It sounds terribly tempting, but I still can't drive. Unless . . .' Julia considered hard before even mentioning the 'F' word. 'Fergus did offer to teach me,' she confessed eventually.

'There you are then. You picked up steering OK in the end. No reason why you couldn't drive. Problem solved.' Julia choked on her ginger tea. 'Oh, before I forget,' Suzy went on. 'How's your home catering business going?'

'It's not. I put postcards up in all the right places, but so far haven't heard a peep.'

Suzy rummaged in her bucket-bag. 'My mother gave you this list of people who would want cooking done for them. You could use the van to do them on the days when there are no bookings for the restaurant. They mostly want dishes in their freezer that they can pass off as home-made.'

'I would have thought your mother's friends would want dinner served to them by a maid in a black dress.'

Suzy shook her head. 'That's my father's business friends. These are Mum's buddies from bridge and flower-arranging. They're much more homespun.'

'Oh damn. It really does sound as if I ought to learn to drive, doesn't it?'

'Definitely. Take Fergus up on his offer. It's the least he can do. He ought to offer to marry you!'

'Oh, he has. Only I won't.'

'Why the bloody hell not? He's perfect for you! Your mother would be thrilled!'

'I know. But she doesn't know he's the father, and won't know if I have anything to do with it. Now' – Julia changed the subject firmly – 'if *Pyramus* is in Oxford, being a restaurant boat, how are you going to get *Thisbe* to where Wayne needs it?'

'Oh, loads of people want to go down there. Ralph put me in touch with a lovely guy, desperate to help me out.'

The rest of the evening was passed looking through the Mothercare catalogue, and, more scarily, a book with pictures of really, really pregnant women in it.

'Will you really look like that? Gross! Oh, sorry,' said Suzy. 'And that big baby's got to come out of that little hole?'

'Don't let's talk about it any more, or I'll change my mind.'

In order to stop herself wondering if letting Fergus teach her to drive was the thin end of the wedge, or the high road to insanity, Julia forced her mind in the direction of her other extremely pressing problem: how to get the papers back to Strange's without admitting she'd ever had them. And sometime between three and five in the morning, she devised a plan.

She would call into Strange's, to see how they were getting on, and while she was there, slip into Darren's office and plant the papers in his desk. That way, none of the girls would get into trouble because they didn't find the papers when the hunt was first on.

Then, when her brother next rang about it (she couldn't ring him, or he'd suspect something) she could say something like: 'Oh for goodness' sake! Ask them if they've looked in such and such a file, in Darren's desk!' End of story.

There were a few minor disadvantages to this plan. Apart from having to explain how she'd left them a hot-shot businesswoman and was returning pregnant and unmarried, there was the faint possibility that they might actually believe she was guilty of industrial espionage and refuse to let her across the threshold. In that case, she'd have to make a plan B. This would necessarily involve her breaking into the office at night and was a very last resort. She could just imagine the headlines: *Pregnant woman discovered breaking into offices to return stolen papers.* She shuddered.

Then there was the question of how she was going to get into Darren's office. She certainly didn't want to see him and planned to visit when he was out. So what excuse could she possibly make for going in there? After chewing this over for some time, she decided to play it by ear. Something would occur to her. She'd got frighteningly adept at prevarication lately.

Julia rang Strange's at five past nine in the morning, knowing Peter Strange wouldn't be in until ten at the earliest. She didn't want to get anyone into trouble if he should overhear their shrieks of 'Julia!'

'Hi, is that Karen? Julia here.'

Julia waited for the sharp inward breath, the throat clearing, or even the phone being slammed down, but she didn't get them. 'Julia! How lovely to hear you! Did you know you're the Wicked Witch of the West, who's sold our secrets to a rival firm?' Karen was obviously delighted to hear from her.

'I know! They're suing me! I couldn't believe it when I got the letter. My brother's handling it all for me. But the reason why I'm ringing is that I wondered if I could pop in and see you all. I've got some news which will make you laugh.' Julia's insistence that she had a long time before she need worry about going through the agony of childbirth and the stress of child-rearing was well known.

'Great! When can you come?'

'Well, naturally when Peter and Darren are out. I don't want to run into either of them. They might have me arrested.'

'They might. They're terribly upset about it. I tried to tell them that Darren had probably just lost the damn papers, but they wouldn't have it.'

'No, well, you can't blame them.' For a second Julia considered coming clean to taking the papers by mistake and just asking Karen to put them in Darren's office for her. But it wouldn't be fair to involve anyone else in her stupidity. Karen, who worked part time, needed a job which fitted in with school, and they were scarce.

They arranged a time when both men would be out of the office and Julia rang off. Then she went upstairs and got the papers out of her briefcase. She couldn't see why they were considered so important. There was a list of clients among them, but it took Julia a few moments to work out what it was. Then she realised. It was the list of clients who were to be invited to the corporate golfing bash, and as lots of their most valuable customers didn't like golf, it was hardly a high security document. Poor Darren, thought Julia, he would have had to work out the golfers from the non-golfers, all by himself.

Julia duly arrived and was exclaimed over and teased mercilessly about her condition.

'It was an accident,' she explained, when she could get a word in.

'You don't have accidents!' said Karen.

'No,' said Michaela. 'You're far too efficient and organised.'

'Not this time, I wasn't. And you are sure that Peter and Darren aren't going to turn up?'

'Yup. They've just gone off to visit a new client. One of

your old ones, actually. They're trying to woo them back. They're both impossible to work with these days. Peter's told Darren that he has to lock his office every time he goes out in case anything else goes missing,' said Karen.

'Oh no!' This was very bad news.

'Exactly! But he's still as absent-minded as ever and either forgets to lock the door, or forgets to bring his keys, so he can't get in.'

'Golly!' This time Julia managed to tone her horror down a bit.

'I got so fed up with it, I had a spare set made. We're both looking for new jobs, aren't we, Mich?'

Michaela nodded. 'But it's hard finding something with reasonable hours.' She leaned closer to Julia. 'You're looking a bit peaky, love. Are you all right?'

'Mmm, well, I do feel a bit queasy. I think I'll just go to the Ladies and splash some water on my face.'

'I'll come with you, make sure you're all right.'

'No need for that!' Julia held up a hand. 'I'll be fine. I know where it is.'

'Please, Darren, don't have locked your office this time,' she entreated softly as she approached his office door. 'God knows how I'll get into Karen's desk for the spare keys if you have.' She was in luck. It yielded as she tried the handle and she slipped inside, closing it behind her.

But his desk drawer was locked, and no amount of tugging or jiggling would persuade it otherwise. She was just approaching the filing cabinet, praying she could get in, when she heard Darren's voice in the passage outside.

Without thinking, she dived under the desk, realising even as she squashed herself uncomfortably into the knee-hole that he was bound to discover her, and it would probably be better just to brazen it out. But it was too late. She shut her eyes as she heard him open the office door and come in.

257

'It's in the filing cabinet, Peter,' called Darren. 'I'll be with you in a moment.'

Julia heard the keys being withdrawn from a pocket and the scrape of metal on metal as he put the key in the lock. Please, please, don't come round behind the desk, Julia prayed to him silently. I know it wasn't your fault about the papers, and I'm sorry for all the trouble I must have caused you. Just stay in that bit of the room.

He seemed to be scrutinising every scrap of paper in his filing cabinet. The baby kicked against the tops of Julia's thighs. Julia transferred her silent conversation to her child. Poor little thing. Fancy being born to a single mother with a criminal record. You'll have no chance of learning to read.

At last Julia heard Darren mutter, 'For Christ's sake, what was that doing in there?' and slam the drawer shut. Please, don't lock it again! Peter's waiting! He hates being kept waiting! Just go now, Darren. Take what you want and go! And *don't*, she thought so loudly she thought he must have heard her, lock the office door behind you! I'll never get out of the window in my condition!

Her mental messages must have been powerful because he didn't relock the cabinet or the door and in another moment she was free to prise herself from under the desk. Sweat poured over her body as she realised the narrowness of her escape. Imagine having to ring Karen and try to convince her that in her confused state she had mistaken Darren's office for the Ladies.

She was still feeling slightly faint as she crossed to the filing cabinet, dragged it open and stuffed her sheaf of papers into a file. So much for placing them strategically, or being able to tell Rupert which file they might be in! She fled to the bathroom feeling genuinely queasy.

'That was a narrow squeak!' said Karen, when she came back in.

'I know! I thought Darren would be bound to come

round and see me!' Julia laughed, relief making her light-hearted. 'I was practically wetting myself!'

'Just as well you were in the Ladies, then,' said Michaela, looking at her oddly.

Her light-heartedness vanished. 'Um, yes. I suddenly had this panic that they might come in. If they're so hooked on security these days.'

Karen and Michaela exchanged glances. Pregnancy really seemed to have gone to poor old Julia's brain.

Fortunately, Julia's brain seemed to have one remaining active cell. She realised that she'd left the most incriminating evidence known to criminal law at the scene of the crime: her handbag.

'I don't suppose I could beg a cup of tea?' she said somewhat hoarsely. 'I've got a herb tea bag – Oops! I've just realised, I've left my bag in the loo. I think what they say about pregnancy making your brain smaller must be true!'

Chapter Twenty-one

By getting Angela to ring her brother, saying that Julia was worried about the case, Rupert duly rang Julia to offer irritated reassurance.

'I told you,' he said impatiently. 'These things take ages to sort out.'

'I just want to make sure you ask them if they've looked in Darren's filing cabinet.'

'For goodness' sake, Julia! Of course they have! It would be the first place they'd look, if they're his papers!'

'I know it seems obvious, but just ask them. Darren's very touchy about who he allows into his files and he's very sloppy. The number of times I've found things where he's sworn he's looked . . .'

'Oh very well. As your solicitor, I can hardly refuse. But why didn't you suggest this earlier?'

Knowing it would be asked, Julia had had the forethought to work out the answer to this question. 'Well, you know how it is. I was on the boats, thinking about an entirely different set of problems. It was only when I got home that I remembered how daffy Darren could be.'

'I don't think Darren's the only one who could be described as "daffy"!'

'Er, no, Rupert,' said Julia humbly. 'Probably not.'

After this fiasco, ringing Fergus was easy, and even the thought of learning to drive no longer seemed particularly stressful – she hadn't yet committed her first traffic offence. Consequently, it was only the Saturday morning after Suzy's visit that Julia found herself waiting for him to come for her first lesson.

'So what made you change your mind?' he asked when he appeared on the doorstep. 'I thought I'd have to bully you into it.'

'I need to drive for a job I've got,' said Julia, before she could wonder if she should tell Fergus about *Pyramus* becoming a restaurant boat for a few weeks. 'And I need to learn as soon as possible.'

'Right, well, we'll do our best then. What's the job?'

'Cooking. On a restaurant boat.' Fergus frowned. 'In Oxford, actually. On the canal.'

'A restaurant boat? Not the *Barge Baguette*?'

'No, that's being repaired. *Pyramus* is understudying for it. I'm doing the cooking. I can do most of the preparation at home, but getting there will be a problem if I can't drive.'

'What about a car?'

'They're lending me the van. But it is vital that I learn to drive as soon as possible. If I have to go about by taxi, it'll cut seriously into my profits.'

'Well, it's a good thing you already had your provisional licence then. I thought it would be a good idea to take you to a disused airfield I know so you can learn the controls with plenty of space around you.'

'Er – yes. Space, yes. A good idea.' Julia lapsed into thought. She'd half expected Fergus to offer her lifts to and from the boat and felt surprisingly put out that he hadn't. Really, it was frightening to think how easily one could become dependent on a man.

'Don't do this if it makes you remotely nervous,' she said. 'This is quite a nice car. I'm sure you don't want it ruined.'

'If I thought you'd ruin it, I wouldn't let you drive it,' said Fergus firmly, and Julia was silenced.

After enjoying the scenery for a few minutes she spoke again. 'I talked to my mother last night,' she said. 'She's trying like mad to find out who the father is.'

'So, did you tell her?'

'No. I put her off the scent by repeating how young the father was, and that was why I wouldn't tell him about it.'

'So why bother to lie? Why not just tell her the truth?'

Why was it that intellectuals were often so stupid? 'Because she'll tell your mother, and what a can of worms that'll open! They'll have us married at Gretna Green!'

'Tell her then. That's what I want, after all.'

Julia was relieved to note that he said this in a fairly detached way. 'I have told you that our mothers have wanted us to get married for years and years, haven't I?'

'Yes, but *not* getting married because it was what our respective mothers wanted is almost as stupid as getting married for the same reason,' said Fergus.

'Well, yes,' Julia was forced to agree. 'But we don't want to – well, *I* don't want to, and you only want to because of the baby, so they'll have to make plans for some other poor couple.'

'I don't think I said I wanted to marry you because of the baby. The baby would just bring the whole thing forward.'

Julia was astonished. 'Are you trying to imply that you would have – wanted to marry me – if I hadn't been pregnant with your child?'

'I don't know. All I'm saying is that I would probably have got in touch when you came off the boats.'

'I don't believe you.'

'Julia! You are pregnant! With my child! Because we made love! We're not animals. One would hope that there was something between us apart from a need to procreate.'

Julia looked out of the window. 'I wish you weren't so pompous sometimes.'

He slowed the car and gave her a look which melted his pomposity and Julia's insides. It was a good thing, she thought, when she had recovered, that he was about to teach her to drive. He would shout and scream at her. That was bound to suppress the feelings of lust which were quite unsuitable for a pregnant woman.

But he didn't shout and scream. He was very patient. And when he explained things, Julia found she understood them, having previously condemned herself as a technophobe. Soon she was happily driving round and round the airfield, changing from first to second gear and back again with very little trouble.

'You're very good at this,' said Fergus, his voice not reflecting the surprise Julia felt. 'But I'm not sure I'll have time to give you lessons often enough. When does *Pyramus* become a restaurant boat?'

'December. They always have November off anyway, but they've got to have a new counter fitted – that's the bit you stand on – and the people running it really want to go away. *Pyramus*'ll do it for December and January. Their busiest times, apparently. We could make lots of money.'

'You might need to change down soon. Oops, too late.' Fergus hung on to the dashboard as the car bounded along. 'Kangaroo petrol.' He grinned.

Julia frowned back at him and changed gear. It wasn't the fact that he grinned at her mistake that bothered her. It was the fact that his grin fazed her more than being in too high a gear did.

'You are doing very well,' he said when they finally swapped seats and he set off home. 'But I do think a few lessons from a professional would speed you up. Do let me pay for them.' He caught her expression. 'Or I could lend you the money and you could pay me back when you're earning the big bucks on *Pyramus*.'

'It's all right. My mother asked was there anything I really needed. I'll ask her to pay for some driving lessons. They'd be far more useful than a new cot or something.'

'True. I do think you ought to tell your mother I'm the father, Julia, to put her mind at rest.'

'I'm sure I will eventually, but I've got other things on my mind.' She was still waiting for Rupert to ring back and tell her the papers had been found.

'You're just making excuses, Julia.'

Julia opened her mouth to protest and then realised she'd have to go into a whole lot of explanations, so she shut it again.

As they approached Julia's cottage Fergus said, 'I've got nothing on tomorrow afternoon. Pick you up about three?'

'Only if you're fully clothed, Fergus,' said Julia, trying to sound carefree. 'I'm not getting into a car with you otherwise.'

Suzy had promised to ring and find out how the lesson had gone. 'So, are you still speaking? Will he ever let you near his car again?'

'It went very well. He's taking me out tomorrow.'

'Wow!'

'But he says I'll need some professional lessons as he won't have time to give me all I need.'

'I'm sure he's right. Plenty of practice is vital. And I think it's excellent that you and Fergus are going to have to spend so much time together. I think you're really well suited.'

'You know, you're going to be just as much of a matchmaker as my mother when you grow up, Suzy.'

'Well, a girl's got to have some hobbies!'

Julia had found her first driving lesson exhilarating, but she was aware that soon her adrenalin would be replaced with exhaustion. Thus, if she wanted to get a parcel of her tenant's possessions posted before Monday, she had better go before her energy ran out.

She set off brightly enough, but when she saw the queue in the post office, she felt her strength drain away. However, there were some forms she needed as well as the parcel so she fought the temptation to find somewhere for a cup of tea and latched herself on to the back of the line of people. Unfortunately, when there were only two people in front of her, too late to duck and run, she saw Oscar joining the back of the queue. She looked the other way, hoping he wouldn't recognise her. But it was no good. She felt a tap on her shoulder which made her jump like a shoplifter caught in the act.

'Julia! It is you, I thought I couldn't be mistaken. My God! You're pregnant!'

It seemed everybody in the post office now looked to see if Oscar's carrying words were true. Julia resisted the childish temptation to look down at her stomach in amazement and say, 'Goodness me! So I am. I never noticed!'

She said, 'Hello, Oscar, how are you? What are you doing here?' Although her voice was calm, she could feel herself blushing.

'Julia! When did this happen? It's that archaeologist, isn't it? Are you going to get married?'

If the baby hadn't been keeping Julia's heart high in her throat, where it burned from time to time, it would have sunk now. If Oscar, who had no imagination at all, guessed that Fergus was the father of her baby, how long could she keep it from other people? She decided to ignore his comments. 'How's work these days? Plenty of business?'

'I'm surprised and very disappointed in you, Julia. It's not the kind of behaviour I expected from you.'

This wasn't the moment to point out that Oscar had always had a quite different image of Julia than she had of herself. Besides, getting pregnant outside marriage wasn't the kind of behaviour she expected of herself either.

'If you need any help persuading him to do the decent thing,' Oscar went on, 'just let me know.' Julia waited for the word 'bounder' but was disappointed.

'Sooty well? And your mother?'

'They're fine. Don't change the subject. I want to talk to

you.' He just managed not to call her 'young lady', which was fortunate, as her feminist honour would have required her to make a nasty scene, and they were already attracting quite enough attention.

'Actually, it's my turn now,' she said with relief. 'Why don't you get in the queue, or you'll be here all day?'

Julia smiled at him, but didn't speak again as she left the post office. Then she went into the chemist and hid behind the breast pumps and nipple shields. He'd never hunt her out there. Unfortunately, she did run into someone she knew vaguely from Strange's. Her name eluded her, but she had done maternity cover for Karen. She was older than Julia and tended to nurse grievances.

'Oh, hello, Julia.' She looked deliberately down at Julia's bump. 'I didn't know you were expecting. Didn't know you were married, actually.' She sniffed, implying she should have been asked to the wedding. 'Did you put it in the local paper?'

'No, because there wasn't a wedding.'

'Oh. I suppose you're "living together".'

'No, but I'm very pleased about the baby,' Julia said firmly with a forced smile.

'Oh.' The woman didn't know whether to be aggrieved that she'd missed an opportunity to wear her hat, or pleased that Julia, usually so efficient, had slipped up so spectacularly. 'Well, I'll be honest with you. I don't approve. I think people should have more consideration for the child. And people expect everything to be handed to them on a plate. Free housing, free dentistry, free I-don't-know-what. Will you have the baby adopted?'

'No, I shall keep it.'

'You have to think what's best for the child, you know. Two loving parents are bound to be better than one. You don't want to disadvantage your baby, do you?'

'But my child will be enormously privileged.' Julia's tense, artificial smile barely disguised her fury. 'He or she

266

will have me for a mother!'

'Glad to hear you sound so positive,' said another, extremely glamorously dressed woman, whom Julia eventually recognised as her midwife, met briefly at her doctor's surgery. 'It's Julia, isn't it? The parentcraft classes start on Tuesday. Seven o'clock. I look forward to seeing you there.'

'Oh, thank you,' said Julia.

'And I think you'll find,' said this grown-up version of Suzy, designer to her last gold earring, to Julia's companion, 'that a lot of single women make better parents than some married women do. It's to do with commitment and unconditional love.' With which somewhat mystifying remark she left Julia staring after her, and her companion tutting crossly.

'Who was that?'

'My midwife,' said Julia, wanting to add: 'as if it's any business of yours'.

'Well, I can't believe she's a real health professional. She isn't wearing uniform. And even if she is a midwife, it doesn't mean she knows everything.'

Julia was horribly reminded of Oscar's mother and then remembered that the woman had had awful trouble with her children. Her married daughter would no longer speak to her. Which meant that in this case, the midwife did know quite a lot.

She stretched her lips still further to simulate goodwill and left the shop. Naturally, she was pleased to know she and her baby were in such good, stylish hands, but she was aware that the attitude of her erstwhile colleague was one she was likely to come across again. Depressed, she started to walk home, pondering that people often did foolish, possibly immoral things, but mostly, these things were kept secret. Only unwise, unprotected sex had such visible consequences. It was a lowering thought.

Oscar's voice, coming from his car, couldn't depress her

any further. When he offered her a lift home, it even cheered her. Her encounters in town had left her completely drained.

'Of course,' said Oscar, when he had ensured that Julia had her seatbelt done up correctly, 'I don't approve of people having babies outside marriage. I suppose you think I'm old-fashioned.' She did, but not for that reason. 'But I hope I'm not so old-fashioned that I don't want to know you any more. I do hope you'll look on me as a friend, someone you can call on if you need a shelf putting up or anything.'

'That's very kind of you, Oscar,' said Julia meekly. She could put up her own shelves, but this wasn't the moment to tell him.

He pulled up in front of her cottage. 'After all, the kid will need a positive male role model in its life.'

Julia got out of the car not knowing whether to hug him or hit him.

That evening, when her mother rang to make sure she was all right, and to ask if there was anything she could do, Julia decided to see if Suzy was right about parents not liking to have all their offers of help refused. 'I'll tell you what would be most awfully useful, if you could manage it . . .' she said.

'What?'

'Driving lessons. Just a few. A friend' – just in time she managed to bite back his name – 'is teaching me mainly, but I need a few lessons with a proper instructor to help me through the test procedure.'

'Darling, don't you think you're a little old to learn to drive?'

'Mother! No, of course not! Besides, didn't that friend of yours learn to drive when she was well over fifty?'

'Well, yes, but she never drives very fast.'

'That's a good thing, surely?' Julia went on, trying to remember she was asking her mother a favour.

'Not if you get stuck behind her in the lane, it isn't. But if driving lessons is what you want, you shall have them. So who's helping you now?'

'Fergus,' said Julia rashly, feeling that keeping one major secret from her mother was enough, without adding smaller, less important ones. 'He is kind, isn't he?'

'Does he know you're pregnant?'

'Of course. It's quite obvious. And besides, you told his mother, so naturally she told him.'

'Oh. I didn't realise Lally was so indiscreet.'

'Didn't you? You told *her*, after all, when some mothers might not have told the world their daughter was pregnant.'

Her mother humphed, obviously feeling guilty. 'Was Fergus very shocked?'

'He was a bit surprised, but once he'd got used to the idea he was very kind and helpful. Which is why he offered to teach me to drive.'

'It's not because he's the –'

'Mother! Fergus and I have never got on! Not when we were young and not much better now!'

'But if you don't get on, why is he teaching you to drive?'

Hoist by the petard of her dishonesty, Julia took a shuddering breath. It was an effort not to shout. 'He's a very kind man, and he thought it would be a useful thing for him to do.'

'Well, I call that kindness beyond the call of duty, if you ask me. Don't impose on him now, will you?'

Julia curled up her toes in rage.

Her next driving lesson with Fergus went very much better than her first. She had been allowed to move from second to third gear, and was beginning to feel far more confident about handling the car.

'So, did you tell your mother?'

269

'No. I've said I will, but not until I'm ready. You should be grateful. Your life will be hell when she finds out.'

'And of course it's just peachy now.'

Julia glanced at him in surprise. What did he have to worry about? He wasn't pregnant; he didn't have to learn to drive.

'Oh never mind,' he said. 'Now turn right. It's time you went on the road. Driving round and round an airfield isn't going to get you through your test.'

At first Julia wanted to dive into the hedge every time anything came up behind her, but eventually she learned to hold her own, only pulling in a little if the road was too narrow for the car to pass safely.

'You're doing extremely well,' said Fergus, after they had successfully skirted a small town. 'Your reactions are quick.'

'Don't sound so surprised. I quite like driving.'

'And did your mother agree to pay for some lessons?'

'Yup. It's very kind of her. She doesn't have much money. I'll pay her back when I'm in a position to.' She stifled a sigh, suddenly feeling tired.

Stifled or not, Fergus noticed, and said, 'I think that's enough for today. You can't learn when you're tired. No one can,' he added, in response to her sudden frown. 'Pull in here and I'll take you home.'

Julia found her lids drooping and realised that she had fallen asleep only when she woke up. They were nearly there.

'Oh goodness, I don't know what made me drop off like that.' She felt terribly bad-mannered. 'Would you like to come in for some tea, or are you in a hurry? I bought a lovely cake from the WI market.'

'That sounds very nice. You make tea, I'll light the fire.'

Hearing him break sticks and scrunch up newspaper while she put on the kettle gave her a repeat of the unsettling feelings she had had when he first called on her, a tiny, piercing yearning for the cosy domesticity of married life. She still hadn't quite got it under control by the time she came back with the tray.

'Something's bothering you,' said Fergus, having examined her over his mug for some unnerving moments. 'What is it?'

'Nothing.' She couldn't tell him how seductive she found this mundane scene, the two of them, the fireside, the tea, and the growing baby. Seeing this was not going to satisfy him, she went on, 'I met an old colleague in the chemist. She asked me if I was going to have the baby adopted.'

'Oh dear.'

'Fortunately the midwife, who is extremely glam, I can tell you, was there and recognised me.'

'What did she say?'

'Oh, she told me when the parentcraft classes started and then she told the woman that single parents often make better mothers than married women do.'

'Is that true?'

'Dunno, but it put the woman in her place. The thing is, I realised I'm going to have to face that kind of attitude.' At that moment she also realised she'd given him a perfect opportunity to go on about marrying her again. 'I know how to deal with it now, of course.'

'Of course,' said Fergus, not taking advantage of her slip. 'I don't suppose you're too happy keeping my identity from your mother, either.'

She studied him. It hadn't been on her mind at that particular moment, but it did bother her, yes. She had always preferred to stand whatever row was forthcoming, than try to deceive her mother. 'Well no. I don't like keeping it from her.'

'Then why don't you tell her?'

'You still don't get it, do you? She'll book a cathedral for us to be married in; she'll be on to your mother, and tell her

271

it's all her fault. Your mother will get on to you and probably give you as hard a time as my mother gave me! And I can't guarantee that my mother won't give you a hard time as well.'

'My back is broad, I can take it. We are adults, you know, Julia. Parental authority doesn't extend much after the age of twenty-one.'

'I *know*! But I don't think we ever will be adults to our mothers. They go on thinking they can tell us what to do for ever. And although it's silly, I've met really strong women who still dread telling their mothers about things they think they'll disapprove of.' She didn't want him thinking she was the only wimp in the world. 'But you are being nice about it. Most men would die rather than expose themselves to the sort of flak you're likely to get.'

'It is my baby too. There's no reason I shouldn't take my share of the "flak", as you put it.'

'Even so.'

Fergus got up. 'I must go. Otherwise I'll drop off too, and then it'll be late.'

'Are you going out tonight?' Julia tried hard not to sound wistful, and almost managed it.

He nodded. 'Dinner with friends,' he said. 'And speak to your mother. It'll make you feel better.'

She shut the door behind him, feeling, quite unjustifiably, like the peasant girl being loved and left by the lord of the manor. She decided to take his advice and ring her mother, not to tell her necessarily, but to help her regain some of her independent spirit.

'Hello, darling. How nice to hear from you.' Her mother actually sounded slightly surprised to hear from her. 'So, darling, how are you?'

'Fine, thank you.'

'Drinking plenty of that raspberry leaf tea I sent you?'

'Well –'

'Darling! It's so good for you just now. It'll help with

272

your labour. And have you thought about it? Would you like me to be there?'

'No!' Julia barely suppressed a scream. The thought of her mother taking over the labour ward as she had the galley on the boat, and any other aspect of her life she'd managed to get her hands on, was desperate. Then, realising how unkind this sounded, she added, 'Actually, Mummy, I thought it ought to tell you who the father is.'

'Oh darling. I know you said he's young, but I do hope it's not that young man on the boats. Quite beautiful, of course, but not father material, not for a few years anyway. What about that young man who was the crew when you first started?'

She was referring to Jason. 'It's Fergus,' confessed Julia, through gritted teeth.

Chapter Twenty-two

There was a clatter as her mother dropped the telephone. 'Mummy? Are you all right?'

'Did you say who I thought you said?'

'Yes.'

There was a silence long enough for Julia to wonder if her mother had fainted. 'Then why did you lead me to believe it was some young – person? And that you and Fergus didn't get on?'

'Because we don't, really.' It sounded incredibly lame, but lately, the truth had.

'Well, that's marvellous news, darling.' Margot decided to set aside Julia's deceit and take a positive attitude.

'Is it?' She knew her mother liked Fergus, but she thought she might have been a bit disappointed to hear he had been so irresponsible as to get her daughter pregnant.

'Of course. Lally will make him marry you.'

'That's a terrible idea!'

'No it's not. It'll be such fun. I can wear a hat. And if you're careful about the wedding dress, no one need know you're pregnant.'

Julia looked down at her stomach which was making inroads into the maternity leggings her sister had lent her. 'We're not getting married.'

'Don't be silly, darling, of course you are. As I said, Lally will make him.'

'But I don't want to get married!'

'Nonsense. Of course you do. Every woman does.'

For a moment Julia recognised that this was probably

true before continuing with her protests to the contrary. 'No they don't! Lots of women elect to bring up babies on their own these days.'

'Not if they've got an alternative.'

'But I haven't!'

'Yes you have! That's what I'm trying to tell you! Lally will make Fergus do the decent thing!'

Julia wanted to scream. 'But I don't want him to! He's offered already, and I've refused.'

'That was silly, but not irrevocable. I'll get on to Lally right away.'

'Mother!' Julia's voice would have reached the Lake District, even without the aid of electronics. 'Do you really want me to end up with someone who was made to marry me by his *mother*?'

Another silence. 'I suppose not. It seems a shame, though, he'd make such a lovely husband.'

'I don't know what makes you say that. He obviously didn't make someone a very lovely husband.'

'We don't know that at all. I gather from Lally that his wife was a dreadfully feminist type. No wonder it broke up.'

Julia shuddered. Never was her resolution not to marry Fergus so strong. 'I must go, Mum. Someone's just rung the doorbell.'

Fergus took her driving on Monday night. As soon as they got out of the town and were on their way to the airfield, so Julia could get a little practice parallel parking with cones, he stopped watching her so intently and started talking.

'So,' he asked casually, showing, in Julia's opinion, far too little interest in what she was doing with his car, 'how did your mother take the news?'

'Maddeningly and typically. She said your mother would make you marry me.' She wanted to check his reaction but didn't dare take her eyes off the road. 'I told her you'd offered and everything. She thinks I'm mad. I expect your mother's been on to you already.'

'She rang me and told me she knew.'

'How did she react?'

'Much the same as your mother. My reputation has suffered enormously by you not marrying me, you know,' he went on calmly. 'Everyone thinks I'm a bastard.'

'You don't seem to mind very much. But I stick up for you at every opportunity. To get you out of trouble, I told Mum how concerned you were, which only made her even more sure I'm mad not to marry you.'

'Well, you know the thing about even hypochondriacs getting sick?'

'Yes . . .'

'Well, even mothers give good advice.'

'That's as may be, but mine, for one, gives me far too much of it. And I have no intention of marrying someone who was made to by his mother!'

Rather to Julia's surprise, he didn't immediately reply. The silence between them grew like an icy balloon, fragile yet tangible. She risked a sideways glance but all she caught sight of was his indomitable profile.

'If and when I marry you, Julia,' said Fergus eventually, 'it will be nothing whatever to do with my mother, or yours.'

Julia couldn't think what to say. Up until now she'd always felt totally safe with Fergus. Now she felt as if she had an unpredictable beast in the car with her. 'It's left here, isn't it?' she asked eventually, reverting to a neutral topic of conversation.

'No, right.' Still in the grip of some unspecified emotion, he took it out on the stream of traffic which was behind them. 'I've changed my mind about the airfield. You can learn to park with real cars, like a real person.'

Flustered, Julia found she had forgotten the procedure

276

for right-hand turns. She drove past the turn he indicated and was rewarded by a hiss of annoyance. This was so unlike Fergus.

'Sorry, I forgot what to do.' Up to now she hadn't found it difficult to ask Fergus questions, but he'd suddenly become unapproachable. 'Could you run it by me again?'

He ran her through the manoeuvres patiently enough, but she felt the kindly Fergus who had been teaching her to drive up to now had abandoned her, leaving her with this stony-faced individual who might bite her head off any moment. The sooner she organised some proper driving lessons the better. Her mother's cheque had arrived, there was nothing stopping her except the daunting process of selecting a driving school.

'Would you like to come in for some tea?' she asked Fergus, when at last the lesson was over, and she could stop going round roundabouts, turning into unbroken streams of traffic and reversing round corners which were also uphill.

'No thank you, I've got things to do. Will Tuesday be all right for your next lesson?'

'No. I've got my first parentcraft class. Wednesday?'

'OK. Six o'clock, then?'

'Fine.'

Julia shuddered, suddenly seeing Fergus in the role of stern parent. How would she cope, she wondered, if their child got into trouble? Would she be able to tolerate someone else telling it off?

Being an unmarried mother no longer carried the stigma it once had. Many women now chose to have babies out of wedlock. Society had got used to the idea, and didn't cast aspersions on the women concerned. At least, that was what Julia tried to persuade herself as she entered the room, which was full of chattering couples. She could picture all the women in wedding dresses and all the men in bought-for-the-occasion suits or hired morning coats. There was one couple who may not have gone up the aisle in white tulle and black worsted: they seemed to have extreme hippy characteristics, which they must have inherited from their parents. They had probably jumped over a bonfire, the ceremony presided over by a white witch, accompanied by chanting and pan pipes. They might look strangely dated in their homespun clothes and coloured sandals, but they were not commitment-phobes. No other woman there was without a partner.

Julia smiled vaguely at people, trying to imply that her husband was away on business, and was too busy to come. Suzy, she thought, ashamed, would have proclaimed her single status with pride. It was, after all, only coincidence that she was the only single mother present. She certainly wasn't the only single mother in existence.

Everyone was seated in a circle, with the glamorous midwife in the middle, when the door opened for a latecomer. It was Fergus.

'Sorry I'm late,' he said to the room at large. 'Sorry, darling,' he said to Julia, as he found a chair and squashed it in beside hers.

She was speechless. What could she say? She couldn't reject him by announcing in a loud voice, 'This man is not my partner,' because no one would believe her. Why should anyone pretend a thing like that? Nor could she pat his arm in a wifely way and whisper, 'Did you manage to get anything to eat?' Or, more satisfyingly, curse him for his lateness by saying, 'Could you *please* put me and our baby before work just for *once*?' – she wasn't wearing the right sort of clothes.

She tried to recall a single instance of Fergus appearing out of the blue (and there had been a few) when her feelings had been entirely unambiguous. Now, she felt justifiably furious with him for appearing uninvited, but also glad not to be on her own among these cosy couples.

It was only the very first time he appeared on the boats, she realised, that her feelings were perfectly clear. And hadn't her instincts to send him away before he even got through the door been spot on?

'Now,' said the midwife, 'I'm Lucasta, and I'm only one of the team of midwives who will be responsible for you all having happy, safe deliveries. Some of you will have met the others already. By the time you have your babies, we'll all be familiar and, we hope, friendly faces.'

Everyone laughed nervously.

'First of all, have you all read the blue book I gave you when you first visited?'

Everyone nodded, except Julia, who had somehow mislaid it.

'Good,' said Lucasta. 'Now, I'm going to go round the room, and I want you to introduce yourselves, tell me when your baby's due, and what sort of births you think you want. Of course, as we go on, you'll learn more about what pain relief is available, but if I just have some idea of your expectations, it'll help me pitch the course at the right level. Right, Sharon and Dan, isn't it? You start. When is your baby due?'

'February.'

'And how would you like to have it?' prompted Lucasta.

'We thought an epidural, didn't we, Dan?' said Sharon.

Julia squirmed in her chair, having counted how many couples there were before it was her turn. Everyone else seemed to know so much about childbirth already, presumably because they'd done their homework. She hadn't, partly because she'd been so busy learning to drive, planning how to support the baby, and generally getting through life, but mostly because she found the idea of giving birth was so terrifying. But if she'd known there was going to be a test, she would have forced herself, so at least she could feel familiar with the jargon. As it was, she'd have to busk it. She ought to be all right – in spite of her pleas with her not to, her sister had given her a contraction-by-contraction account of all three births. A few fragments floated to the surface: Pethidine only made you go to sleep, gas and air worked a bit, and there was some machine or other. Before she'd formed a sensible-sounding sentence in her mind, it was her turn.

'I'm Julia –'

'And I'm Fergus.'

'The baby's due in early February,' said Julia, trying to ignore Fergus and finding it impossible. Lucasta seemed to be looking at them both very intently. She was probably trying to work out if they had had a reconciliation of some sort, and she need no longer class Julia as a single parent.

'And what sort of birth would you like?'

Julia froze. She wanted to say: 'For someone else to do it for me,' but the atmosphere was rather too serious for jokes. She couldn't think of a single sensible thing to say, and was still reeling from the shock of Fergus's appearance. To come here without telling her, to come here at all, was too bad. But planning her revenge was not going to make Lucasta turn her attention to the next couple. She opened her mouth, 'Well . . .'

'We don't know much about it,' said Fergus. 'But while we would like to have the baby as naturally as possible, we don't want to block our chances of effective pain relief should it prove necessary.'

'Good answer,' said Lucasta. 'We'd all like to have our babies squatting in a wigwam by candlelight aided only by herbs thrown on to the fire' – she cast an eye in the direction of the hippies – 'but most of us need a little help.'

The hippy couple blushed. It was their turn. 'I'm Ayrian,' said the man.

'And I'm Thrush . . . after the bird,' she clarified, seconds too late for Julia, who had already assumed it was after something else.

'And we don't want any drugs that are likely to cross to the placenta,' said Ayrian.

'I'd like a birthing pool, acupuncture, and my best friend there, as well as Ayrian, of course.' Thrush squeezed her partner's hand.

'Good point,' said Lucasta. 'You should think very carefully about whether or not you want your partners present. It can bring you very close as a couple, but if either of you feels reluctant, no one's going to make you.'

'If you think you're going to be there,' said Julia from between clenched teeth, 'you've got another think coming.'

Fergus pretended not to hear.

At last the circle was complete. The desire for pain relief varied between one woman, who wanted every drug in the book, including a general anaesthetic if she was allowed, through epidurals, to those who only wanted a bit of gas and air. Then there were Ayrian and Thrush. They had read more about how children were born in obscure corners of the earth than most anthropologists and this was their chance to share their knowledge.

It was all too much for one brave soul, a man with a very short haircut and a very broad wedding ring, who had listened, squirming, to accounts of women who bit off the umbilical cord and ate the placenta ('for all the minerals and vitamins which are usually just thrown away'). 'Why,' he asked, 'if you're into all that natural childbirth crap, did you come to the bog-standard National Health classes, instead of something more' – he sought for a word, rejected 'disgusting' and settled for – 'more way out?'

'Thrush runs a dream workshop on Mondays,' explained Ayrian. 'And I've got my welding course on Wednesdays. Thursdays it's Tantric Yoga, and on Fridays we go to a "Harmony and Happiness" circle. This is the only class we could both come to.'

'No chance of keeping up with Coronation Street, then,'

said a very young, pretty girl, with a hairstyle dependent on a lot of hair-wax and kirby grips.

'We don't have television. We like to spend our time creatively.' He looked around defensively. 'While we would have preferred a class which was less alopathically based, we're not going to submit to unnecessary intervention, or drugs we don't need.'

'Well, I hope you won't need any drugs, Ayrian,' said Lucasta briskly. 'And I think you'll find the much beleaguered National Health can deliver babies perfectly well. It's not all stirrups, stitches and episiotomies nowadays.'

'What's an episiotomy?' asked someone.

Julia distracted herself from the answer by whispering to Fergus, forgetting for a moment that she wasn't speaking to him now, nor ever again, 'Wouldn't my mother just love those two?'

'She probably knows them already.'

Lucasta's brilliant blue eyes silently reproached them for talking.

'Right, now we've got to know each other a little, I suggest we have a few games to relax us further.' She handed out sheets of paper. 'Anagrams,' she declared. 'All of words you're going to become very familiar with over the next months. Now, get into teams with the people next to you.'

Somehow, they were paired up with Ayrian and Thrush. By now, Julia was grateful for Fergus's presence. She wasn't particularly good at word games and she hadn't brought a pen. Neither had Ayrian and Thrush. Depending heavily on Fergus's Rollerball, somehow they got through without disgracing themselves.

'Now,' went on Lucasta, her enthusiasm undimmed. 'After tea or coffee, we're going on to something more practical.'

The tea and coffee were bad enough, Julia having gone

violently off one, and become fussy about the other. But the 'something more practical' was worse. It involved a plastic pelvis, like the middle section of a skeleton, and a doll which looked as if it had come off the front of a dustcart. It had a plastic head and cloth limbs and was distinctly grubby.

'Now I'm going to demonstrate the various ways which a baby can present itself, and the three stages of labour, so you'll know what's happening.'

'That's why I want a general anaesthetic,' said the *Coronation Street* fan, 'so I won't know. Do you think they'd let me have an elective Caesarean?'

'Probably not on the National Health,' said Julia. 'You'll have to pray that your baby's a breech.'

Like a puppeteer, Lucasta moved the baby's limbs into position, but when she angled the head, so it was about to enter the birth canal, most people there refused to believe it would ever go through the tiny space available.

'No way will that great big head go through that little gap. And if it does, I definitely want a Caesarean,' muttered Julia's ally.

'It does seem incredible, but yes, it will.' Lucasta turned the baby's head sideways, and out it came. 'See? Easy as pie. Later on you'll see videos of seven different kinds of birth. It won't be so scary when you're more used to the idea.'

'I could see a million videos,' the girl went on, endearing herself to Julia more and more, 'it won't change my mind. Pain-free birth is what I'm after.'

'But surely,' said Ayrian, who didn't have to go through it, 'you want the whole experience of childbirth? How will you feel like a proper mother if you haven't had any pain?'

'Just the same way you'll feel like a father, although you won't have had any pain either,' said the girl.

Julia clapped; one or two of the others joined in.

'But if the baby doesn't come out through the birth

canal,' said Thrush, 'it'll have to be rebirthed as an adult.'

'Boll – rubbish,' said the girl, looking scathingly at Thrush.

Lucasta intervened. 'I'm certainly not going to tell you that childbirth is painless,' she said. 'But it is pain with a purpose, and very few mothers ever feel that it wasn't worth every bit of it. If you end up with a healthy baby, what you went through to get it is nothing. It's a pain you always forget. So they tell me,' she added quickly.

'Yeah, well. No one gives out medals for the amount of agony having your baby took,' went on Julia's chum. 'Perhaps I should go private!'

Everyone laughed, and Julia felt the parentcraft classes would be bearable as long as that woman kept on coming. 'That was pretty gruelling,' she declared to Fergus, when, two hours later, they were allowed to go home. She got into Fergus's car without thinking. 'Do I really have to go back? Can't I just make it up as I go along? Ignorance is bliss, after all.'

'I don't think childbirth is likely to be bliss, ignorant or not, and I do think a little information would be a good idea.'

'Well, I'm not watching the videos. I'm not watching a baby being born. My sister told me it's quite unnecessary. She's had three and she's never seen anything.'

'I'll watch it, and tell you anything I think you ought to know.'

Julia suddenly realised she was being driven home, instead of walking, which was how she had come. Somehow, since his appearance at the class, they had become a couple, linked by medical anagrams and a plastic pelvis. It would never do. It was the slippery slope it would be so easy to slither down. If she let herself get seduced into domesticity, so it felt normal and right, how would she cope when everything fell apart?

'Fergus,' she said, just before they arrived at her cottage.

284

'I don't think you understand. I'm having this baby, not you. You're not my "partner".' She said the word with a grimace, having heard it *ad nauseum* all evening.

'I'm the father of your child. I'm entitled to do anything which will make that child's arrival into the world as easy and safe as possible.'

Julia suddenly felt tired and bad-tempered. It had been a long evening. 'Sometimes I get the impression that this is more your baby than mine.'

'Oh do you? Now you know how it feels!'

'You may not have noticed, but the baby *is* more my baby than yours. It's in my stomach. I'm the one who's going to have to go through the labour.'

'I'm perfectly aware of that.'

'So I'd be obliged if you would just let me get on with it and stop interfering.'

'Fine. If that's the way you want it, it'll save me a whole lot of time.'

'Good.'

Fergus drew up outside Julia's cottage. 'So, do you still want driving lessons? Or does that qualify as "interfering" too?'

Julia undid her seatbelt and fingered the door catch. 'Actually, I'm going to have proper lessons.'

'Fine.' He stared straight ahead, waiting for her to get out.

Too late, she remembered how much he had done for her so far. 'Not that I'm not extremely grateful for all the lessons I've had already, but I can't impose on your good nature any longer.'

'Whatever you think is best. Now if you wouldn't mind getting out, I would like to get home. I do have a life of my own to lead.'

She started clambering out of the car. 'I'm so sorry to have taken up so much of your time already, Fergus,' she said as she got on to the pavement. 'Please rest assured it won't happen again!' She slammed the door and stalked away.

Bloody Fergus! He was the one who offered all the help. She hadn't asked him. And now he was throwing it back in her face! Well, she'd learn to drive without his help. And she'd have the baby without him too. She went upstairs to the bathroom and started to run herself a bath, tipping in a large dollop of bath-oil, to stop herself dwelling on the realisation that she needed to be able to drive in less than a month, and doing it without Fergus would be very difficult indeed. But not impossible, she told herself, ripping off her clothes. 'Do we need him, Baby? No we don't!'

The baby kicked in agreement. 'There's a good girl,' said Julia. 'You be on Mummy's side.'

Then she lit a soothing phalanx of scented candles and thought about names.

Chapter Twenty-three

Julia's brother Rupert rang her ten minutes before her first driving lesson was due. She'd sorted through the dozens of ads in the *Yellow Pages* and finally come up with an instructor who was willing to teach her. But she felt if she heard the expression, 'You need a lesson for every year of your life' again she would scream: she couldn't afford that many.

'Oh Rupert, I can't chat, I've got a driving lesson.'

'Really? Oh. Well, I never do chat. We've got to sort something out about this business with Strange's.'

'Ah . . . Did they look where I suggested?'

'Yes, and they found them. What they want to know is how you knew they were there. And I must say, I think it's a fair question.'

Of course it was fair. It was just a pity it was damn impossible to answer. 'Oh well, I'm glad they found everything. And I didn't *know* they were there. I just thought they might be. Darren lost something once before which turned up in his filing cabinet.'

'Well, apparently the girls in the office said they'd looked there before. It seemed to them, and to me, highly suspicious.'

'Rupert?' Julia filled her voice with icy incredulity. 'Are you suggesting that I somehow placed the papers in Darren's filing cabinet? That I'd had them all along, and somehow contrived to put them back? If so, I'd be fascinated to hear how I am supposed to have done it. Broken in at the dead of night, I suppose? Disabled the burglar alarm, made copies of all the keys, and just "put them back". I hate to ask you, Rupert old chap, but what are you on?'

'I only asked, Ju.'

Julia put the phone down in triumph. Having had a deeply sarcastic headmistress came in useful when you were really in a spot. She was so delighted with having got away with her dastardly crime, and disposed of her brother's perfectly accurate suspicions, that she forgot to be nervous about her driving lesson.

'You drive quite well, don't you?'

Julia switched off the ignition and waited for the caveat, 'for a woman, a pregnant one at that', but it didn't come.

'Whoever you had lessons with before didn't do a bad job.' Mike smiled at her.

He was, Julia had come to realise, really rather nice. He took her to Oxford, by the canal, every lesson, until she knew the route by heart. Now that she felt confident about the journey she would be making daily, which was the real-life reason for her needing to drive, the thought of the actual test became less terrifying.

She had had four two-hour lessons before the next parentcraft class was due. Her confidence had increased along with her driving ability. Mike had already put her in for her test. Julia decided she was finally going to put Fergus in his place. On Tuesday afternoon, she rang him up. His answerphone replied.

'It's Julia. I just rang to tell you that I think it would be better if you didn't come to the parentcraft class tonight, it's too confusing for everyone and I really don't want you there. No need to ring back. Bye.'

'That should sort him,' she said to herself when she'd put down the receiver.

It did, but she was disappointed to note how many times during the evening she glanced at the door, to see if he really wasn't going to turn up.

She was not surprised when Lucasta asked if she would wait behind after the others had gone. The class had spent the evening watching videos of childbirth. Julia had kept her eyes closed.

'So, what's the score with Fergus?' demanded Lucasta in a very un-health-professional way. 'I take it he's the father?'

'Yes, and he has offered to marry me, and I've refused. He wants to be a lot more involved with the baby than I want him to be.'

'Why?'

'Because he wants children and his first wife put her career first and wouldn't have them.'

'No, I meant, why don't you want him involved? It's nice to have a friend there with you, you know.'

'I'm sure, it would be nice to have a man to go to hospital with and everything.' For a moment she allowed herself to think about the other couples in the class, who were real couples, not just people briefly connected. 'But if we did get married, it couldn't possibly last and I feel it's better not to start anything that's going to end in tears.'

Julia expected a lot more argument, but Lucasta just said, 'Pity, he seemed a nice man.'

'He is a nice man. I'll give you his telephone number if you like,' said Julia.

Lucasta laughed. 'No, sorry. I'm spoken for. Look at this.' And she drew from the neck of her blouse a gold chain from which dangled a diamond ring of spectacular size and brilliance. 'I can't wear it at work in case I cut someone, but isn't it heaven? We're getting married in the spring.'

'Wow,' said Julia. 'It's stunning.'

'Sometimes,' said Lucasta, mysteriously, 'commitment is worth it.'

The day before Julia sat the written part of the driving

test, Mike presented her with a book of the questions she was likely to be asked. That night she read it through and through, forcing the information into her tired brain like minced meat into a sausage-skin.

'It's a doddle,' said Mike after Julia had parked, very neatly, in front of the test centre. 'You don't have to stay once you've finished. Just come out and we'll get on with teaching you to drive. Did I tell you? Your test date's come through? You got a cancellation. Next week.'

This piece of information shook Julia somewhat, but she didn't find the questions difficult. Multiple choice always seemed an easy option, possibly because she'd done so many of them as a teenager, trying to learn about herself. *Test Yourself for Sensuality – How much of a Sex-Kitten Are You?* and *Good Friend, or Good-Time Friend? Would you let down your mate if there was a bloke involved?* You could always tell the answer which would make you come out on top.

'Go OK?' asked Mike as Julia came out. Julia nodded. 'Good, I thought we'd go to Swindon today.'

'Swindon? Is that specially hard?'

'Nah. Something I need to buy there.'

'So I'm just taking you shopping?'

'That's it. Don't hang about.'

Julia didn't feel unduly nervous before her test. Of course she would be terribly disappointed if she failed, but she was expecting it. And knowing she was going to be driving a car with dual controls, so it was unlikely she would either kill or be killed, helped. She knew the test route as well as she knew the route from her house to *Pyramus* in Oxford, which, last time she'd visited, had been tied up, ready for its career change. Her parallel parking was unparalleled.

'So, when's the baby due?' asked her examiner, eyeing her bump uncertainly. He was a kindly middle-aged man. 'I've got four of my own.'

'Not till early February, so don't worry. I won't have it today.'

'All the same, I don't think we'll do the emergency stop at high speed. When you're ready, move away from the kerb . . .'

Julia finished her round of telephone calls and her ear was sore from hearing congratulations on passing her test shouted down it. But she was aware that the one person she really wanted to tell, who deserved to hear more than anyone else, was Fergus. Julia knew that it was the good start he'd given her which made it possible for her to get through the test so quickly. So why couldn't she just be adult about it and thank him?

Well she could, she just couldn't ring him up and tell him. She didn't really want to talk to him, nor did she want to leave a message on his machine. She decided on a card.

It was fortunate that she had a whole packet of notelets left over from several Christmases ago, tastefully decorated with baby animals in endearing poses, because every time she started to write she went wrong and had to cross it out and start again. She only had two cards left before she realised that the thing to do was to write out what she wanted to say on a piece of paper, and then copy it out, in her best writing, on to the picture of the kitten with a bow round its neck, peeping out of a basket of blue roses. Eventually, she came up with:

Dear Fergus, I am just writing to tell you that I passed my driving test and to thank you for all your help in this matter.

It wasn't perfect, the picture would probably make him sick, but it was OK. What she would have said, if she'd been able to admit it to herself, was that she missed him and would have liked to give him a nice meal as a thank you for all his time and trouble. It was the least she owed him. Eventually, she decided to invite him for one on the boat, when she'd settled into the routine.

'There you are, love. One van, safely delivered.'

It was pitch-dark and raining, and the man who was now dangling the keys, expecting her to take them, was wearing black leather motorbike gear. His friend had followed him on a Harley Davidson, the lights of which illuminated the scene.

'Thank you.' Julia took the keys as if they were dangerous. Having car keys in her possession seemed too big a responsibility.

'There are some menus and stuff in that folder on the front seat. Now, I could run round the block with you, tell you the van's little ways' – Julia opened her mouth to take him up on this offer – 'but it's not really necessary. She goes really well. The only thing is the fuel gauge. It says it's half empty the minute it's not full, so you've got to keep a note of the mileage. So, no probs then?'

Realising she had nothing to gain by declaring that she'd only just passed her test, it was dark and raining and she was pregnant, she said, 'No. It's fine. I'll be all right, thank you. You go now. Are you the boatman?'

He nodded. 'Yeah. I'll be there when you start. Tuesday evening, isn't it?'

'That's right.'

'I'll see you then, then.' He gave her a cheery waggle of his fingers and flung himself across the saddle of the Harley. His friend hurled a few hundred decibels and a large quantity of fossil fuel into the air, and they roared away.

Julia regarded her new responsibility. The yellow sodium streetlight didn't allow her to tell what colour it was, but she could see it was painted in traditional narrow-boat style, with sweeping serpentine lettering and a few garlands of roses and daisies around the name. It was a shame that it said, *La Barge Baguette* on it instead of *Pyramus*, but that couldn't be helped.

She jangled the keys in her hands. She had heard the words. 'Where are my car keys?' so often. Now she would say it. She would have to keep them hanging on a special hook, so she wouldn't lose them.

A bubble of excitement pushed past her anxiety. She had learned to drive, now, via a bit of cooking on a restaurant boat, she was going to earn lots of money.

Julia considered her options. She could take the menus and the other bits of information about how to do it from the van, and study them inside. Or she could do what she half dreaded, and half longed to do, which was to get in the van and drive it. The baby moved encouragingly. It seemed to be telling her to stop being a coward. Julia checked that she had her house keys and the door was shut, got into the van and tentatively inserted the ignition key.

She moved the seat forward, stretched the seatbelt over her bump, fiddled with the mirrors, then she switched on.

At first she couldn't believe she was allowed to drive on her own. And the van was very different from the two cars she had driven previously, but after a few minutes it started to feel more familiar. A feeling of achievement soothed her aching back and calmed her anxiety about cooking again after a couple of months away from it. She could drive; she was a proper, grown-up person. She had Life Skills.

Julia had arranged to meet Suzy on the boat and it was lovely to see her again. Suzy had a new haircut, very short and chic, and was looking prettier than ever. She hugged Julia.

'It's just like old times! Except I can't believe how big you are! This is so exciting! You will let me be a godmother, won't you? I'm longing to give it unsuitable presents and take it to films that are too old for it.'

Julia hugged her back. 'Of course. I wouldn't have anyone else. It's such fun to be back on *Pyramus* again, working together.' Julia pushed her way through to the galley and looked about her.

'It is a bit of a mess,' said Suzy. 'I tried to have a go at it, but you know, I'm pony at cleaning.' She said the word 'pony' with a slightly self-conscious air.

'You're what?'

'Pony. It's rhyming slang. Wayne picked it up at college.' Julia was still looking bemused. 'Pony and trap . . .?'

'Oh yes,' said Julia. 'I see. So how is Wayne getting on?'

'He said the course was pony at first, and wanted to leave, but I told him it would get better soon, and I was right.'

Julia smiled. 'So you're quite a mother to him, then?'

'Not at all. Just wifely, or partnerly, whatever it is. Speaking of which, how's Fergus?'

Realising this was a conversation which wouldn't go away, Julia sighed. 'OK. I'll tell you all the gory details if we clean while we talk. We've got our first booking tomorrow, you know.'

'Of course I know! I arranged it!'

They were still a team. By the time the guests arrived the following evening, the boat was looking fit for a visit from the Health Inspector or Oscar's mother. And the smells from the galley would have seduced anyone away from their diet.

Julia had read all the menus, adjusted them to make them personal, and had done a lot of the cooking at home, where she had more space and more mod cons (Suzy having presented her with a food-processor in lieu of knitting for the baby). She had made brandy-snap baskets; she'd marinated lamb; she'd spent hours making individual onion tartlets, cutting smoked salmon into squares, and all manner of other fun, fiddly things she would never have had time to do during the summer. She was surprised how much she enjoyed herself. Cooking dinner was fun when you hadn't previously cooked breakfast, lunch and tea, and cleaned eight cabins, and three pump-out toilets.

Moving around in the galley was harder. Unlike Julia, the galley hadn't got any wider since they'd last met, and it felt a great deal narrower. Her tummy, she discovered, kept getting wet in a way it never had before, possibly because she had to lean over to wash up, and she seemed not to realise just how far it extended. Her balance was not as good as it had been, and she found herself falling off her haunches on to the floor a few times while she got things out of the low cupboards.

But she was more than ready for the first set of guests, a pre-booked party of college types.

'Sod's law Fergus will be among this lot,' she said to Suzy as she saw the first couple of cars drive up.

'Well, will it matter? I thought you and he were perfectly amicable.'

'Well, sort of, and no, of course it won't *matter*, it's just if I prepare myself for him coming, he won't.' She peered out of the window, her hands round her face to block out the light. 'Oh my God, I'm sure that's his car, or one very like it.'

The guests all arrived punctually, and Julia's suspicions were right: Fergus was among them. The boat set off on its cruise. Quite what anyone thought they'd see in the wildlife and scenery line, Julia didn't know, but she had to admit that moving along in the darkness, with the lights of Oxford passing, added something to the evening.

Julia knew it was pointless trying to avoid Fergus, but she did it anyway. She kept her head down as she handed out the dishes, and she never looked over the stable door, although she longed to see if people were enjoying themselves. She contemplated getting off at a bridge-hole after she'd served the puddings, but decided that she wasn't as nimble as she had been, and it would be a long muddy walk down the tow-path to the van.

So, although in a way she was ready for him when he left his companions and came into the galley, she wasn't prepared for the rush of emotion the sight of him produced. She wiped her hair off her face to hide her sudden desire to fling herself into his arms.

'So, you're here,' he said.

'As you see. As planned. I wasn't expecting to see you. Although you must have known you were coming when I first told you about it.'

'I know you won't believe me, but I didn't know then. I just knew I was booked for dinner with colleagues. By the time I found out you weren't speaking to me.'

'So you didn't come to check up on me?'

'Of course not.' He looked affronted, as if he had never made stipulations about her preparations for motherhood, nor commented on her lack of life skills. 'You've got bigger,' he added.

'I expect I have.' Julia found herself examining his expression for signs of distaste. She couldn't see any, but then, with Fergus, you couldn't be sure. 'It's what happens.'

'I know. But I wasn't expecting to notice the change. It hasn't been that long, has it?'

'I'm not sure.' Actually, it had been a lifetime, but she would hardly admit it, even to herself.

Fergus made another stab at conversation. 'Thank you for telling me you passed your driving test.'

This was her opportunity to really thank him, but she never found thanking Fergus easy. 'I'm sorry it was such an awful card, but it was all I had . . . I couldn't have done it without you,' she added gruffly, her gaze fixed on his stomach. No sign of middle-aged spread or incipient fatherhood there, she noted.

'I'm sure you could have.'

'It would have taken lots longer.' She raised her eyes; she must look silly staring at his midriff. 'But as you see, I can drive now, and I'm really enjoying getting back into food again. When *La Barge Baguette* comes back into service, I've got lots of contacts for dinner-party cooking, and things like that.'

'What you're saying is that you and the baby will be fine, and you don't need me to help out?'

Julia's gaze slid away from the expression in his eyes. Even if she'd studied it, she never would have been able to tell what he was thinking, so she didn't give him the chance to observe how muddled her feelings were. 'That's about it. I can earn enough for both of us.'

'I see. Well, I won't take up any more of your time. I can see you're busy.'

'Frightfully. I've got all this washing-up to do.'

'I won't offer to help you with it.'

'No, don't. I couldn't possibly allow a paying passenger to wash up.'

'Right. Goodnight then, Julia.'

'Goodnight.' She turned away so he wouldn't see her cry.

The restaurant boat was closed on Christmas Day and Boxing Day. Julia was going to spend the time with her sister, who was also having her mother. Her brother and his family were coming over for Christmas lunch. Everyone was going over to his house for tea on Boxing Day. Julia was dreading it. She'd spoken to her brother only on the phone since becoming pregnant and she had never liked his wife, a thin, nervy woman who nagged her children continually.

It was lovely seeing her mother and sister though, and together they peeled potatoes and sprouts, designed a new stuffing, influenced by a dozen cookery books, and spiked the pudding with pound coins. That was the best part of Christmas for Julia, the rest just seemed hard work.

Her brother's children had eyed her stomach with awe, obviously warned not to mention it. Julia promptly asked them what they felt about having a new cousin, and would they like to feel it move? By the time Christmas Day was declared over, and they had piled back into Rupert's company car, Julia was aware that she was not number one in the eyes of her brother and sister-in-law, but had gone up a couple of notches with their children.

'You don't have to go home today,' said her sister, watching disapprovingly as Julia loaded her luggage into the van, the day after Boxing Day. 'Why not stay another night? It's still Christmas, really.'

'No, you need some time alone with your family.'

'I've got Mum, I might as well have you as well.'

'No. I want to get used to being alone on public holidays.' She was joking, but as she heard the words, she realised that it was true.

Her sister nearly wept. 'Never, while I live and breathe, will you spend Christmas on your own.'

'OK, OK, no need to make such a fuss. Now I must go and say goodbye to Mum.'

This farewell took a long time, although they would be together again as soon as the baby was born. Margot was coming to look after Julia when she came out of hospital.

'Now are you sure you don't want me there?' Margot said, for the umpteenth time.

'Quite sure. Angela's going to take me in and look after me. You can leap in the car as soon as she rings to say I've had it.'

The 'Are you sures?' went on for some time, but eventually, Julia got away.

'Dear little van,' she said, patting its dashboard. 'I do

love you. When I have to give you back, I must get myself another one.'

She had had a bath, put on the enormous red fleece dressing gown her mother had given her for Christmas (in spite of saying that the driving lessons were her present), lit a fire, and prepared for a cosy night in. She had planned to start reading the glacial-sounding novel which had been a present from her sister-in-law, accompanied by the Christmas Specials on television, when there was a knock on the door.

Julia thought twice about opening it. Who would be calling at this time of night, in the middle of the Christmas holidays? She put the chain on the door, and opened it gingerly. It was Fergus.

'Oh Julia, thank goodness you're here. I thought you might be a house-sitter, or a security device which turns the lights on and off.'

She fumbled at the door chain and got the door open. Fergus staggered in. He was soaking wet. 'What on earth's the matter?'

'One bloody thing after another! First, the flat above mine's pipes burst while we were both away. His flat's flooded and so is mine. He hasn't come back yet, but I got through the door to find everything soaked. I spent an absolute fortune on an emergency plumber who insisted on being paid in cash, but the place is still uninhabitable.' He paused.

'So?'

'I thought I'd inflict myself on some friends, but none of them are in. The only ones that are live miles away. And I ran out of petrol.'

'That's not like you, surely?'

'Don't rub it in. So I was walking to see if I could find a garage that was open, when I saw your lights on . . .'

'And?'

'I thought you might give me a drink.'

'Well I would, of course. But won't you be driving later?'

'Just put the kettle on.'

Disguising her pleasure, Julia reached up for his coat.

Chapter Twenty-four

Julia fluttered round him, boiling kettles, building up the fire, and turfing a pile of magazines about pregnancy off the rocking chair so he could use it as a footstool. It felt wonderful to be rescuing him, instead of the other way round.

But she wished she could go up and put on some make-up. Behaving like his mother was one thing, looking like her was another.

'I'd offer you a bath,' she said, feeling she should explain her extra red and shiny cheeks, 'only I've just had one and used most of the hot water.'

'Oh. A bath would have been brilliant. I've been staying with some friends who had a lot of other people there too. They didn't have a shower and baths were at a premium.'

'Well actually . . .' Was this the moment to confess that the bath water was still in the tub? One of the many advantages of living alone, in Julia's opinion, was not having to clean the bath the moment you got out of it or tidy your dirty clothes away. You could leave the washing-up until next morning too.

'What?'

'I haven't actually let it out. But you probably wouldn't want my dirty water anyway.'

'Oh yes I would. I don't expect it's really dirty.'

'But what would you change into? There's no point in having a bath if you've got to put wet clothes on afterwards.'

'Oh, I've got my suitcase in the car. Still unpacked.'

'But your car is quite far away, isn't it?'

'Not too far to sprint back to.'

In her turn, Julia sprinted – rather slowly – up to the bathroom to remove her used underwear, her soggy magazine, the candles which surrounded the bath (to make up for the otherwise harsh lighting) and generally make her bathroom respectable. While she did so, she was aware that something wasn't quite ringing true about Fergus's story. She wasn't quite sure what. It *had* been cold, people's pipes *did* burst, particularly when they were away and the heating was off. And people did run out of petrol. So why did she think he was lying? It was the last thing anyone would make up.

However, it was lovely to be able to repay some of Fergus's kindness. Having removed the less savoury trappings of femininity from the bathroom, she went downstairs to boil a kettle, in case the water wasn't hot enough. If it was, she could use it to make a hot toddy. Fergus drinking and driving was not her problem, and although she personally felt she couldn't eat a liqueur chocolate and drive, for all she knew a small amount of whisky in among a lot of hot water and lemon juice might not even touch the breathalyser.

Fergus was gone long enough to dispel Julia's doubts about his story. No one would walk for twenty minutes, two ways, in foul weather, unless they had a very good reason. When he finally did appear, he was wetter than ever. 'It's starting to snow. I don't suppose it'll amount to much, but it has got much colder.'

'Would you like a drink first, or a bath?'

'Bath, please.' He was shivering.

'I'll just add a kettleful of water to give it a boost. I've put a towel out for you.'

While he was in the bath, she decided to investigate the spare room. She hadn't actually invited him to stay, but she felt it was inevitable that she would. It was a foul night, and her chastity, or what remained of it, would hardly be threatened, after all. Only the most devoted and 'in-love' husband would fancy a woman who was not only the same size and shape as Father Christmas but wore the same clothes. And Fergus was neither her husband, nor in love.

She had forgotten how untidy the spare room was. She hadn't been able to face sorting it out since her dreadful discovery of the papers, and not only was the bed still covered with the cardboard boxes and plastic bags, but the floor was covered with sticky tape and scraps of paper covered with cheery robins and overweight snowmen.

'Do I really have to tackle this now?' she muttered under her breath. 'Would it be too cruel to send him out into the snow' – her heart gave a little skip at the thought that there was snow – 'and make him trudge for miles looking for a twenty-four-hour, three-hundred-and-sixty-five-day garage?'

She decided she couldn't let him get warm and dry and then make him get wet and cold again.

But although her spirit of goodwill was still strong, her energy had deserted her. She felt very tired and very pregnant. She forced herself to the airing cupboard to look for clean sheets and a duvet, but was further weakened by the unidentifiable heaps of bed linen which confronted her. She went back downstairs and decided she would try and avoid offering him a bed for the night. She could ask if he wanted to siphon some petrol out of the van. The trouble was, she wasn't sure how much was in there, owing to the vagaries of its fuel gauge.

She lay with her feet up on the sofa to get her strength back. There were still several weeks before the baby was due, but Julia was having twinges. She was sure they were Braxton Hicks contractions, nothing to worry about, just the body preparing itself for the ordeal ahead, but when Fergus reappeared in the sitting room, she didn't get up.

'Are you all right?' he demanded instantly.

'Fine, just a bit tired.' Mention any form of contractions to Fergus and he would squash her into the van and carry her off to hospital. There would then follow a lengthy enrolment process, involving a hundred forms, blood pressure tests and intimate examinations, which would result in her being sent home for another month. 'How are you?'

'That was a wonderful bath. I hope no one notices if I smell of jasmine bath-oil.'

'It was a present from my sister. I really like it.'

'Oh so do I, but not so much on me.' He smiled. 'Can I get you something?'

'No. You're the guest. I should get you things.' Julia tried to stir, but her limbs didn't receive the message sent by her brain. She felt welded to the sofa. 'I'll get up in a minute. Do you need to stay the night? Or I could lend you some money, or even give you some petrol, then you could go on to your friends.'

'Money isn't a problem, I've got my credit card, but I don't really want to go back out there. I might have to walk miles to find a garage that's open. And doesn't your van use diesel?'

'Oh. Yes. It does. I haven't actually put the wrong stuff in yet, but I always think of it as petrol.' There was no alternative then. She would have to keep him. Just then, a particularly vicious gust of wind rattled against the window.

'Do you feel awkward about me staying?'

She shook her head. 'Not awkward; lazy. The spare room is a tip and I can't bear the thought of clearing it.'

The anxiety left his expression. 'Well, if that's all, I can easily do what needs doing. I only need a bed, not an empty chest of drawers, or a wardrobe.'

Julia smiled in relief. 'My mother says a lady always unpacks, and gets very indignant when she hasn't anything to unpack into. I never take anything out of my case in case I leave it behind.'

'Well, don't worry about me. It's very kind of you to take me in. If you point me in the right direction, I'm quite capable of climbing into a sleeping bag or something.'

Julia shook her head. 'No sleeping bag, I'm afraid, but I do have plenty of bedding, it's just it's in the linen cupboard which is in chaos at the moment.' It always was, but no need to tell him that. 'Having someone else living here disrupted my storage space.' That at least was true.

'I'm sure I can manage. You just stay here while I sort it out, and then I'll make you a nice drink.'

Julia's instincts of hospitality were appalled by this suggestion. Her body was delighted. 'And I'll make you a sandwich,' she countered, not wanting to be outdone.

She'd actually dozed off, and woke up, momentarily surprised to see him. 'Oh, it's you. Did you find everything you need?'

'Yup. But right now, I need to sit next to you. Shove up.'

'I was going to make you a sandwich.'

'Not hungry. Unless you are?'

Julia shook her head and shifted along the sofa. Somehow, she found herself lying along the sofa with her feet on a cushion and her head on Fergus's chest. It was blissfully comfortable.

'Now, where's the remote?' said Fergus. 'There's quite a good film on about now.'

He pressed buttons on the remote control until he found the film. It was one she'd looked forward to seeing herself, one of the reasons, in fact, she had decided to leave her sister's house today, rather than spending another night, so she could watch the film in peace, without the ribald comments of her brother-in-law. The opening credits went up. She slept.

'Come on, up to bed now.' Julia felt herself being heaved from behind. 'I've made you a hot-water bottle. All you have to do is brush your teeth and go to bed.'

'I brushed my teeth when I had a bath, and I haven't eaten anything since. In fact,' she frowned, 'I'm starving!'

'What do you want?'

'Cheese sandwiches and a glass of milk. Please.'

'In bed then. Come on.'

While she'd been asleep, there'd been a velvet revolution: Julia had been deposed from her role of carer and was now the cared-for. She hauled herself up the stairs and got into bed. While she adjusted her pillows, a task which took a long time, she wondered how she felt about it. Grateful, was her conclusion, when, after she was tucked up in bed, Fergus brought her a plate of sandwiches and some milk.

'Now all you need to do is read me a story,' she said, smiling at him over the mug of milk.

'OK then. What are you reading? This?' He picked up the glacial novel which she'd tidied away earlier. 'Appropriate, as it's snowing. Snuggle down, then.'

'Fergus, I was joking!'

'Well, I wasn't. Now shut up and listen. I won't be offended if you go to sleep.'

Which was just as well.

Julia awoke to hear movement in the kitchen. Fergus was up before her, damn! Falling asleep to the sound of his voice – he did read aloud well – was a great show of weakness, allowable only because of her condition. But still to be in bed when her guest was up and about was unforgivable. She got out of bed and eyed her dressing gown, lying temptingly on the chair. She ignored its siren call. She didn't want to remain a Father Christmas figure for ever in Fergus's mind. She put on the velvet leggings and overshirt which constituted her best maternity clothes, brushed her hair and did her face carefully. Last night she'd been a lump who had to be waited on. This morning she would be a dynamic young woman in charge of her destiny – her stomach tightened for a few moments – who happened to be pregnant. She went downstairs, wondering what on earth she could cook him for breakfast.

He had lit the fire. 'Oh! Good morning!' she said, surprised to see the fireplace full of crackling flames.

'I hope you don't mind, but it's snowy outside and it's Christmas.' He looked sheepish for a moment in his enormous and slightly misshapen sweater covered with reindeer which might just as well have had 'Christmas present' knitted into the pattern. Then he noticed her outfit. 'What are you doing dressed? I was going to bring you breakfast in bed!'

'I was going to say exactly the same thing,' Julia bent the truth slightly. 'You're the guest, after all.'

'But I'm not Oscar's mother. I don't need breakfast in bed.'

'Nor am I.'

They both laughed.

'Oh look!' said Fergus suddenly, glancing down. 'I saw it move, the baby!'

Julia looked down at the now familiar, but always wonderful, evidence of her baby's health and strength. They both spent several moments watching the outline of a tiny hand or foot moving inside Julia's stomach. 'May I?' Fergus asked. Then he put his hand on the place.

It was an awkward situation. It was his baby, after all, presumably he had a right to feel it move, but it was in her stomach, and in order to feel it, he had to feel her too. Julia felt herself blush. Somehow this was too intimate. Even over her clothes, his hand on her body had a disturbing effect.

'Shall I make breakfast?' she said, when she could endure it no longer.

'What's wrong? Are you in pain?'

'No, I'm fine. I'm just hungry, that's all.' She tried a grin;

it came out a sort of lopsided smirk.

'That's not it, is it?'

There was concern in his eyes, but any minute it would turn to frustration. Julia could sympathise, it was annoying when people were obviously upset and wouldn't say why. But how could she possibly tell him? 'I just feel a bit awkward about you touching me.'

He stepped back, stung. 'I'm sorry. I didn't mean to offend you. I was just so excited about feeling the baby move, that's all.'

'Oh I know. I didn't read anything into it, I promise.' Julia felt near to tears. It was all such a muddle.

'Well perhaps you should have done. I'm by no means indifferent to you as a woman. Being pregnant doesn't make you asexual, you know.'

This was not what she wanted to hear, although it should have been: she'd gone to considerable trouble with her appearance. And being pregnant didn't stop her sexual feelings, either.

'I still want you,' he went on. 'But as you obviously don't –' He stopped. Julia had started to cry. Tears were welling at the corners of her eyes and pouring down her cheeks, making her face wet and cold. 'Oh Julia!' he said crossly, and suddenly Julia found herself enveloped in the home-made sweater, and the next second, Fergus's lips were on hers.

All her mixed-up feelings were polarised into that kiss. Wild plans of asking him to marry her, taking her chance that he'd love her as well as the baby, whirled round in her head like the stars and black dots which warn you that you are going to faint. For a few moments, she forgot the baby, forgot everything and just melted into the sensation. But the baby moved again, he felt it, and he pulled away. 'I'm sorry,' he said. 'I shouldn't have done that. It's taking unfair advantage.'

'That's all right,' said Julia, aware she must have been

far more deeply involved in the kiss than he had been. 'Build up the fire and I'll go and make some toast.'

Fergus did as he was told but joined her in the kitchen. 'I do wish you'd tell me what the matter is. I'm not psychic but I can tell you're upset.'

'I'm fine, really. When you're pregnant, your hormones go up the shoot. It makes you burst into tears when you're not remotely sad.'

'Is that why you didn't want me to touch you? Because of your hormones?'

'I don't know, really. Why did you kiss me?'

He frowned. 'Because I'm human and you were crying. That, and the fact that you're an attractive woman. Pregnancy suits you. But I really didn't mean to offend you.'

'That's all right. I'm not offended.' Heartbroken, desolate, and unspeakably depressed maybe, but not offended. She smiled weakly. 'Do you like tea or coffee?'

'I take it you're still off coffee?' Touched that he'd remembered, she nodded. 'Then I like tea.'

They ate breakfast in front of the fire, and as they chatted, Julia began to feel less tense. But her reasons for not wanting him to marry her still remained. He wanted the baby more than he wanted her, and second place was nowhere. Equal first was the least she'd settle for.

'More toast?' she asked.

'Yes please. I'm surprised you still have time to make your own bread.'

'I do it while I'm doing other cooking. As long as you're there anyway, it doesn't take up much time.'

'But I don't suppose you'll be able to do it after the baby comes.'

'No, I don't suppose I will.'

'Julia, are you absolutely sure you don't want us to get married?'

'Yes.'

'Why?'

'You know why. I really don't want to go over it all again.'

'And you haven't changed your mind?'

'No. Why should I have?'

'I just thought this time together might prove to you that our marriage would have as good a chance as anyone's.'

'What do you mean: "this time together"? Didn't your pipes burst and your car run out of petrol?'

'Yes of course,' he said quickly, examining his finger-nails. 'But I did just wonder if, having spent time together and I think, enjoyed each other's company, you wouldn't reconsider?'

Of course Julia had enjoyed his company; even when he was driving her mad she'd rather be with him than anyone else. Of course she knew that the best marriages consisted of the sort of cosy companionship they had enjoyed last night. But unreasonable or not, she wanted passion as well. At least to begin with, even if it couldn't last for ever.

He insisted on washing up. He also insisted on putting all the bags and boxes up in the loft for her, and doing all sorts of other jobs about the house. All of which, she insisted, she was perfectly capable of doing herself.

'I know you can do them yourself,' he argued. 'But I want to prove to you that I can do them too.'

She chuckled. 'But that's silly, doing jobs just to prove a point!'

'Yes it is, but it's amazing what silly things people do, just to prove a point.'

'Isn't it? Now, I think we ought to get you some more petrol, before it gets too late.'

Fergus regarded her steadily for several unnerving seconds. 'I think I'm being thrown out.'

Julia was appalled. 'Of course not! I may not be very like her, but I am my mother's daughter! I would never throw a guest out!'

'Not even one who invited himself under rather dubious circumstances?'

'Not even one of those. Now get your coat on and I'll show you how well I drive these days.'

Thanks to Fergus's straightforward attitude, they spent the rest of the morning together without awkwardness. But because she wasn't entirely convinced by Fergus's tale of running out of petrol, she avoided being around to see him pour the can they had bought into the tank, in case it overflowed.

He came back into the house to wash his hands. 'I'm going to make sure you have plenty of logs cut before I go. It's what I'd do if I was staying with your mother, after all.'

For some reason she couldn't explain she didn't tell him she ran the fire mostly on coal these days, the logs were just for a nice blaze, so she didn't need any chopping done. She was rewarded for her duplicity by the sight of him talking to her neighbours over the fence. She watched with tenderness touched with dismay as he went into their garden and start chopping logs for them too.

'Well, you've certainly paid for your board and lodging,' she said, when he came in, looking incredibly healthy, not to say attractive, after so much exercise. 'Next time your flat floods, you can stay with Daisy and Dan. They'd take you in like a shot.'

'Sweet as they are, I really wouldn't want to stay with Daisy and Dan if you were next door.'

'Oh?'

'No. Now, goodbye, Julia. You won't forget to tell me when you go into labour, will you?'

'I don't want you at the birth, Fergus.'

'I still want to know, so I can pace around.'

'I will tell you when we – when I've had the baby, I promise.'

'I know, but I want to know when you're having it.'

'If I've time, I promise I'll let you know.'

'I suppose I have to be satisfied with that.'

She nodded.

Looking far from satisfied, he kissed her hard on the mouth, got into his car, now parked in front of the cottage, and drove away.

Julia felt she had blown her last chance of happiness, but knew it was her only choice.

Chapter Twenty-five

Julia had to work very hard at not being depressed in the days after Fergus left her, even though she was sure she was doing the right thing by not marrying him. Her sister had been unequivocal on the subject over Christmas, despite having been instructed by their mother to try and change Julia's mind.

'There's no getting away from it. Having a baby puts a terrible strain on a marriage, even a really happy one. It's not that Andrew and I didn't both dote on the babies one hundred per cent, but when you're neither of you getting a good night's sleep, ever, you do get scratchy. And as for sex' – she gave a hollow laugh – 'any time spent in bed not sleeping just seems a wicked waste. Don't get married for the sake of the baby.'

The restaurant was re-opening the following night, and she had earning a living to think about. At least she didn't want to marry Fergus so she wouldn't have to work.

The mirage of domestic bliss firmly banished from her mind, Julia concentrated on food: anything that didn't include fowl or dried fruit was her choice for those dreary days after New Year. Shopping, and using her new food-processor, exploiting all its sophisticated gadgetry, cheered her somewhat, as did a call from Suzy telling her that as Wayne was still at home with his parents in Tewkesbury, she would be on the boat the following night.

'We can have a post-Christmas therapy session: "How was it for you?"' she added. 'Although mine was better than it could have been. I missed Wayne terribly, but he came to stay the day after Boxing Day.'

'How did he get on with your father?'

'Terribly. He was perfectly nice and Mummy thought he was lovely, but Dad, well, Dad was Dad, terribly Alpha Male and territorial. Wayne only stayed one night. I expect Daddy will come round in the end.'

Julia thought what Suzy meant was that she expected she could twist her father round her little finger in the end.

It was good to get back to work, where she knew how she felt and what she was doing. The galley seemed to have got awfully dusty since she'd left it, but, with an energy she hadn't had for a long time, she wiped every surface. She set the table just so, and redid all the decorations so they didn't look jaded and post-Christmas like the rest of the world.

She did feel a bit tired, having done all that, and wondered if she ought to ask Suzy to lift the big china dish covered in foil into the oven for her. But Suzy was sluicing down the outside of the boat.

As she straightened up, Julia resolved she *would* call Suzy when it was time to take the dish out. The Braxton Hicks contractions which were now so much part of her life seemed to require pauses to deal with them, when before she had carried on with what she was doing. A little flutter of excitement made her bite her lip. Could this be the moment she had been waiting for for so long? But then sense prevailed. There were weeks still before the baby was actually due, and as everyone told her that first babies are always late, she couldn't allow herself to get excited.

Any excitement which may have been lurking was swept away by the sight of Mrs Anstruther, Oscar's mother, climbing daintily on board on the arm of a silver-haired charmer who looked, to Julia, like a crook.

'I have been on this boat before, you know, Arnold. Dear Oscar – he means so well – was involved with a frightful woman. We had the most ghastly . . .' Julia removed herself before she could be seen. Suzy would have to cope with this dilemma on her own.

Suzy thought differently. 'It's Mrs Anstruther! What's she doing here? I can't deal with her. You'll have to.'

'I'm cooking, Suze, and I'm pregnant. And it's your fault she's here. You arranged the booking.'

'They call themselves the Antiques Club! I thought it was a club for people who *collected* them.'

'Well, she's with a man who I'm sure is after her money. Perhaps you could ring Oscar and warn him his inheritance is about to be blown. He might come and take his mother away.'

'I doubt it. Don't you worry about it, Julia. I'll handle this completely on my own and let you hide in here in the kitchen –'

'Doing the cooking, having a baby . . .'

'What?'

'I mean – soon.'

'Oh that's all right. I thought you meant you were in labour!'

Julia managed a merry laugh.

In spite of trying to hide in the kitchen, Julia did come face to face with Mrs Anstruther. The look of horror on Mrs Anstruther's face almost made up for all the anxiety and discomfort Julia had suffered during her pregnancy.

'And did you hear what she said?' demanded Suzy, who had just served the starters. '"How can she let herself be seen in that condition?" Then she went quiet! She must have suddenly wondered if it was Oscar's!'

The meal was eaten and thoroughly enjoyed by most of the guests, the washing-up was under way, and Julia was putting coffee cups on to a tray when water started seeping down her legs. At first she thought the battle against incontinence had finally been lost, but then she realised that her waters had broken. Suddenly, having a baby just then didn't seem such a good idea. She'd really rather wait until February, when she had nothing else much planned. She went to the loo to sort herself out and have a little think.

They were fifteen minutes away from the mooring, and it would mean a long trot down a muddy tow-path to get to civilisation, but she knew she should contact her midwife, or go into hospital immediately, in case of infection. But she couldn't believe an hour or two would make a huge difference. Surely there was time to run home and get her things? Having decided not to say anything to Suzy but just go home quickly, she came out of the loo, and had a contraction which made her gasp. Suzy noticed.

'Are you all right?' she demanded sharply.

Julia shook her head. 'Not really,' she said after a moment's heavy breathing. 'My waters have broken and I think the contractions have started.'

Suzy gave a little scream of fright and then her organisational skills kicked in. 'Right, well, you should go to hospital immediately. Handy that you're already in Oxford, so you won't waste any time. I'll call an ambulance the minute we tie up.'

Julia shook her head. 'Hang on, Suzy. The baby won't come for hours and hours, and if I go into hospital now, I'll get bored out of my skull. They'll put me in a gown that doesn't do up at the back and I won't be able to move.'

'Why will they do that?'

'Because, sweetheart' – Julia withheld a sharper epithet – 'I happen to be dressed for work and I'm not giving birth in my best silk shirt! But at home, I've got two bags packed, one for me, and one for the baby, and my one has got a secret package of goodies in it that my sister gave me for Christmas. It's to keep me going during labour. She wouldn't let me open it before. I really don't want to go into hospital without it.'

316

'Your sister's going to be with you for the birth, isn't she?' demanded Suzy.

Julia nodded. 'Then ring her and get her to bring your stuff. Your neighbours have got a key, haven't they?'

'Well, yes, but really, I don't want to go to hospital on my own and be there for hours with nothing to do and nothing happening.'

'But something *is* happening.'

'Yes, but labour pains aren't very entertaining. I need jolly company.'

'I could come with you.'

This was a kind offer, but Julia could see it was one Suzy didn't want taken up. 'No, really. You've got enough to do here and it's not necessary. I've got plenty of time to go home, get my stuff, ring my sister and wait for her to bring me in. Honestly. Everyone I've spoken to in the last month has told me that all first babies are late, and they all take hours to be born.'

'But your first baby isn't being late, it's being early,' Suzy pointed out. 'It may not take hours to be born, either. Ring your sister on the mobile.'

'Honestly, I've heard so many stories of twenty-four-hour labours . . .'

Suzy thrust the phone in Julia's face. 'Ring her!'

'Oh, Ju!' Her sister sounded distraught. 'It's you. I'm afraid I can't chat right now. Andrew's out and Petal's ill, I'm waiting for the doctor.' There was a pause. 'I really hope you're not ringing because you've started. You haven't, have you? It's not due for ages!'

'Well . . .'

'Oh my goodness. Would you believe it?'

'Is Petal really ill?'

'It's probably just a "sponge her down, give her Calpol and ring in the morning if she's not better" job. But there's been a lot of meningitis about lately, and I can't leave her with my neighbour when she's like this.'

317

'No, of course not. I was just ringing for a chat anyway,' said Julia, trying to sound nonchalant. 'But I won't keep you.'

'You're in labour, aren't you? Come on, admit it!'

'Possibly.'

'What do you mean possibly? What signs have you had?'

'My waters have broken and I think . . .' There was a longish pause while Julia breathed very carefully. 'My contractions have started.'

'Hell! Why does bloody Andrew have to be out? He's not going to be long but, by the sounds of it, you shouldn't wait for me to get to hospital. Get an ambulance.'

'I'm on the boat.'

'Still get an ambulance. I'll pick up your stuff and bring it in as soon as the doctor's been and Andrew's back. There'll probably still be lots of time.' She softened her tone. 'I won't let you have it on your own, I promise.'

'It's not that I'm worried about. It's being there for hours and hours with nothing to read in a hospital gown. I want my own things, Ange.'

'I know how you feel. It's silly, but I felt just the same. Don't worry, I'll make sure you get them.'

'So is your sister coming?' asked Suzy.

'Not immediately. Her baby's ill and her husband's not there.'

'You're not going to like this, but I've made arrangements.'

'What!'

'I mentioned to Mrs Anstruther, very tactfully, of course, that you were in labour.'

This news brought on a strong contraction.

'And after she'd nearly fainted, her partner said that Oscar was coming to pick them up. He'll take you to hospital. One of the other women says ambulances take ages and they might not be able to find us.'

'Have you told *all* the passengers that I'm in here, having a baby?'

'Had to, honey, what else could I do? They're all very excited about it.'

'Well, *you* can tell Oscar he's got to take his ex-fiancée to hospital to have another man's baby.'

'He'll be fine about it, Ju! No man objects to being the hero of the hour!'

Now her secret was out, the members of the Antiques Club, with the exception of Mrs Anstruther, insisted that Julia come and sit in the dining area with them. It was not exactly what she would have chosen, sitting making polite conversation with strangers in between contractions, but it helped to pass the time.

Soon they docked. Most of the passengers disembarked and, eventually, Oscar arrived. Julia retreated behind the stable doors, hiding her pregnant bit.

'Evening, everyone,' said Oscar jovially. 'Sorry I'm late.'

'Oscar!' Mrs Anstruther was on the verge of hysterics. 'Thank God you're here. That Woman' – she pointed at Julia with a trembling finger which should have had ice crystals issuing from it – 'is having a baby. Right here! Now! And they want *you* to take her to hospital! It's an outrage!'

'Oh! Julia! Is this true?'

'Well, no,' Julia began. 'I mean, I am having a baby, but an ambulance would be fine . . .'

'And it's not even your child! How dare she expect you to pick up the pieces for her like this!'

'I don't really,' Julia protested. 'I can easily call an ambulance.'

'Nonsense,' broke in Suzy. 'You know what that woman said. You could have had the baby by the time the ambulance finds us.'

'I think I can decide what I want to do,' said Oscar, unwilling, as Suzy had predicted, to let slip an opportunity to be a hero. 'I shall certainly take Julia to the hospital. You, Mother, can call a cab!'

'Oscar! Your first duty is to me! Not that . . . har –'

'Mother! How dare you speak about Julia like that! Ring for a taxi and get – get –'

'Arnold,' provided Mrs Anstruther's escort.

'Arnold to take you home. My duty is to Julia!'

'How can you say that after the way she treated you? She left you heartbroken! And obviously lost no time in finding another man to take your place! Wasn't it her fault you lost your best golfing partner? Because she stole some papers or something?'

'Really, everyone. Please don't fight. Just ring an ambulance,' pleaded Julia. The prospect of giving birth in one no longer seemed such a terrible idea.

'Nonsense!' Oscar turned to Julia. 'If that other bastard has let you down, I would consider it a privilege to take you to hospital.'

Another contraction prevented Julia from protesting at this defamation of Fergus. Mrs Anstruther was in shock from hearing her son use language like that in her presence, and Arnold, Mrs Anstruther's escort, was getting agitated.

'If there's likely to be blood,' he said, 'I'd rather not be here. I'm very happy to take your mother home,' he said to Oscar, not looking convinced, 'but it will have to be soon.'

'I've rung a cab,' said Suzy. 'They'll probably be here before the ambulance, which I've also rung.'

'You shouldn't have done that!' said Oscar. 'I've said I'll take her!'

'Well, if the cab comes first,' said Julia, 'I could have that. Mrs Anstruther and – er –'

'Arnold,' said Arnold.

'Could have the ambulance.'

'This is no time for flippancy!' declared Oscar. 'Cancel the ambulance immediately!'

'I wasn't being flippant,' protested Julia to Suzy. 'I meant it!'

'Right!' said Suzy. 'Julia, Oscar, into the car. Mrs Anstruther, Arnold, sit there and wait for the cab! And have a brandy while you're doing it,' she added, less fiercely.

Oscar took hold of Julia's elbow and, as he hindered her progress off the boat, Julia heard his mother say, 'Frightfully common, this practise of saying "*a* brandy" or "*a* coffee" when they should just say "some"!'

'I do hope Suzy isn't expecting any further business from your mother,' said Julia, on dry land at last. 'Because, somehow, I don't think she's doing to get it.'

'I'm afraid m'mother overreacted, somewhat. She's a bit squeamish about anything medical.'

'Can't say I blame her,' said Julia, after panting her way through a strong contraction. 'I've gone right off the idea of childbirth myself.'

'If you just drop me here, the nurses will look after me from now on,' she said as the car drew up at the entrance to the hospital. 'They won't let you park here, anyway.'

'Don't worry, my dear. I'm here to look after you now. I'm not going to desert you in your hour of need.'

'Oh, don't overdramatise, Oscar! It's not "my hour of need". You don't have to come in with me.' She hadn't had a contraction for a while and now it seemed terribly melodramatic to have been rushed to hospital like this.

Oscar was about the argue when he saw a notice saying 'Wheel Clamps in Operation'. 'I'll be with you as soon as I've parked the car. If there is anywhere to damn well park it.'

It obviously took him some time to find a car-park, because Julia had nearly completed her explanations at the desk when she heard a commotion at her back. She turned round to see Oscar and Fergus confronting each other, both inside the revolving doors. There were a few farcical moments while they both tried to get into the building first. Fergus won.

'Julia! Are you all right?' he demanded, forgetting in his anxiety that they were in a hospital.

'What's it to do with you?' stormed Oscar. 'Where were you when she needed you?'

'I happen to be the father of the child!' announced Fergus to the woman who was trying to take down Julia's particulars – and to anyone else who happened to be in the lobby.

'If you'd married her you might have the right to say that!' Oscar went on, joining them at the desk. 'As it is, you're no better than a tom cat! I'm taking care of Julia now!'

There was a muffled roar from Fergus and Julia turned round just in time to see Fergus draw back his arm and land a punch on Oscar's jutting chin.

As if in slow motion, she saw Oscar lose his balance, his arms whirling, and topple on to the floor.

'Gentlemen!' said the receptionist. 'If you're going to fight, you can do it outside, or I'll call the police!'

'Sorry!' Abashed, Fergus saw the sprawling Oscar. 'Here, let me give you a hand up.'

Oscar took hold of Fergus's arm, but instead of helping himself up with it, he pulled hard, trying to bring Fergus to join him on the floor. Julia shut her eyes and took refuge in a contraction. She did a lot of audible panting, hoo-hooing through pursed lips, partly to ease the pain, but mostly to give everyone the impression that she was about to have the baby at that very moment, so that Fergus and Oscar would come to their senses. They were both looking decidedly shame-faced when she opened her eyes again.

'I have never been so embarrassed in my life!' she said. 'Now go home both of you, before you get thrown out!'

'I'm not leaving you with that man,' said Oscar, nursing

his chin and giving said man a wide berth.

'And I'm the father. I've got every right to be here,' growled Fergus.

Julia appealed to the receptionist. '*Could* you have them thrown out? They're both mad. I don't want either of them near me.'

'Well, I could, but it might take some time. We don't often have a call for security guards in Maternity.'

'It's all right!' Oscar decided that honour was satisfied. 'There's no need for any of that. But if you need me, Julia, I'll stay.'

Julia shook her head. 'You wouldn't like it. You go home and put some arnica on that jaw.'

Oscar had almost decided to go, but then saw how entrenched Fergus was, and changed his mind. 'What about him? Is he going?'

'Of course he is! I've said I don't want either of you here. Oh –'

'I've brought you some things,' said Fergus calmly, when Julia had finished panting. 'Suzy told me that you'd had to go to hospital without anything.'

'That's really kind, Fergus, I'm extremely grateful. But I don't want you to stay.'

Fergus scowled. 'I'll just help with the checking-in process,' he said to Oscar. 'After all, I came to the classes, I know the answers to a lot of the questions.'

'Actually, it was only one class,' muttered Julia, inaudibly.

But Oscar at last was ready to admit defeat, and fought his way back out of the revolving doors.

'Really, Fergus,' said Julia. 'I can manage this bit fine without you. There's no earthly need for you to stay.'

'I only said that to get rid of Oscar,' said Fergus. 'I've no intention of leaving.'

'Would you like a wheelchair, or can you walk?' asked the nurse. She produced a wheelchair.

Julia was tempted. It seemed awfully lazy, but it would mean she wouldn't have to keep stopping for contractions. She looked round for a burly porter to push it, but then realised it would be the slip of a nurse who had to do the work.

She dithered.

'Sit in the chair, I'll push,' said Fergus, reading her mind in that annoying way of his. He dumped a couple of carrier bags on her knee and set off.

With the nurse trotting along beside them, Julia didn't really feel she could send Fergus out of her life for ever, it would be so ungrateful.

'Where did you find a shop open at this time of night?' she asked, clutching the bags.

'The sales are still on. The big department stores are open really late.'

'Oh.' It was a funny thing about Fergus, she pondered (her mind veering away from thoughts of incipient pain), whenever he was there, she tried to send him away, and whenever he wasn't there, she wanted him desperately.

They went up in the lift and when the doors opened they were greeted by Lucasta.

'Julia! You're a bit early aren't you? How lucky! All my mums tell me the last few weeks are the worst. And you've got Fergus with you. How nice.'

'Lucasta! How lovely to see you!' Her midwife's glamorous figure lifted her spirits. She turned to Fergus. 'I won't need you now, Lucasta is here.'

'Only by chance. I was checking up on a baby I delivered yesterday.'

'But you will stay?' Julia knew the chances of getting Lucasta for the birth were one in five, but it would be too cruel if Lucasta were snatched away from her now.

'Of course. You two go into the labour ward and this nurse'll make you comfortable while I make some calls. See you in a bit.'

Fergus waited outside while the nurse helped Julia investigate the bags. In the first there was a cotton nightie – far too good to give birth in, Julia felt – a selection of paperback books, and an enormous bottle of Chanel No 19.

'Hmm. Weren't you given a list of what to bring? What's in the other bag?' The nurse sounded critical.

There were a pack of three babygrows, size nought to three months, some baby oil and a packet of terry nappies.

'Doesn't your husband have a clue about what you and baby need?'

'He's not my husband and I think he's done very well! He must have rushed round getting these things like a mad thing! I only went into labour an hour and a half ago!'

'You should have got your things ready before this,' the nurse persisted. 'Weren't you told to pack a bag for yourself and a bag for your baby?'

Julia was prevented from answering by another contraction, during which Lucasta came in. 'Mmm,' she said knowingly. 'Slip along to the bathroom and have a shower. We'll find you a hospital nightie, that one is far too glamorous for the moment, then I'll have a look.'

Clean, and without the nurse, Julia felt more relaxed when Lucasta examined her.

'Mmm,' she said again. 'Six centimetres dilated. You left it a bit late, didn't you?'

Julia shook her head through her panting. The pain was getting to the stage when she wondered if she should have something for it. But her sister had advised her to leave pain relief as long as possible, so she would feel the benefit when things were really tough.

'You'll be more comfortable if you stop lying down now I've examined you,' said Lucasta. 'I'll get Fergus in and he can support you if you want to walk about a bit.'

'I don't really want him here,' insisted Julia. 'He just turned up with some things. He punched Oscar. It was really most embarrassing. Besides, I feel I must get used to being a single parent right from the beginning. I don't want to start depending on him!'

'Keep him now he's here. He can make himself useful, and when you're in transition and you really want to lash out, you can do it to him and not me.'

'I don't want him around when I'm actually giving birth. We really don't know each other that well.'

Lucasta chuckled. 'I'll get him in now. He's probably getting anxious out there in the corridor.'

'Are you all right? Shouldn't you be in bed?' demanded Fergus when he saw Julia standing in the corner of the room, looking out of the window.

'I thought you knew about labour and childbirth.'

'I do,' he said, sounding hurt. 'I know all about it. But the films I watched mostly showed the bit when the mother's on her back yelling like mad.'

Julia smiled. 'There's a lot of wandering about and huffing before you get to that part. You will have gone long before.'

'No I won't. I'm going to stay until I know you and the baby are both safe.' Julia started to argue but was stopped by a very long contraction. 'And there's nothing you can do to stop me.' She looked at him balefully. 'Would you like me to rub your back?' he asked in a placatory way. 'I brought baby oil.'

'No!' she said, when she could speak again. 'I want you to go home. I don't want you here!'

'Why not? You'll need someone to hold your hand and tell you when to push.'

'My sister's coming. She's going to do all that.'

'All right. I'll stay until your sister gets here. What about that?'

'OK. But isn't there something you'd rather be doing? A film you're longing to see?' He shook his head. 'I'll tell you what,' she confided. 'I'd rather turn out the cupboard

326

under the stairs, just now.'

'Have you rung your sister?'

'From the boat. She was going to be a little delayed. One of her children is ill. Poor little Petal. I do hope she's not really ill.'

'If you could get to a phone, you could ring to find out. There's one just down the hall.'

'Good idea!' She slipped off the bed where she had been perching between contractions. 'I'll just see if I've got some change.' She rummaged fruitlessly in her purse until Fergus dug his hand in his pocket and produced a handful of coins. 'I'll just trot along and phone her.'

She had a contraction while trotting and so felt free to speak to Angela for two minutes. Angela was pleased to hear that Julia was safely in hospital. 'I'll be with you as soon as I can, but although Andrew's home and Petal's got some antibiotics, she's still crying.'

'I can hear. Poor little thing. Is she very ill?'

'The doctor doesn't think it's anything serious, just an ear infection. She should settle soon, and I'll be with you like a shot.'

Petal didn't sound at all as if she was going to settle soon. 'Listen, Ange. Don't bother to come. I'll be fine without you and I really wouldn't feel happy making you leave Petal at a time like this.'

Angela screamed. 'But, Ju! Talk about a time like this! I can't leave you alone! You need someone on your side, however good the midwives and stuff are.'

Julia took a deep breath. 'I'm not on my own. I've got Lucasta, who's lovely, not like a midwife at all. And Fergus is here.'

Angela screamed again. 'Fergus? How on earth? Did you tell him?'

'No. Suzy did. He brought me a nightie and stuff, so I'll let him stay until things really get going. Then I'll be fine with Lucasta, she's really great. So don't you worry about me, just make sure you're there when I ring to say what I've had.'

'Well, if you're sure, Julia . . . Julia? Are you all right?'

Panting hard, Julia had hung up.

Chapter Twenty-six

꒰ঌ❀໒꒱

'I think I need the gas and air, now,' Julia gasped.

What seemed like hours had passed. Somehow she had never got round to sending Fergus away – fortunately, because, man-like, he had been unable to resist technology and so had listened to Lucasta's instructions, and thoroughly checked out the gas and air machine. He hadn't gone so far as to have a whiff of it himself, but now she had asked for it, he knew exactly what to do.

'If this isn't enough, you must say. It isn't a competition for how much pain you can endure.' He sounded as if he was quoting from a childbirth magazine.

'It's all right. At the moment I feel if I just concentrate on the pain as if it's something I'm doing, rather than something that's happening to me, I'll be all right.' There was a long, pain-filled pause. 'But it does depend on how long all this goes on for.'

Several more hours seemed to pass, although Fergus, when applied to, in between reading her novel to her and rubbing her back, said that they hadn't.

'You're fully dilated now,' said Lucasta, after the next inspection. 'You'll be ready to push soon.'

Julia felt she'd been in a dream, a warm, pain-filled world where only she and Fergus and the coming baby existed. Time moved very slowly, but she wasn't bored. Now a sense of urgency entered the room, along with another midwife, and equipment she didn't have time or inclination to look at. Knowing the baby, which had been decades arriving, was nearly there was exciting; the thought that the pain, which was getting beyond her control, was nearly over was a heartfelt relief.

'I think I need something stronger for the pain now,' she breathed, when she could.

'I'm afraid you've left it a bit late. Nothing you have now will have time to work,' said Lucasta.

'But that's ridiculous!' said Fergus angrily. 'She's in pain, damn it! She's been through all this without anything stronger than gas and air, and now you say it's too late!'

'There's really no point in giving her anything now. The baby will be born before it has time to take effect,' Lucasta explained patiently. 'And anything she took now would cross the placenta. You wouldn't want that, would you?'

'I want what's best for Julia!'

'Really, Fergus, I don't need you to run interference for me! If Lucasta says I'm managing, I'm managing!' snapped Julia. 'What are you doing here anyway? I said I didn't want you here for the birth!'

'She's also in transition,' said Lucasta to Fergus. 'Hell hath no fury etc., so don't you dare leave. Time to start pushing.'

A part of Julia decided it was like a tug of war – a team effort, with lots of shouting from the crowd. Intellectually she knew she was the only one actually pushing the baby out, but Fergus and Lucasta were working just as hard.

'Come on, darling, you're doing so well! I'm so proud of you!' said Fergus.

Julia had one foot against his chest, and the other against Lucasta. They leaned in towards her and she pushed back against them. She was aware of not wanting to push so hard against Lucasta, who, she noted, looked as *soignée* as ever, even in her uniform. Fergus looked strong enough to withstand an oak-tree being rammed into him.

'I don't want an episiotomy,' said Julia. 'I don't want to be cut.'

330

'No reason for you to have one,' said Lucasta calmly. 'Even if you do tear a little, it'll heal up quite well on its own. Now don't you worry about that, just keep your mind on the job.'

'I can see the head!' shouted Fergus. 'It's got hair!'

'Stop pushing and pant through the next contraction. When the head's out, you can sit up and deliver the baby, Julia.'

'Don't want to.' She was already sitting up, but she felt too far away to reach down and touch her baby.

'Fergus then? But make up your mind. There's not long.'

'Julia?'

'If you want to.'

'Here's the head. And the cord is fine.'

'Come on, darling, nearly there now. It's coming, I can see it . . . It's a boy!' said Fergus. 'Oh my goodness.'

'Well caught, Fergus! And that's the umbilical cord,' said Lucasta, 'but yes, it is a baby boy. Do you want him now or shall I clean him up?'

'Now please,' said Julia. A moment later her baby was in her arms, rooting for her breast. She found that she was crying and laughing at the same time. Emotion tumbled about her. She felt she was nearer life or death than she had ever been, and had life stirring in her arms. She felt so full of love for this small but perfect person who now looked up at her, eyes wide open, she seemed to have enough to spare for the whole world.

She looked up at Fergus. 'We did it, didn't we?' she chuckled. 'And he looks just like you.'

'You did it, Julia. I just ran interference. But I'm so, so proud of you.'

'You delivered him. You're practically a midwife.' Julia wanted to cry again and concentrated on being flippant and on the tiny form in her arms, complete and perfect in every detail, even down to his fingernails.

'What are you going to call him?' asked Lucasta.

'Don't know,' said Julia. 'Something will come to me.'

'Well, if you could let me have him back now, I'll weigh him, check him over, and put some clothes on him and you three can get to know each other.'

'Perhaps I should go and make some phone calls,' said Fergus. 'You must have a list of people you want told. Your sister . . .'

'No point in telling people if you don't know how much he weighs,' said Lucasta. 'It's the first thing people ask after the sex. Do you want his weight in metric or imperial?'

'Pounds and ounces,' said Julia.

'Then it's exactly seven and a half pounds. Well done. That's a good size for an early baby. Although boys do tend to be a bit heavier than girls. Now I'll just make sure he's OK, though a healthier little thing I've rarely had the pleasure to meet.'

It seemed ages before the baby was returned to them once more. 'Now you just relax together for a bit.' The baby, who still had no name, was put into Julia's arms. 'There'll be plenty of time for telephone calls later.'

'I expect Julia would like this time alone with the baby,' said Fergus.

Julia, although in some altered state, was aware of the bleakness in his tone and knew she couldn't let him leave now.

'Don't go, Fergus. Stay with me and get to know your son.'

Fergus half sat, half lay on the bed beside her, and took the baby into his arms when Julia offered him. 'I just didn't believe I'd ever hear those words.'

'Are you glad it's a boy?'

Fergus shook his head. 'I'm just glad it's a baby.'

'Yes, having a kitten or a puppy would make us stand out rather from other parents.'

He scowled at her and Julia saw he had been crying. She

wished, how she wished, that she could ask him to stay with her for ever. But she knew decisions taken at such a high point of bliss would bound to be ones they would regret later.

At last Lucasta came back. 'I've had an anxious Angela Wilton on the phone, saying she can't get in and will the baby wait until she can. I told her she was too late and that she already had a new nephew. I hope that's all right. I'm not supposed to pass on confidential details.'

'It's fine. She'll tell my mother and everyone else.'

'If we get you settled down in the ward, I can bring a phone to you if you want to ring her yourself.'

Julia, Fergus and their baby processed down the corridor to the ward. 'Now, I'm going to send you away Fergus, so we can get Julia cleaned up and into that heavenly nightdress.'

'It's time I was going anyway,' said Fergus, pleased to hear his present described as heavenly. 'I'll be in to see you in the morning.'

'Afternoon please,' said Lucasta. 'We like our mums to rest in the mornings. Childbirth is a very tiring business.'

He grinned, looking remarkably schoolboyish. 'The afternoon it is, then.'

The following morning, a woman wearing the sort of clothes and expression you didn't argue with came to visit Julia. 'Good morning, dear. Lovely baby. A little boy? Wonderful. Now, it says on your form that you're a single parent.' She tried to gloss over her disapproval (it wasn't her job to make value judgements) but somehow, it was evident.

'That's right,' said Julia cheerfully.

'But the midwife tells me that your partner was with you for the birth?'

'Right again.'

'But you're not living together?'

'No. I really am a single parent.'

'Oh. And there's no chance of a reconciliation?'

'No. There isn't anything to reconcile. We're not enemies or anything. We're just not a couple.'

The woman pursed her lips to keep from making 'for the sake of the child' noises, made a note on her clipboard and left.

Shortly afterwards the nurse came in. 'You're all in luck. We're one of the few hospitals to offer a registry service. The registrar's here, if any of you want to register your babies.'

'Oh, I do,' said Julia.

'Mum's absolutely thrilled, of course,' said Angela, gazing at her nephew with eyes which would have made her husband anxious, had he been there. 'She's coming down first thing tomorrow and they'll probably let you go home when she's got here. She would have come tonight, only she had things to do, and I persuaded her you needed a little time to get used to the idea of being a mother, without having twenty-four-hour responsibility.'

Julia considered. 'I would like to learn how to bath him without dropping him, but otherwise I'm dying to get home. Not that the food's marvellous or anything but it's nice not to have to worry about cooking and stuff.'

'Have you told Fergus it's a boy?'

Julia picked up the baby and gooed at it for a little. 'Actually, he told me.'

Angela shrieked. 'What? I thought he was going to go before things got going?'

Julia shook her head. 'I tried to make him, but he wouldn't. He delivered David.'

'And you're not even married? You didn't have to refuse ever to have sex with him again if he didn't stay?'

'Certainly not!'

Angela sighed. 'Well done, that man. A lot of men are reluctant to see their wives in that much pain. But I feel that since it's as much their fault as yours that you're in pain, they shouldn't be allowed to pace about outside just to spare themselves seeing you suffer.'

'Well, anyway, he was there.'

'What a hero.'

'He didn't seem to mind.' Julia was indignant that Fergus was getting brownie points for doing something he wanted to do.

'Even so. Did he send you Birnam Wood? You've got more flowers than anyone else.'

'Suzy sent the lilies, but he sent the others.'

'What a sweetie. Andrew completely forgot. I was the only mother on the ward without any. I felt like a single parent. Oh. Sorry.'

'Don't worry.' Julia laughed. 'I am a single parent, but I have got flowers, so that's all right.'

'I didn't mean to be tactless. Gosh, who owns this wonderful man? The one coming down the corridor?'

'That's Fergus, Angela. Don't you remember?'

'Not looking like that. He's filled out nicely, hasn't he?'

'Shut up. He'll hear you.'

Fergus loomed up and put a big box of chocolates on the bedside cabinet. 'Hello, Julia. How are you?'

'Fine! And thank you so much for the flowers. It's the biggest bouquet in the ward. I don't think you've met my sister for a few years . . .'

'A few years and several incarnations,' said Angela. 'How do you do?'

Fergus kissed her cheek. 'We are old friends, after all.'

'Practically relations,' agreed Angela.

Julia frowned. 'Have a look at David.'

'David? Is that what you've called him? That's a good name, nice and straightforward. Can I pick him up?'

'He's your baby, too.'

Angela got to her feet. 'Well, I'd better get back and tell the children about their new cousin. Mum'll probably be with you tomorrow evening. Then you can go home.'

It seemed natural that Fergus should half sit and half lie next to Julia, holding David, just as they had lain after he was born. 'So your mother's coming down to look after you?'

'Yes. They won't let you leave unless you've got someone. They're extra picky about single mothers.'

'No, well. There's a lot to do. Can I unwrap the chocolates for you?'

'Yes please. Although chocolate's supposed to make the babies constipated.'

'Don't let them eat it, then,' said Fergus.

'I didn't mean . . .'

'I know you didn't. How is the feeding going?'

'The milk doesn't come in until three days after you've had the baby, but he's sucking well at what there is. It hurts though.'

'So do you want to change your mind and bottle feed after he's had the colostrum?'

Julia frowned. 'Honestly, Fergus, isn't there any aspect of childbirth you haven't researched?'

'Sorry,' he said meekly. 'So do you?'

'No. Angela told me if you persevere for two weeks, you might as well go on. According to her, if you bottle feed you never get to sit down, because other people can give it a bottle, but you don't trust them to make up the feeds. So instead of lying about reading and watching television while you feed the baby, you rush around levelling off spoons with knives. And later on you can take it for picnics.'

Fergus remained silent for a moment. 'But I can't.'

'You can! You just have to take me as well. You can take us punting.' She said this to cheer Fergus up, but it didn't work. He was still bleak.

Just then a woman in a white coat bustled up. 'Good morning, Mr and Mrs . . .'

336

'Miss Fairfax. I'm a single parent,' said Julia firmly.

'Oh. Well, I'm the paediatrician. That means I look after children,' she said, smiling kindly.

'Oh really?' said Fergus, with one eyebrow raised. 'I was going to ask you to cut my toenails.'

The woman looked confused and then slightly abashed as she realised. 'Well, not all our parents know what a paediatrician is. But anyway, I just want you to know that your baby's fine.'

'I know that, too,' said Fergus, who had obviously taken against her, saving Julia from the trouble. 'I read the notes.'

'So as far as I'm concerned, you can go home as soon as you like.'

'Oh good,' said Julia.

'As long as you've got someone at home to look after you.' She looked chummily at Fergus, which made them both wince. 'She'll need a bit of waiting on, so not too long in the pub with your mates.'

'We are not a couple,' said Julia. 'If Fergus wants to live in the pub with his mates, it's fine with me.'

'Oh. So you're not living together?'

'No,' said Julia. 'We're not.'

'So who's going to look after you?'

'My mother. She's coming down from the Lake District tomorrow.'

'Oh good.'

'Now if you don't mind, my baby's crying. I need to feed him.'

'That's not really crying, dear. If you pick him up every time he whimpers, you'll be making a rod for your own back.'

'Really?' she said disbelievingly and the woman bustled off.

'She's not right, is she?' asked Fergus, hating the idea that she might be.

'Not according to Angela, who is a bit Mother-Earthy, I must admit. She can't bear to hear her babies cry, so she just carries them around a lot. It really develops the muscles in your arms. She's amazingly strong now.'

'That doesn't sound a bad thing.'

'No it isn't.'

'Well, I'd better go. I must do some work.'

'Have you told anyone you're a new father?'

'It's not easy explaining the situation. It does put me in a very poor light.' There was an awkward pause. 'Anyway, I must be off. I'll be back again as soon as possible, if that's all right.'

'Of course.'

Her next visitor was Suzy: black-leather clad, clutching a bottle of champagne and a box of truffles from Fortnum and Mason.

'Why don't you open it?' suggested Julia. 'I can't drink much, but a little shouldn't do David any harm.'

'Oh no. Keep it for later. You might need it. Have a chocolate instead. Isn't he sweet?' she added, peering into the cot which looked like an aquarium.

'Do you want to hold him?' Julia reached over and picked up the sleeping form.

'Not particularly. I do want children myself one day, of course, but not just now.'

'Holding your godson won't make you pregnant.'

Suzy laughed and agreed to take the bundle. 'He's not very heavy, is he?'

'He weighed seven and a half pounds at birth, that's quite a lot for an early baby.'

'Is it? But I must admit, he is gorgeous. I can't wait for him to be big enough to play with. Wayne's looking forward to seeing him. He's staying with us at the moment. Daddy's behaving like a stag at bay. Every time he sees Wayne, he sort of roars.'

Suzy stayed until she saw Julia begin to droop, and then

she kissed her warmly and left, promising to be back with more goodies the moment she was at home.

When Fergus returned, he was looking terrifyingly purposeful. Julia was glad her baby had given her a chance to have a long nap.

'Do you know if there's anyone in the day room?' said Fergus. 'I need to speak to you alone.'

'Do you? Well, I'm afraid I haven't a clue.'

'I'll go and see.'

He was back in a moment and shepherded Julia and David, complete with aquarium, along the corridor.

'Well, what have you got to say which can't be said in a ward full of nursing mothers and their visitors?' asked Julia, not totally thrilled at being moved from the cosy temperature of the ward to the chillier one of the day room.

'Your mother rang me.'

'Why you and not me?' demanded Julia, suddenly furious.

'She can't get down here before next week. She's snowed in.'

'Oh.' Disappointment replaced the anger like a blanket. There wasn't anything wrong with the hospital, but she had been counting the hours before she could go home.

'They won't let you go home without someone there to look after you,' said Fergus.

'I know. That's why my mother was supposed to be coming.' Julia suddenly felt tearful. She felt abandoned, like a Victorian servant girl made pregnant by the master and then thrown out into the snow. 'I'm bored with being in hospital. Everyone's being very kind and everything, but I just want to go home.'

'Your mother will be here as soon as she can get along the lane. Angela can't come, with her youngest still poorly – possibly infectious,' he hurried on, before Julia could suggest Angela brought Petal with her. 'So you'll just have to stay put. Unless . . .'

'Unless what?'

'I look after you.'

'Oh Fergus, would you? That would be so kind. But how would you manage to get time off work and stuff? With me not being your wife, you can hardly ask for paternity leave.'

'No I can't. But on the other hand, I could get time off if you were my fiancée.'

'Could you? Well that's all right then. You could just pretend.' He seemed to lack enthusiasm for this idea. 'You'd do that for me, wouldn't you?'

Fergus, who had been so supportive, particularly during David's arrival, looked very uncompromising. 'No. Why should I?'

'So David and I can go home, of course.'

'What good does that do me?'

'Fergus! What's the matter with you? Ever since you've known I was pregnant you've wanted the best for me and David. Why are you being so difficult now?'

'I'm not being difficult. I'm just not prepared to perjure myself merely to get you out of hospital.'

'Then why did you even suggest that you could look after me!'

'Because I'm more than willing to do so. But on my terms.'

'Well, what are your terms? Interest free for the first six months, but you end up paying for ever?'

'Something like that. You have to promise to marry me.'

Julia felt quite weak. 'But that's blackmail.'

'Yes it is. But I don't know what else I can do to make you see sense.'

Julia huddled in the armchair and closed her eyes, too tired to go through the arguments again.

'I love you, Julia, and I want to spend the rest of my life looking after you. I've tried proving to you that we can live happily with each other, that I care for you and not just our baby, but you don't seem able to believe me.'

One eye opened. 'What are you talking about?'

'When I broke down outside your house.'

'You didn't break down!' She was giving the matter her full attention now. 'You ran out of petrol!'

'Is that what I said? I can't even remember my own lies. But I actually had plenty of petrol.'

'And wasn't your flat flooded?'

'Well, the fridge had leaked a bit, but nothing that a bit of kitchen towel couldn't cope with.'

'Fergus!' She was appalled. Goody-goody law-abiding Fergus, being so underhand and deceitful. 'Why?'

'I wanted to prove my love for you in a practical way, by really looking after you.' He took hold of her hands. 'I know that you won't want me near you for weeks and weeks, but if we were together, with David, you might learn to love me like I love you. It may not be all hearts and flowers and romantic, but it would be a real-life kind of love, the kind that survives in spite of not having gourmet sex and gourmet food every night. You are beautiful to me when you're wearing your dressing gown and you've just got out of the bath. I want you to learn to feel about me like that. I want us to be together for ever, for *us*, not for David, although he is part of us. Blackmail seemed my only weapon.'

Julia couldn't think what to say. Her heart was somer-saulting in her chest.

'And before you say that the whole thing is out of the question, and that you'd rather wait in hospital for ever than go home with me, I saw the name you gave him.'

'I called him David!' What was this to do with the price of fish?

'David Fergus. You must feel something for me if you call your baby after me.'

The 'something' she felt was threatening to make her very emotional. 'He's not my baby, he's our baby.'

341

Fergus grinned suddenly. 'Does that mean you agree? You'll marry me? Let me love and cherish you until death us do part?'

She nodded, determined to keep her act together. 'I don't have much choice, do I? If I ever want to get out of hospital.'

He hugged her until she winced with pain as her swollen breasts got crushed by his passion. 'I've loved you since I first saw you on the boat. You looked so grumpy, my heart just flipped.'

'You're so contrary,' she murmured, clutching the edge of his jacket. 'How could you love someone bad-tempered?'

'Because you're not really bad-tempered, and I find you impossibly sexy.'

'Impossibly is the case for a while, I'm afraid.'

'Perhaps we'd better wait until we're married,' he suggested. 'Rather sweetly old-fashioned, don't you think?'

Julia couldn't think. Her brain was roller-coastering around like a kid on a skateboard. Fergus really wanted her for *her*, and didn't just want to marry her because he'd made her pregnant. It took some getting used to.

'So are we engaged? Will you marry me?' Julia nodded. 'Then I'd better give you this – make it official.'

He produced from his pocket a jeweller's box. Inside was a ring with three large diamonds set in gold.

'This must have cost a fortune!' she breathed, vulgarly, as Fergus detached it from its case and slipped it on to her finger.

'It's all right. It's second-hand – well, twentieth-hand probably. It's antique.'

She gasped. 'Think of all the things we could have bought for the baby with the money.'

'I wanted to prove that I love you and not just the baby, though of course I'm dotty about him too. If I'd bought an expensive pram or something you would never believe that I want to marry you for yourself and not just because you're the mother of my son.' Julia turned her finger this way and that, seeing the diamonds sparkle. 'Apparently some men give their wives eternity rings on the birth of their first child. Well, that's not appropriate for us, so I just gave you an extra flashy engagement ring. It's not too much, is it? You do like it?'

'Like' didn't really cover it. 'It's wonderful.'

'I took Suzy with me to help me choose it. She has very expensive tastes and assured me that it was money well spent.'

'Hmm. They say the only thing that's harder than a diamond is paying for it. And this ring has three! You must have put yourself hideously in debt. It's just as well I can keep my baby without assistance from his father,' said Julia.

'If you've got time, after you've planned a wedding.'

'And a christening. Might as well get it all over in one.'

Lucasta found them a little while later indulging in a group hug with their baby. She saw the ring and swore, softly. 'That makes mine look like a glass chip. It must have cost a fortune.'

'Julia's worth a fortune. David and I both think so.'

Later, Julia was watching television with another new mother. It was the weather forecast. Rather to Julia's surprise, there was no mention of snow in the North. In fact, they seemed to have been having milder weather than they were in the South-west.

'Would you marry a man who had lied to you, at least twice?' Julia asked her companion.

'If he gave me a ring like that, sure I would.'

'Mmm,' said Julia. 'Then so will I.'